Isr...

JEWISH VALUES

KETER BOOKS

This book is compiled from material originally published in the *Encyclopaedia Judaica*

Cat. No. 25073

ISBN 0 7065 1332 0

Printed in Israel

CONTENTS

CONTRIBUTORS

Israel Abrahams *(deceased)*, M.A., Rabbi: Professor of
Hebrew, the University of Capetown: Chief Rabbi of
Cape Province, South Africa

Alexander Altmann, Ph.D., D.H.L., Rabbi: Professor of
Jewish Philosophy, Brandeis University, U.S.A.

Gershon Bacon, M.H.L., New York

Saul Berman, M.A., M.H.L., Rabbi: Brookline, Mas-
sachusetts, U.S.A.

José Faur, Ph.D.: Associate Professor of Rabbinics, the
Jewish Theological Seminary of America, New York

Marvin Fox, Ph.D., Rabbi: Professor of Philosophy,
Ohio State University, Columbia, U.S.A.

Moshe Greenberg, Ph.D., Rabbi: Professor of Bible, the
Hebrew University of Jerusalem

Yehoshua M. Grintz, Ph.D.: Professor of Biblical Studies,
Tel Aviv University

Warren Harvey, M.A.: New York

Moshe David Herr, Ph.D.: Lecturer in Jewish History,
the Hebrew University of Jerusalem

Louis Jacobs, Ph.D., Rabbi: scholar, London

Zvi Kaplan, Jerusalem

Baruch A. Levine, Ph.D., Prof. of Hebrew, New York
University, New York

Jacob Licht, Ph.D.: Associate Professor of Biblical Studies,
Tel Aviv University

André Neher, Dr. Phil., M.D., Rabbi: Professor of Jewish
History and Philosophy, the University of Strasbourg
and Tel Aviv University

Raphael Posner, D.H.L., Rabbi: Assistant Professor of
Rabbinics, the Jewish Theological Seminary of

America, Jerusalem

Louis Isaac Rabinowitz, Ph.D., Rabbi: Former Chief Rabbi of the Transvaal and Former Professor of Hebrew, the University of Witwatersrand, Johannesburg; Jerusalem

Gershom Scholem, Dr. Phil.: Emeritus Professor of Jewish Mysticism, the Hebrew University of Jerusalem

Steven S. Schwarzschild, D.H.L., Rabbi: Professor of Jewish Philosophy, Washington University, St. Louis, Missouri

Eliezer Schweid Ph.D.; Senior Lecturer in Jewish Philosophy the Hebrew University of Jerusalem.

Manfred H. Vogel, Ph.D.: Associate Professor of History and Literature of Religions, Northwestern University, Evanston, Illinois

Leon J. Yagod, D.H.L., Rabbi: Irvington, New Jersey

PREFACE

The all-embracing nature of the Jewish religion is one of its unique characteristics. It also explains why Judaism is so hard to describe succinctly. Its basis is a faith—but that faith is only the starting-point for a way of life and a complete culture. Indeed, there are Jews in the modern world who accept the culture but question the faith.

The fundament of the faith is the concept of God, and from this stems the entire ideology. Also basic is the concept of Holiness which extends from God to those who accept His revelation. From this develops an entire ethical system. The quintessential Ten Commandments are seen by the Rabbis as consisting of two sets of five—five commandments regulating man's relations to God and five regulating his relations to his fellowman.

Jewish theology cannot be seen in a detached vacuum—and, indeed, abstract theological speculation is a late development in Judaism. The relationship to God implies a complete set of imperatives and necessitates a life regime implementing in practice the implications of that relationship. In Jewish tradition, this was held to have been dictated by the Divine Will as expressed in the 613 Commandments, but full allowance was made for developments and later traditions in what was conceived to be the spirit of that Will. Thus theory and practice were inseparable.

This book on "Jewish Values" is necessarily eclectic. An overall description of the ideology of Judaism is contained in the entries "Judaism" and "Articles of Faith" while the practical obligations are contained in full in "The 613 Commandments". But only a selection of subjects have been developed in the chapters following each general survey. Readers wishing to pursue amplification of other topics are referred to the *Encyclopaedia Judaica*.

Notwithstanding the difficulty of encompassing the subject in a single volume, we have in this book endeavored to trace Jewish values in all major contexts. First comes Jewish belief. Judaism was not promulgated as an ordered system and thousands of years passed before it was felt necessary to suggest a creed. But although not systematized, there was, of course, a consensus of belief. This was based at the very outset on the monotheistic vision and faith in the revelation at Sinai, expressed in the Torah. Ideological values, then, form the subject of Parts One and Two.

Jewish values in practice—the relations between man and man—are described in Parts Three and Four. The ethics of Judaism and its stress on social justice have profoundly influenced the Western world. The brotherhood of man—a corollary of the fatherhood of God— was a pioneering Jewish vision which evoked a moral philosophy of timeless applicability. The practical aspects are also expressed in the Law—both in the broad moral concept of Justice, which has played so significant a role in the Jewish personality, and in the detailed codification of the laws governing everyday living.

The religious imperatives translated into everyday terms involve not only man's conduct toward his fellow-creatures but his conduct toward God. This is expressed through the prescribed ritual and prayer. The ritual ensures that even the most trivial action will be sanctified— and also that there should be regular occasions on which man communes with God. One of Judaism's great contributions to mankind is its Sabbath—a day of rest from mundane matters to be devoted to spiritual affairs. These aspects are treated in Part Five, which also includes a chapter on Study, another elemental Jewish value, expressed through the intense concentration on the study of sacred literature, the reverence for the scholar, and the supreme stress on education among Jews in all societies.

Finally, there is an essay on a vital aspect of Jewish historiosophical values. By virtue of their Covenant with God, the Jews have seen themselves as chosen to embody His word. This has been expressed in their historical role among the nations and also in their Divinely prescribed link with the Land of Israel by virtue of which that Land became a Holy Land and its capital city, Jerusalem, a Holy City. The attachment to the Land of Israel, even during the many centuries when they were precluded from living in it, must be understood as one of the most compelling of Jewish values.

In conclusion, it should be noted that Judaism is not monolithic. Its mainstream evolved as a result of frequent internal dissensions. In some instances, dissension led to lasting splits and the formation of sects (such as the Karaites): in other cases—such as the violent controversy over the teachings of Maimonides—compromises were reached without damaging the structure of the community. In modern times, too, there has been a major ideological split with the rise of Reform Judaism, which has reinterpreted many ideological and practical premises. It has challenged the fundamentalism of the Orthodox and does not accept, for example, the continuing validity of much of Orthodox ritual practice. Where relevant, reference is made to modifications introduced by the reformers. And notwithstanding the differences, it will readily be seen that there is a broad common base of Jewish values accepted by all Jews.

Geoffrey Wigoder
Editor "Israel Pocket Library"

Part One:

INTRODUCTION

1 JUDAISM

DEFINITION

The term Judaism is first found among the Greek-speaking Jews of the first century C.E. (*Judaismes,* see II Macc. 2:21; 8:1; 14:38; Gal. 1:13–14). Its Hebrew equivalent, *Yahadut,* found only occasionally in medieval literature (e.g., Ibn Ezra to Deut. 21:13), but used frequently in modern times, has parallels neither in the Bible (but see Esth. 8:17, *mityahadim,* "became Jews") nor in the rabbinic literature. (The term *dat Yehudit,* found in Ket. 7:6, means no more than the Jewish law, custom, or practice in a particular instance, e.g., that a married woman should not spin or have her head uncovered in the street.)

The Term "Torah." The term generally used in the classical sources for the whole body of Jewish teaching is Torah, "doctrine," "teaching." Thus the Talmud (Shab. 31a) tells the story of a heathen who wished to be converted to the Jewish faith but only on the understanding that he would be taught the whole of the Torah while standing on one leg. Hillel accepted him, and in response to his request replied: "That which is hateful unto thee do not do unto thy neighbor. This is the whole of the Torah. The rest is commentary. Go and study." Presumably if the Greek-speaking Jews had told the story they would have made the prospective convert demand to be taught "Judaism" while standing on one leg.

Modern Distinctions Between "Judaism" and "Torah." In modern usage the terms "Judaism" and "Torah" are virtually interchangeable, but the former has on the whole a 3

Hillel teaching the Torah to a heathen, who is standing on one foot. Detail from the *menorah* by Benno Elkan at the Knesset, Jerusalem. Photo Yiẓḥak Amit, Kibbutz Zorah.

more humanistic nuance while "Torah" calls attention to the divine, revelatory aspects. The term "secular Judaism"—used to describe the philosophy of Jews who accept specific Jewish values but who reject the Jewish religion—is not, therefore, self-contradictory as the term "secular Torah" would be. (In modern Hebrew, however, the word *torah* is also used for "doctrine" or "theory" (e.g., "the Marxist theory"), and in this sense it would also be logically possible to speak of a secular *torah*. In English transliteration the two meanings might be distinguished by using a capital *T* for the one and a small *t* for the other, but this is not possible in Hebrew which knows of no distinction between small and capital letters.)

A further difference in nuance, stemming from the first, is that "Torah" refers to the eternal, static elements in Jewish life and thought while "Judaism" refers to the more creative, dynamic elements as manifested in the varied civilizations and cultures of the Jews at the different stages of their history, such as Hellenistic Judaism, rabbinic Judaism, medieval Judaism, and, from the 19th century, Orthodox, Conservative, and Reform Judaism. (The term *Yidishkeyt* is the Yiddish equivalent of "Judaism" but has a less universalistic connotation and refers more specifically to the folk elements of the faith.)

It is usually considered to be anachronistic to refer to the biblical religion (the "religion of Israel") as "Judaism" both because there were no Jews (i.e., "those belonging to the tribe of Judah") in the formative period of the Bible, and because there are distinctive features which mark off later Judaism from the earlier forms, ideas, and worship. For all that, most Jews would recognize sufficient continuity to reject as unwarranted the description of Judaism as a completely different religion from the biblical.

THE ESSENCE OF JUDAISM

The Hebrew writer Aḥad Ha-Am (*Al Parashat Derakhim,* 4 (Berlin ed. 1924), 42) observed that if Hillel's convert (see above) had come to him demanding to be 5 taught the whole of the Torah while standing on one leg, he would have replied: " 'Thou shalt not make unto thee a graven image, nor any manner of likeness' (Ex. 20:4). This is the whole of the Torah. The rest is commentary," i.e., that the essence of Judaism consists in the elevation of the ideal above all material or physical forms or conceptions.

Aḥad Ha-Am's was only one of the latest attempts at discovering the essence of Judaism, its main idea or ideas, its particular viewpoint wherein it differs from other religions and philosophies. This is an extremely difficult—some would say impossible—task, since the differing civilizations, Egyptian, Canaanite, Babylonian, Persian, Greek, Roman, Christian, Muslim, with which Jews came into contact, have made their influence felt on Jews and through them on Judaism itself. It is precarious to think of Judaism in monolithic terms. Developed and adapted to changing circumstances throughout its long history, it naturally contains varying emphases as well as outright contradictions. Belief in the transmigration of souls, for example, was strongly upheld by some Jewish teachers and vehemently rejected by others. Yet the quest has rarely ceased for certain distinctive viewpoints which make Judaism what it is. Some of these must here be mentioned.

Talmudic Attempts to State Essence. In a talmudic passage (Mak. 23b–24a) it is said that God gave to Moses 613 precepts, but that later seers and prophets reduced these to certain basic principles: David to eleven (Ps. 15); Isaiah to six (Isa. 33:15–16); Micah to three (Micah 6:8); Isaiah, again, to two (Isa. 56:1); and, finally, Habakkuk to one: "The righteous shall live by his faith" (Hab. 2:4). This would make trust in God Judaism's guiding principle.

In another passage the second-century rabbis ruled at the council of Lydda that although the other precepts of the Torah can be set aside in order to save life, martyrdom is demanded when life can only be saved by committing murder, by worshiping idols, or by offending against the laws governing forbidden sexual relations (e.g., those against adultery and incest). The historian Heinrich Graetz (in JQR, 1 (1889), 4–13) deduces from this ruling that there are two elements in the essence of Judaism: the ethical and the religious. The ethical includes in its positive side, love of mankind, benevolence, humility, justice, holiness in thought and deed, and in its negative aspects, care against unchastity, subdual of selfishness and the beast in man. The religious element includes the prohibition of worshiping a transient being as God and insists that all idolatry is vain and must be rejected entirely. The positive side is to regard the highest Being as one and unique, to worship it as the Godhead and as the essence of all ethical perfections.

Modern Trends. In modern times two new factors have been operative in the search for the essence of Judaism, one making the task more difficult, the other more urgent. The first is the rise of the Wissenschaft des Judentums movement in the 19th century. This had as its aim the objective historical investigation into the sources and history of Judaism. Its practitioners succeeded in demonstrating the complexity of Jewish thought and the fact that it developed in response to outside stimuli, so that there could no longer be any question of seeing Judaism as a self-contained unchanging entity consistent in all its parts. The second new factor was the emancipation of the Jew and his emergence into Western society, calling for a fresh adaptation of Judaism so as to make it viable and relevant in the new situation. The historical movement had demonstrated the developing nature of Judaism and seemed, therefore, to offer encouragement to those thinkers who wished to develop the faith further in accord with the new ideals and challenges. Yet this very demonstration made it far more difficult to detect that which is permanent in Judaism when so much is seen to be fluid and subject to change. Among modern thinkers, Leo Baeck was so convinced that the quest was not futile that his book carries the revealing title, *The Essence of Judaism* (1948[2]). Acknowledging the rich variety of forms and differing phenomena in Judaism's history, Baeck still feels able to declare: "The essence is characterized by what has been gained and preserved. And such *constancy,* such *essence,* Judaism possesses despite its many varieties and the shifting phases of its long career. In virtue of that essence they all have something in common, a unity of thought and feeling, and an inward bond."

The Concept of "Normative Judaism." Jewish thinkers who hold that an essence of Judaism can be perceived tend to speak of "normative Judaism," with the implication that at the heart of the Jewish faith there is a hard, imperishable core, to be externally preserved, together with numerous peripheral ideas, expressed to be sure by great Jewish thinkers in different ages but not really essential to the faith, which could be dismissed if necessary as deviations.

Unfortunately for this line of thinking no criteria are available for distinguishing the essential from the ephemeral, so that a strong element of subjectivity is present in this whole approach. Almost invariably the process ends in a particular thinker's embracing ideas he holds to be true and valuable, discovering these reflected in the tradition and hence belonging to the "normative," while rejecting ideas he holds to be harmful or valueless as peripheral to Judaism, even though they are found in the tradition. Nor is the statistical approach helpful. An idea occurring very frequently in the traditional sources may be rejected by some thinkers on the grounds that it is untrue or irrelevant, while one hardly mentioned in the sources may assume fresh significance in a new situation, to say nothing of the difficulties in deciding which sources are to be considered the more authoritative. The absurdities which can result from the "normative Judaism" approach can be seen when, for example, contemporary thinkers with a dislike for asceticism, who wish at the same time to speak in the name of Judaism, virtually read out of the faith ascetics such as Baḥya ibn Paquda and Moses Ḥayyim Luzzatto (see, for instance, Abba Hillel Silver, *Where Judaism Differed* (1957), 182–223).

Recognition of Constant Ideas. However, if due caution is exercised and no exaggerated claims made, the idea of a normative Judaism is not without value in that it calls attention to the undeniable fact that for all the variety of moods in Judaism's history there does emerge among the faithful a kind of consensus on the main issues. It has always been recognized, for instance, after the rise of Christianity and Islam, that these two religions are incompatible with Judaism and that no Jew can consistently embrace them while remaining an adherent of Judaism. The same applies to the Far Eastern religions. This, of course, is very different from affirming that there are no points of contact between Judaism and other faiths, or no common concerns. Nor has the idea of a Judaism divorced from the peoplehood of Israel ever made much headway, even in circles in which the doctrine of Israel's chosenness is a source of embarrassment. Nor does Jewish history know of a Torah-less Judaism, even though the interpretations of what is meant by Torah differ widely. The most important work of Jewish mysticism, the Zohar, speaks of three grades or stages bound one to the other—God, the Torah, and Israel (Zohar, Lev. 73a–b). Historically considered it is true that Judaism is an amalgam of three ideas—belief in God, God's revelation of the Torah to Israel, and Israel as the people which lives by the Torah in obedience to God. The interpretation of these ideas has varied from age to age, but the ideas themselves have remained constant.

THE DEVELOPMENT OF JUDAISM

The Biblical Period. Any account of the development of Judaism must begin with the Bible as the record of those ideas, practices, and institutions which became prominent in the faith. With regard to the biblical record, as with regard to Judaism itself, the monolithic view has yielded among modern scholars to that of development and change, so that it is unsatisfactory to speak of the faith of the Bible, as if the Bible were a unit rather than a collection of books produced over a period of many hundreds of years and stemming from diverse circles with divergent views. The opinions of biblical criticism are frequently at variance with the traditional viewpoint on such questions as whether the biblical accounts of the lives of the patriarchs are factually accurate, or whether all the legislation attributed to Moses really goes back to the great lawgiver or was fathered by him. Nevertheless, it is possible to trace certain key ideas which eventually assumed importance in the Bible and which were influential in shaping Judaism.

MONOTHEISM. The usual description of the biblical faith is ethical monotheism. Whether, as a minority of scholars suggest (e.g. Y. Kaufmann), monotheism erupted spontaneously among the people in ancient Israel or whether, as the majority would have it, there can be traced a gradual progress from polytheism through henotheism to complete monotheism (see the survey and critique by H. H. Rowley, *From Moses to Qumran* (1963), 35–63), the doctrine that there is one God, Lord of the universe, is clearly taught in a large number of biblical passages (e.g., Gen. 1:1–2:3; 5:1–2; 6:1–7; 9:1–8; 11:1–9; 14:18–22; Ex. 19:5; 20:1–14; Deut. 4:15–19; 5:6–8; 10:14; 32:8; I Kings 8:27; Isa. 2:1–4; 11; 45:5–8; 66:1–2; Jer. 32:17–19; Amos 5:8; Jonah 1:9; Micah 1:2; Hab. 3:3; Zech. 8:20–23; 14:9; Mal. 1:11; Ps. 8:2–4; 33:8–11; 47:6–9; 67:2–5; 86:9; 90:1–4; 96:5; 104; 113:4–6; 115:16; 136; 139:7–18; 145; 148; Job 38; 39; 40). What later became Israel's declaration of faith—the *Shema*—is found in Deuteronomy 6:4: "Hear, O Israel: The Lord our God, the Lord is one." The probable meaning of *eḥad* ("one") in this verse is not only "not many" but also "unique." God is transcendent and different from all His creatures (S. R. Driver, ICC, *Deuteronomy* (1896²) 89–91). From the critical standpoint these passages are comparatively late, but they are present in the Bible and were consequently adopted by Judaism.

CHARACTERISTICS OF THE ONE GOD. This one God is holy (Lev. 19:2; Isa. 6:3) and demands holiness (Ex. 22:30; Lev. 19:2), righteousness, and justice from His people (Gen. 18:19; Ex. 23:2; Deut. 16:18–20) and from all mankind (Gen. 6:13; Amos 1; 2:1–3). He has compassion over all His creatures (Ps. 145:9), and man can respond to

His love in love and fear of Him (Deut. 6:5; 10:20). This God, Lord of all the earth, has chosen the people of Israel, the descendants of Abraham, Isaac, and Jacob, to serve as a "nation of priests" (Ex. 19:6) and to assist in the fulfillment of His purposes (Isa. 43:10; Zech. 8:23). It is incorrect to see the biblical idea of Israel's choice in terms of the relationship between the god of a tribe and the tribe: a tribal god cannot choose; his destiny is bound up with that of his people. When the tribe is vanquished he, too, suffers defeat. In the biblical record it is the God of all the earth who chooses Israel (Heinemann, in *Sinai,* 16 (1944/45), 17–30). God has given Israel the holy land as its place of abode (Gen. 28:13; 50:24; Ex. 6:8; Deut. 26:15). The special place in which God is to be worshiped by the sacrifices is the Temple (Deut. 12:11–14; I Kings 8).

CEREMONIAL AND ETHICAL LAWS. Prominent among the ceremonial laws are the observance of the Sabbath (Ex. 20:8–11; 31:12–17; Lev. 25:1ff.; Deut. 5:12–15), the New Moon feast (Num. 28:11–15; Amos 8:5; Hos. 2:13; Isa. 1:14; II Kings 4:23), and the celebration of the festivals of Passover (Ex. 12:14–20; 23:15; Lev. 23:5–8; Deut. 16:1–8), Shavuot (Ex. 23:16; Lev. 23:15–21), and Sukkot (Ex. 23:16; Lev. 23:33–43). Males were to be circumcised eight days after birth as a sign of the covenant made with Abraham (Gen. 17:9–27; 34:13–15; Josh. 5:2–8). The dietary laws (Lev. 11:1–23; Deut. 14:3–21) were to be observed as well as laws governing dress (Deut. 22:11; Num. 15:37:41; Lev. 19:27) and agriculture (Lev. 19:9–10; 23:22; Num. 18:8–32). Numerous are the laws governing human relationships and social justice (Ex. 21; 22; 23:1–9; Lev. 19; Deut. 22; 23; 24; 25).

SPIRITUAL LEADERS. The spiritual leaders of the people were of different kinds: the priest *(kohen)* who served in the Temple and was the custodian of the law (Lev. 21; 22:1–25; Deut. 17:8–13); the prophet *(navi)* who brought a particular message from God to the people (Deut. 18:18; I Sam. 9:9); and the sage *(ḥakham),* the teacher of worldly wisdom and good conduct (Jer. 9:22; Eccles. 7:4–5).

MESSIANIC BELIEFS. The belief became more and more pronounced that a day would eventually dawn when God's kingdom would be established over all the earth and war would be banished (Isa. 2:1-4; 11:1-10; Micah 4:1-4; Zech. 14:9). After the destruction of the Temple and the exile of the people to Babylon, this hope became associated with that of national restoration under a Davidic ruler, later called the Messiah, and the resurrection of the dead (Dan. 12:2).

UNIVERSALISM AND PARTICULARISM. Israel, it was taught, had been chosen to be a light unto the nations (Isa. 42:6; 49:6) and to be God's special treasure (Ex. 19:5). But both universalism and particularism are found in the Bible with all the tensions inseparable from belief in God as Father and King of all men and belief in His special concern with Israel. This people were to lead lives of absolute faithfulness to God. The greatest sin they could, and did, commit was idolatry.

There are many prayers in the Bible but these are private and individualistic. Communal prayer was a later development (see Prayer).

The Pre-Rabbinic Age. The period after the return from Babylon is shrouded in obscurity, but some of the main lines of development can be traced. Not later than the fifth century B.C.E. the Pentateuch had become the Torah, sacred Scripture, with the prophetic books and the books of the Hagiographa being added later on as holy writ. The process of canonization of the biblical books, other than the Pentateuch, was a lengthy one, the full acceptance of all 24 books which constitute the Hebrew Bible, taking place as late as the second century C.E.

THE RISE OF ORAL TRADITION. The concept of Torah was, of course, known in the earlier biblical period, but there it referred to groups of laws taught by the priests (Lev. 6:2, 7; 7:11, 37; 13:59; 14:2; 15:32; Num. 5:29-30; 6:13, 21) or to general "teaching" or "doctrine" (Isa. 2:3). In this period, for the first time, the new idea of the Torah (i.e., the Pentateuch) as a sacred text came to the fore. The regular reading of the Torah in assembly began at this period. Out of these assemblies the synagogue and the whole system of public worship evolved. The reading of the Torah was accompanied by its exposition and its application to new situations as they appeared and developed. It is commonly assumed that the notion of an Oral Law, as distinct from the Written Law, was the invention of the Pharisees in their determination to make Judaism viable by freeing it from the bonds of a text written down in former ages. It is said, further, that the Sadducees rejected the whole notion of an Oral Law. While it is undoubtedly true that the full development of the Oral Law idea was the work of the Pharisees, the issue must not be oversimplified. The Sadducees, too, must have had some traditions of Torah interpretation, if only because the literal reading of the Torah text cries out for further amplification. Buying and selling, for instance, are referred to in the Torah, but no indications are given there as to how the transfer of property is to be effected. There are references in the Torah to keeping the Sabbath, but hardly any indication of what is involved in Sabbath work.

PERSIAN AND GREEK INFLUENCES. The two civilizations with which the Jews came into contact at this period, first the Persian then the Greek, made their influence felt on Jewish beliefs. Under Babylonian and Persian influence there came into Jewish life and thought the notion of angels as identifiable, sentient, but not necessarily corporeal beings, each with his own name and sometimes particular function: Michael, Gabriel, Raphael and so forth. The personification of the evil in the universe as Satan probably owes much to Persia, as do the beliefs in demons and the resurrection of the dead. It was probably under Greek influence that the doctrine of the immortality of the soul came into Judaism. The doctrine of the resurrection also established itself, possibly at the time of the Hasmoneans when young men were dying for their religion, so that the older solutions to the problem of suffering, in terms of worldly recompense, became increasingly untenable. There are no doubt indications of this belief in the earlier period, but it had not at that time obtained a complete foothold in the faith. Basically the two beliefs of resurrection and the soul's immortality are contradictory. The one refers to a collective resurrection at the end of days, i.e., that the dead sleeping in the earth will arise from the grave, while the other refers to the state of the soul after the death of the body. When both ideas became incorporated into Judaism it was held that when the individual died his soul still lived on in another realm (this gave rise to all the beliefs regarding heaven and hell) while his body lay in the grave to await the physical resurrection of all the dead here on earth. However, the pronounced this-worldly emphasis of the early biblical period was not abandoned completely. This life was still held to be good in itself as a gift from God. But the thought took shape that, in addition, this life was a kind of school, a time of preparation for eternal life.

ESCHATOLOGICAL ELEMENTS. Toward the end of the Second Temple period, when ominous clouds of complete national catastrophe began to gather, the eschatological note was sounded particularly loud. Speculations were rife regarding the end of days and hope for a new era to be ushered in by direct divine intervention. The doctrine of the Messiah and the messianic age, heralded by the prophets, was seen as a hope shortly to be realized. Some groups of Jews fled into the desert there to await the coming of the Messiah, as is evidenced by the sect of Qumran (held by most scholars to be identical with the Essenes).

CHALLENGES FROM OTHER RELIGIONS. From the time of Judaism's contact with Zoroastrianism, faith in the unity of God had to be defended against dualistic theories that there were two gods, one of light and goodness, the other of darkness and evil. With the rise of Christianity the challenge came from the doctrines of the incarnation and the trinity. These challenges took the place of the polytheism and idolatry of the earlier biblical period, though, of course, idolatry continued to exist in the form of the Greek and Roman gods, and made polemics and legislation against *avodah zarah* ("strange worship") all but academic.

The Rabbinic Period. Rabbinic Judaism, the heir to all these tendencies, emerged at the beginning of the present era and lasted until the year 500, but many of the ideas put forward by the great rabbis had their origin in an earlier age. In the rabbinic literature there is a fairly consistent treatment of the three ideas of God, Torah, and Israel, with much debate among the rabbis on this or that detail.

PARTICULARISTIC TENDENCIES. With regard to the doctrine of Jewish peoplehood, the greater the degradation and the more intense the feelings of national rejection, the stronger became the need for national consolation and the assurance that God still cared. All the poignancy of Israel's hope against hope is expressed in the typically rabbinic, imaginary dialogue between God and Israel, in which Israel complains that she has been forgotten by God, and God replies "My daughter, 12 constellations have I created in the firmament, and for each constellation I have created 30 hosts, and for each host I have created 30 legions, and for each legion I have created 30 cohorts, and for each cohort I have created 30 maniples, and for each maniple I have created 30 camps, and to each camp I have attached 365 thousands of myriads of stars, corresponding to the days of the solar year, and all of them I have created only for thy sake, and thou sayest that I have forgotten thee" (Ber. 32b). It can hardly be accidental that the groupings are taken from the divisions of the Roman army. The universalistic tendencies in Judaism are apt to become obscured by the particulars in this period. Nevertheless, conversion to Judaism is possible. The biblical *ger* ("sojourner") had long been interpreted to mean a proselyte to the Jewish faith, and the equal rights demanded in the Bible for the *ger* are applied. "Our rabbis taught: If at the present time a man wishes to become a convert, he is to be addressed as follows: 'What reason have you for wishing to become a convert; do you not know that Israel at the present time is persecuted and oppressed, despised, harassed, and overcome by afflictions?' If he replies 'I know and yet am unworthy,' he is accepted forthwith, and is given instruction in some of the minor and some of the major commandments" (Yev. 47a).

DOMINANT VALUE OF TORAH STUDY. The study of the Torah is now the supreme religious duty, the closest approach to God, the Pharisaic form of the beatific vision (R. Travers Herford, *The Ethics of the Talmud, Sayings of the Fathers* (1962), 15). Typical is the saying in the Mishnah (Pe'ah 1:1): "These are the things whose fruits a man enjoys in this world while the capital is laid up for him in the world to come: honoring father and mother, deeds of lovingkindness, making peace between a man and his fellow; but the study of the Torah is equal to them all." When a rabbi took an unduly long time over his prayers it was not considered incongruous for his colleague to rebuke him: "They neglect eternal life [Torah study] and engage in temporal existence [prayer]" (Shab. 10a). Only such devotion to Torah study can explain the remarkable ruling in the Mishnah (BM 2:11): "If a man is called upon to seek the lost property of his father and that of his teacher, his teacher's comes first—for his father only brought him into this world but his teacher, that taught him wisdom, brings him into the world to come; but if his father was also a sage, his father's comes first. If his father and his teacher each bore a burden, he must first relieve his teacher and afterward his father. If his father and his teacher were taken captive, he must first ransom his teacher and afterward his father; but if his father was also a sage he must first ransom his father and afterward ransom his teacher." The reference to wisdom in this passage comes at the end of a long process in which wisdom no longer means, as it does in the Bible, worldly knowledge and practical philosophy but the wisdom of the Torah. Moreover Torah is no longer the province of the priest but the heritage of all the people.

ANTHROPOMORPHISM. Anthropomorphic descriptions of God abound in the rabbinic literature but when excessively bold are generally qualified by the term *kivyakhol* ("as it were"). The two most popular names for God in this literature are *Ribbono shel olam* ("Lord of the universe"), used in direct speech, and *ha-Kadosh barukh Hu* ("the Holy One, blessed be He"), used in indirect speech.

THIS WORLD AND THE WORLD TO COME. The idea of this life as a preparation for eternal bliss in the hereafter looms very large in rabbinic thinking, yet the value of this life as good in itself is not overshadowed. The second-century teacher, R. Jacob, said: "Better is one hour of repentance and good deeds in this world than the whole life of the world to come; but better is one hour of bliss in the world to come than the whole life of this world" (Avot 4:17). The same teacher said (Avot 4:16): "This world is like a vestibule before the world to come: prepare thyself in the vestibule that thou mayest enter the banqueting hall." In the same vein is the saying that this world is like the eve of Sabbath and the world to come like the Sabbath. Only one who prepares adequately on the eve of the Sabbath can enjoy the delights of the Sabbath (Av. Zar. 3a). Bliss in the hereafter is not limited to Jews. The view of R. Joshua, against that of R. Eliezer, was adopted that the righteous of all nations have a share in the world to come (Tosef., Sanh. 13:2).

The Middle Ages. During the Middle Ages Judaism was confronted with the challenge of Greek philosophy in its Arabic garb. The Jews mainly affected were those of Spain and Islamic lands. The French and German Jews were more remote from the new trends, and their work is chiefly a continuation of the rabbinic modes of thinking. The impact of Greek thought demanded both a more systematic presentation of the truths of the faith and a fresh consideration of what these were in the light of the new ideas. A good deal of the conflict was in the realm of particularism. There is definite hostility in much of Greek thought to the notion of truths capable of being perceived only by a special group. Truth is universal and for all men. There is a marked tendency in medieval Jewish thought to play down Jewish particularism. This is not to say that

Judaism was held to be only relatively true, but that the doctrine of Israel's chosenness had become especially difficult to comprehend philosophically. The greatest thinker of this period, Maimonides, hardly touches on the question of the chosen people and, significantly enough, does not number the doctrine among his principles of the faith. For most of the thinkers of this age a burning problem was the relationship between reason and revelation. What need is there for a special revelation of the truth if truth is universal and can be attained by man's unaided reason?

In rabbinic times, wisdom is synonymous with Torah. The tendency in medieval thought is to give wisdom its head but to incorporate this, too, under the heading of Torah. Greek physics and metaphysics thus not only become legitimate fields of study for the Jew but part of the Torah (Maim. Yad, Yesodei ha-Torah, 2:5).

LAW CODES AND BIBLICAL EXEGESIS. The great codes of Jewish law were compiled in this period, partly in response to the new demand for great systemization, partly because the laws were scattered through the voluminous talmudic literature and required to be brought together, so that the *posekim* could easily find the sources of their decisions. A further aim was to render decisions in cases of doubt.

In addition to the incorporation of secular learning into Torah, the scope of Torah studies proper was widened considerably. The Karaites were responsible for a new flowering of biblical scholarship. The Kabbalah was born, its devotees engaging in theosophical reflection on the biblical texts. According to the Kabbalah every detail of the precepts mirrored the supernal mysteries and the performance of the precepts consequently had the power of influencing the higher worlds. In the writings of the later kabbalists, Judaism becomes a mystery religion, its magical powers known only to the mystical adepts.

THEOLOGICAL SPECULATIONS. Under the impact of Greek thought the emphasis in medieval Jewish thinking among the philosophers is on the impersonal aspects of the

Deity. Not only is anthropomorphism rejected but the whole question of the divine attributes—of what can and cannot be said about God—receives the closest scrutiny. Baḥya ibn Paquda (*Duties of the Heart, Sha'ar ha-Yiḥud,* 10) and Maimonides (*Guide,* 1:31–60) allow only negative attributes to be used of the Deity; to say that God is wise is to say no more than that He is not ignorant. It is not to say anything about the reality of the divine nature in itself which must always remain utterly incomprehensible. In reaction to the philosophers' depersonalization of the Deity, the kabbalists, evidently under Gnostic influence, developed the doctrine of the *Sefirot,* the ten divine emanations by which the world is governed, though among the kabbalists, too, in the doctrine of *Ein Sof* ("the Limitless"), God as He is in Himself—the Neoplatonic idea of *deus absconditus*—is preserved. Indeed, from one point of view, the Kabbalah is more radical than the philosophers in that it negates all language from *Ein Sof.* The utterly impersonal ground is not mentioned in the Bible. Of it nothing can be said at all. No name can be given it except the negative one of "Nothing" (because of it, nothing can be postulated). By thus affirming both the impersonal ground and the dynamic life of the *Sefirot,* the kabbalists endeavor to satisfy the philosophical mind while catering to the popular need for the God of Abraham, Isaac, and Jacob.

The Period of Transition. The 18th century was a period of great ferment in Jewish life, the old world dying, the new not yet coming to birth. The pioneer Jewish historian Zunz correctly sees the Jewish Middle Ages as lasting until the end of this century. The repercussions following on the adventures of the pseudo-messiah Shabbetai Ẓevi caused Jewish leaders to retreat into the past. There was a fear of new tendencies in Jewish thought and a pronounced suspicion of mystical fervor. Yet revivalist tendencies were in the air, and not only among Jews. The century which saw the phenomenal successes of a Wesley in England, and movements addicted to what Father Ronald Knox calls "enthusiasm" in America and the European continent, also witnessed the rise of Ḥasidism. The three towering Jewish figures of this age each represented a prominent trend important at the time and influential for the future. R. Elijah b. Solomon, the Gaon of Vilna (1720–97), "the last great theologian of classical Rabbinism" (L. Ginzberg, *Students, Scholars and Saints* (1928), 125), spent his days and nights shut up in his study with drawn shutters and setting standards of utter devotion to Torah study in the classical sense as man's noblest pursuit. In the 16th century, Poland had become a home of Torah. The complete devotion there to talmudic studies on the part of so many was unparalleled. The Gaon was an outstanding but not untypical product of this type of hermit-like dedication. The old teaching (Avot 6:4), "This is the way of the Torah. Thou shalt eat bread with salt and thou shalt drink water by measure, and on the ground shalt thou sleep and thou shalt lead a life of suffering the while thou toilest in the Torah," became, in large measure through the Gaon's influence, the pattern for many thousands of talmudists in Russia, Poland, and Lithuania.

ḤASIDISM. It is extremely difficult to disentangle fact from legend in studying the life and work of R. Israel Ba'al Shem Tov (d. c. 1760), but Ḥasidism, the movement he founded—with its message that simple faith is superior to scholasticism untouched with fervor, that joy is to be invoked in God's service, and that there are "holy sparks" in all things to be redeemed by a life of sanctity—spread so rapidly, despite the most powerful opposition of established rabbinic authorities, that by the end of the 18th century it had won over to its side numerous Jewish communities in Galicia, the Ukraine, Poland, and Belorussia.

MENDELSSOHN AND THE ENLIGHTENMENT. Moses Mendelssohn (1729–86) is rightly looked upon as the pioneer in bringing the Jewish people face to face with the modern world. Religious truth, taught Mendelssohn, was universal and could be attained by the exercise of the free human reason. No special revelation was required. The Torah, for

Mendelssohn, is not revealed religion but revealed legislation. The eternal truths that there is a God, that He is good, and that man's soul is immortal are revealed in all places and at all times. Mendelssohn, thus speaking as a child of the Enlightenment, succeeded in paving the way for those Jews—and they were many—who wished to eat of its fruits. But Mendelssohn was not able to explain adequately why a special revelation to Israel was necessary if the basic truths were attainable by all men. What was the purpose of this special revealed legislation and, if it had value, why was this confined to a special group? He speaks of "a special favor" for "very special reasons," but nowhere states what these reasons were (M. A. Meyer, *The Origins of the Modern Jew* (1967), 37). Moreover his advice to his fellow Jews to comply with the customs and civil constitutions of the countries in which they lived while, at the same time, being constant to the faith of their forefathers, was easier said than done. Nevertheless no modern Jew is immune from Mendelssohn's influence, and, by the same token, opponents of any kind of modernism in the Jewish camp have laid all the ills of subsequent Jewish faithlessness at Mendelssohn's door.

With the possible exception of the Oriental communities, every Jew in the post-emancipation era, insofar as he strove to remain Jewishly committed, was a disciple of the Gaon, or the Ba'al Shem, or Mendelssohn, with many Jews disciples of more than one of these great figures at the same time.

The Emancipation. The entrance of the Jew into Western society at the beginning of the 19th century presented Judaism with a direct confrontation with modern thought without the long period of preparation and adjustment that had been available to Christendom since the Renaissance. On the practical side there were the problems connected with the new social conditions. How, for example, were Jews to participate in life in a non-Jewish environment without surrendering their distinctiveness and the claims of their ancient past? How were they to avoid being dubbed antisocial or outlandish? How were they to earn a living if they refused to work on the Sabbath? How were they to mix freely with their neighbors and keep the dietary laws? On the intellectual plane fresh challenges were being presented to the ancient faith by the new scientific viewpoints, by modern philosophy, by art, music, and literature, cultivated independently of any dogmatic considerations, and later, by the historical investigations into the Bible and Jewish origins. It was in Germany that Judaism had to bear the brunt of the new thinking, though, as evidenced by the emergence of a Russian Haskalah movement, other Jewries were not unaffected by the revolutionary trends.

THEOLOGICAL CHALLENGES. It is not surprising that atheism and agnosticism had their unprecedented appeal for some Jews, and Christianity in one form or another for others. But among the faithful, traditional theism remained the accepted philosophy of life until more recent years when a number of Jewish thinkers began to explore the possibility of a radical reinterpretation of theism in naturalistic terms. The main tensions, however, in post-emancipation Judaism centered on the ideas of Torah and Israel rather than God.

THE NATIONALISTIC QUESTION. With regard to Jewish peoplehood, the Zionist movement at the end of the century posed in acute form a problem which had agitated Jewish minds from the beginning of the century—the role of nationalism in Judaism. Were the Jews merely adherents of a common religion—as it was put, Germans, Frenchmen, Englishmen of the Mosaic persuasion—or were they a nation? Was Judaism dependent for its fullest realization on residence in the Holy Land, or was it desirable that Jews be dispersed in many lands to further there the "mission of Israel" in bringing God to mankind in the purest form of teaching? These questions were being asked, and the replies varied considerably. The early Reformers deleted from the prayer book all references to national restoration. Exile was not seen as an evil to be redressed but as an essential step in the fulfillment of the divine purpose.

22   The Reformers were not alone in their opposition to a

nationalistic interpretation of Judaism. When political Zionism became a practical policy for Jews, many of the Orthodox opposed it as a denial of Jewish messianism according to which, it was believed, the redemption would come through direct divine intervention, not at the hands of men. There were not lacking, however, religious leaders who advocated a form of religious Zionism, claiming that, as in other spheres, the divine blessing follows on prior human effort.

With the actual establishment of the State of Israel the older attitudes became academic. With the exception of the fringe groups of the Neturei Karta (Orthodox) and the American Council for Judaism (Reform), the majority of Jews now accept the special role the new state has to play as a spiritual center (over and above the haven of refuge it provides), while generally acknowledging that to uncover the full implications of this concept requires a good deal of fresh thinking. Some Orthodox thinkers have taken refuge in the notion of the establishment of the State of Israel as *athalta di-ge'ullah* ("the beginning of the redemption"), i.e., that while complete redemption is at the hands of God through the Messiah, the present life of the State still has messianic overtones and belongs in a realm far removed from the secular. Some see this as an unsuccessful attempt literally to have the best of both worlds.

THE QUESTION OF HALAKHAH. The great divide between Orthodoxy and Reform was on the question of Jewish law *(halakhah)*. According to the Orthodox position the traditional doctrine of *Torah min ha-Shamayim* ("the Torah is from Heaven") means that both the Written and the Oral Laws were communicated by God to Moses and that, therefore, all the Pentateuchal laws, in their interpretation as found in the rabbinic literature, are binding upon Jews by divine fiat. The Sabbath, for instance, is to be kept in the manner set forth in detail in the Talmud; the dietary laws are to be observed in all their minutiae. On this view nothing in the law is trivial or unworthy or out-of-date since every law is a direct command of God for all time. Reform

23

Judaism rejects the idea of a permanently binding religious law. In the Reform view, the moral law alone is eternally valid together with those religious ceremonies which are still capable of inspiring contemporary Jews to appreciate the beauty, dignity, and supreme worth of a God-orientated life. A middle of the road position was advocated by the followers of the historical school in Germany and later by the Conservative movement in the United States. On this view, Reform is in error in rejecting the *halakhah*, but Orthodoxy is also mistaken in wedding adherence to *halakhah* to a fundamentalism which recognizes no change or development in Jewish law.

Contemporary Judaism. There are a number of groupings in contemporary Orthodox Judaism. Reform has made little headway among Sephardi or Oriental Jews, and the majority of these, if religious, are at least Orthodox with many of their own rites and customs.

ORTHODOXY OF THE LITHUANIAN PATTERN. Among the Ashkenazim, possibly the most prominent Orthodox group is that represented by the yeshivot of the Lithuanian pattern and the rabbis educated in these institutions, most of them in Israel and the U.S. The main emphasis here is on Torah study, to the virtual exclusion of all else, and the carrying out of the detailed practical observances. In this group the stress is on intellectual comprehension, particularly of the difficult logic and reasoning of the Talmud, the most admired figure being the *lamdan,* the man proficient in these studies. Religious feeling and ethical content is provided by the Musar movement, which succeeded in capturing the Lithuanian yeshivot at the end of the last century. Secular learning is either entirely frowned upon or treated as necessary for earning a living, and little more.

NEO-ORTHODOXY. Neo-Orthodoxy (not generally called by this name) has a far more positive attitude to secular learning, with a particular fondness for the physical sciences. In this group are the followers of the Samson Raphael Hirsch school, which aims at combining Torah (i.e., strict adherence to *halakhah*) with *derekh erez* ("the way of the earth," in this context, the values of Western civilization). In this group, too, are the majority of Orthodox synagogues in the U.S. (the rabbis mainly alumni of Yeshiva University) and Great Britain (the rabbis mainly alumni of Jews College).

ḤASIDISM. The Ḥasidim still owe their allegiance to various dynasties of rabbis. Ḥasidism is emotional and mystical. Most of the Ḥasidim wear a special garb, consisting of a girdle for prayer, a long black coat, and fur hat. Beards are generally worn long and earlocks *(pe'ot)* cultivated. Ritual immersion plays an important part in ḥasidic life. The best-known ḥasidic rabbis with large followings today are the Lubavicher and the Satmarer in New York, and the Gerer, Viznitzer, and Belzer in Israel. Neo-Ḥasidism, as presented in the writings of Martin Buber, is not a movement but a mood of sympathy with some of the ḥasidic values as relevant to the spiritual predicament of Western man.

The two major world groupings of Orthodoxy, embracing members of all preceding groups, are the Zionist Mizrachi movement and the more right-wing Agudat Israel.

CONSERVATIVE JUDAISM. This movement is especially strong in the U.S. with its teaching center at the Jewish Theological Seminary in New York. It is organized in the United Synagogue of America and has sympathizers in other parts of the Jewish world. It has been said that while contemporary Reform stresses the God idea and contemporary Orthodoxy, the idea of Torah, Conservative Judaism stresses that of Israel (i.e., Jewish peoplehood). This is too much of a generalization, but it is true that an important plank in the Conservative platform is the unity of the Jewish people amid its diversity.

REFORM JUDAISM. This movement is strong in the U.S., with its teaching headquarters at the Hebrew Union College in Cincinnati, but with followers in other parts of the Jewish world. Reform congregations are loosely organized in the World Union of Progressive Synagogues. (The term "Traditional Judaism" is used, nowadays, to denote either Orthodox or Conservative Judaism. The term "Torah-true Judaism" is used by some of the Orthodox as a synonym for Orthodoxy in order to avoid the possible pejorative implications of the latter term as suggesting reaction or obscurantism. "Liberal Judaism" is the term used in Great Britain for the Reform position, though there are in Great Britain both Liberal and Reform congregations, with the Liberals more to the left.)

There are very few Reform or Conservative congregations in the State of Israel. Orthodoxy is the official religious position in Israel with the majority of the rabbis belonging to the old school of talmudic jurists. Here and there in recent years a number of small groups have emerged with the aim of seeking a religiously orientated outlook, but one not necessarily Orthodox.

2 ARTICLES OF FAITH

The term "dogma" which is so extensively and definitely expounded in Christianity has as such no place in Judaism. In Judaism the need for a profession of belief did not arise and rabbinic synods saw no necessity for drawing up concise formulas expressing Jewish beliefs. Theologically speaking, every Jew is born into God's covenant with the people of Israel, and membership in the community does not depend on credal affirmations of a formal character. Jewish beliefs are voiced in the form of prayer and in the twice-daily recital of the *Shema*.

In Rabbinic Literature. Outside the liturgy, formulations of specific aspects of the Jewish faith abound in rabbinic literature from the Mishnah onward. The need to define the Jewish position vis-à-vis heretical views even in talmudic times occasioned the statement of the Mishnah (Sanh. 10:1) that, while all Israelites have a share in the world to come, it is withheld from those who deny the resurrection of the dead, the divine origin of the Torah, and from the "Epicurean." This statement comes close to formulating "dogmas" of Judaism, yet it is neither couched in the form of a credal affirmation nor is it comprehensive enough to serve as a total expression of Jewish beliefs. However, its insertion into the Mishnah invests it with authority, and it can readily be seen why Maimonides' famous formulation of 13 principles of Judaism was offered as a kind of elaboration of this particular passage. The formulation of articles of Jewish faith is largely a medieval development, even though Philo (first century C.E.) had spoken of eight essential principles of scriptural religion: (1) existence of God; (2) His unity; (3) divine providence; (4) creation of 27 the world; (5) unity of the world; (6) the existence of incorporeal ideas; (7) the revelation of the Law; and (8) its eternity (H. A. Wolfson, *Philo, Foundations of Religious Philosophy*, 1 (1947), 164ff.). In the Middle Ages it arose from the theological discussions which had started in Muslim *Kalām* and which then had spread to Jewish circles. The term *ikkarim* (lit. "roots"), the most widely used Hebrew term denoting the "principles" of Judaism, is a literal translation of the Arabic *uṣūl* denoting the "roots" of various disciplines (*Kalām;* the science of *Ḥadīth* or "tradition"; jurisprudence). The term *uṣūl al-dīn* ("the roots of religion") is synonymous with *Kalām*. In this sense Maimonides refers to the theologians employing the methods of *Kalām* as people concerned with *uṣūl al-dīn* (*ikkarei ha-dat; Guide* 3:51). Maimonides' formulation of articles of faith was not without precedent. Hananel b. Ḥushi'el declared that faith is fourfold: belief (1) in God; (2) in the prophets; (3) in the world to come; and (4) in the advent of the Messiah. Among the Karaites the first enumeration of fundamental Jewish beliefs is found in Judah Hadassi's (middle of the 12th century) *Eshkol ha-Kofer*. This author lists ten articles *(ishurim)* of faith: (1) God's unity and wisdom; (2) His eternity and unlikeness to any other being; (3) He is the Creator of the world; (4) Moses and the rest of the prophets were sent by God; (5) the Torah which has been given through Moses is true; (6) the Jews are obliged to study the Hebrew language in order to be able to understand the Torah fully; (7) the holy Temple in Jerusalem was chosen by God as the eternal dwelling place of His glory; (8) the dead will be resurrected; (9) there will be a Divine judgement; and (10) God will mete out reward and punishment. It is not clear whether Judah Hadassi offered this statement as an innovation on his part or whether he followed earlier authorities.

Maimonides. Maimonides' "Thirteen Principles" are set down in his commentary on the Mishnah by way of introducing his comments on *Sanhedrin* 10. Writing in Arabic, Maimonides presents these articles of faith as *uṣūl* ("roots") and *qawāʿid* ("fundamentals") of Jewish beliefs *(iʿtiqādāt)* and of the Law *(sharīʿa)*. The Hebrew versions render *uṣūl* by *ikkarim* and *qawāʿid* by either *yesodot* or *ikkarim*. The term *uṣūl* acquires here a new meaning: it no longer denotes the topics of the *Kalām* investigations, but the fundamental tenets of faith or the concise abstracts of religion as seen through the eyes of a philosopher. Maimonides undertook such a presentation to teach the rank and file of the community the true spiritual meaning of the belief in the world to come *(ha-olam ha-ba)* and to disabuse their minds of crude, materialistic notions. Since the ultimate felicity of man depends on the possession of true concepts concerning God, the formulation and brief exposition of true notions in the realm of faith is meant to help the multitude to avoid error and to purify belief. The "fundamentals" listed by Maimonides are: (1) The existence of God which is perfect and sufficient unto itself and which is the cause of the existence of all other beings. (2) God's unity which is unlike all other kinds of unity. (3) God must not be conceived in bodily terms, and the anthropomorphic expressions applied to God in Scripture have to be understood in a metaphorical sense. (4) God is eternal. (5) God alone is to be worshiped and obeyed. There are no mediating powers able freely to grant man's petitions, and intermediaries must not be invoked. (6) Prophecy. (7) Moses is unsurpassed by any other prophet. (8) The entire Torah was given to Moses. (9) Moses' Torah will not be abrogated or superseded by another divine law nor will anything be added to, or taken away from it. (10) God knows the actions of men. (11) God rewards those who fulfill the commandments of the Torah, and punishes those who transgress them. (12) The coming of the Messiah. (13) The resurrection of the dead.

In a postscript Maimonides distinguishes between the "sinners of Israel" who, while having yielded to their passions, are not thereby excluded from the Jewish community or the world to come, and one who "has denied a root principle" *(kafar be-ikkar)*. Such an individual has excluded himself from the community and is called a heretic (*min*) and Epicurean. Maimonides thus attempted to invest his principles with the character of dogma, by making them criteria of orthodoxy and membership in the community of Israel; but it should be noted that his statement was a personal one and remained open to criticism and revision.

In their credal form ("I believe with perfect faith that . . . ") Maimonides' "Thirteen Principles" appeared first probably in the Venice *Haggadah* of 1566. They are found in the Ashkenazi prayer book as an appendix to the regular morning service. Of the many poetic versions, the best known is the popular *Yigdal* hymn (c. 1300). This hymn has been adopted in practically all rites.

Maimonides' "Thirteen Principles" became the prototype of a succession of formulations of the Jewish creed which first merely varied in the number, order, and the articles of belief selected, but which eventually (in the 15th century) introduced methodological criteria for determining whether a certain belief could be regarded as fundamental. The discussion was at no time purely academic. It was stimulated to the controversy over the allegorical interpretations of traditional beliefs according to Aristotelian doctrine, and it focused on such articles of faith as *creatio ex nihilo*, individual providence, etc. The formulation of *ikkarim* was designed to accentuate the vital beliefs of Judaism and to strengthen Orthodoxy. It was also meant to define the position of the Jewish faith as regards to Christianity.

The Thirteenth and Fourteenth Centuries. In the 13th century David b. Samuel d'Estella and Abba Mari Astruc b. Moses b. Joseph of Lunel offered fresh formulations of the creed. David d'Estella in his (unpublished) *Migdal David* uses the term *ikkarim* to refer to the three elements of Judaism: (1) commandments; (2) beliefs; and (3) the duty to engage in philosophical speculation in order fully to understand the Torah (M. Steinschneider, *Hebr. Bibliographie*, 8 (1865), 63, 100–3). The "beliefs" are outlined in great detail under seven heads called "pillars" (*ammudim*) of the faith: (1) creation of the world; (2) freedom of the will; (3) divine providence; (4) divine origin of the Torah; (5) reward and punishment; (6) the coming of the Redeemer; and (7) resurrection. The author claims that these articles follow a logical order. Abba Mari, a defender of Orthodoxy in the Maimonidean controversy, arranged, in his *Minhat Kena'ot* (ed. by M. Bisliches, 1838), Jewish beliefs under three principles: (1) God is eternal, incorporeal, and His unity is absolute simplicity (7–11); (2) *creatio ex nihilo* and its corollary, miracles (11–16); (3) God's individual providence (17–19). In the 14th century, Shemariah of Negropont (Crete), an Italian philosopher and exegete (d. after 1352), chiefly known for his efforts to reconcile Karaites and Rabbanites, presented five principles of Judaism relating to the existence of God: (1) incorporeality; (2) absolute unity; (3) creation; (4) creation in time; and (5) by a divine *fiat* (M. Steinschneider, *Catalogue . . . Muenchen*, no. 210). Another philosophical writer, David b. Yom Tov ibn Bilia of Portugal, in a treatise called *Yesodot ha-Maskil* (published in E. Ashkenazi's *Divrei Ḥakhamim* (1849), no. 8) supplemented Maimonides' 13 articles by 13 of his own. These additional principles include such dogmas as belief in angels, in the superiority of the Torah over philosophy, in the canonicity of the text of the Torah, and in good actions as a reward in themselves. In spite of their stress on the superiority of the Torah they bear a highly intellectual flavor.

Fifteenth and Sixteenth Centuries. The 15th century and the beginning of the 16th are particularly rich in works on Jewish dogmatics. Some of them are based on strictly methodological considerations, while others stress the purely revelational character of Jewish beliefs. To the first category belong the writings of Ḥasdai Crescas, Simeon b. Ẓemaḥ Duran, Joseph Albo, and Elijah Delmedigo; to the second, those of Isaac Arama, Joseph Jabez and Isaac Abrabanel.

ḤASDAI CRESCAS. Crescas' *Or Adonai* (completed in 1410) is essentially a treatise on dogmatics, the structure of which is determined by a sharp differentiation between various categories of belief. (1) The existence, (2) unity, and (3) incorporeality of God (1:3) form the three root principles (shoresh ve-hathalah) of Judaism. A second group of beliefs comprises the six fundamentals (yesodot) or pillars (ammudim) of the Jewish faith without whose recognition the concept of Torah loses its meaning (2: 1–6): (1) God's knowledge of all beings; (2) His providence; (3) His omnipotence; (4) prophecy; (5) free will; and (6) the purpose of the Torah as instilling in man the love of God and thereby helping him to achieve eternal felicity. The third group represents true beliefs characteristic of Judaism and indispensable for Orthodoxy, yet not fundamental (3:1–8; part 2:1–3). Eight in number, they are: (1) creation of the world; (2) immortality of the soul; (3) reward and punishment; (4) resurrection; (5) immutability of the Torah; (6) supremacy of Moses' prophecy; (7) divine instruction of the high priests by way of the Urim and Thummim; and (8) the coming of the Messiah. In addition there are three true beliefs connected with specific commandments: (1) prayers are answered by God; (2) repentance is acceptable to God; and (3) the Day of Atonement and the holy seasons are ordained by God. Finally Crescas lists 13 problems concerning which reason is the arbiter; these include such questions as: will the world last forever; are there more worlds than one; are the celestial spheres animate and rational; do the motions of the celestial bodies influence the affairs of men; are amulets and magic efficacious?

SIMEON BEN ZEMAH DURAN. Simeon b. Zemah Duran deals with the problem of dogmatics in his *Ohev Mishpat* (written in 1405; published, Venice, 1589) and *Magen Avot* (3 parts, Leghorn, 1785). He arranges Maimonides' 13 articles under three principles (ikkarim): (1) existence of God (implying His unity, incorporeality, eternity, and His being the only object of rightful worship); (2) revelation (implying prophecy, Moses' supremacy as a prophet, the divine origin of the Torah and its immutability); (3) reward and punishment (implying God's knowledge of things, providence, the coming of the Messiah, resurrection). He finds these three dogmas indicated in the statement of the Mishnah Sanhedrin 10:1 (see above). He also mentions earlier attempts to reduce the dogmas to three, and draws a distinction between basic principles of the Torah and other beliefs, the denial of which do not constitute heresy but mere error.

JOSEPH ALBO. Albo's *Sefer ha-Ikkarim*, the most popular work on Jewish dogmatics, is indebted to both Crescas and Duran. Albo criticizes Maimonides' selection of principles, and finds some fault also with Crescas. Like Duran he finds his basic articles in three "root principles" *(ikkarim)*. (1) existence of God; (2) divine origin of the Torah; and (3) reward and punishment. From these "root principles" stem derivative "roots" *(shorashim)* which, together with the former, constitute the divine Law. The existence of God implies His unity, incorporeality, independence of time, and freedom from defects. The divine origin of the Torah implies God's knowledge, prophecy, and the authenticity of divine messengers or lawgivers. Reward and punishment implies individual (in addition to general) providence (1:13-15). Of lower rank, although obligatory, are six beliefs *(emunot)*, the denial of which does not constitute heresy: (1) the creation of the world in time and *ex nihilo;* (2) the supremacy of Moses' prophecy; (3) the immutability of the Torah; (4) the attainment of the bliss of the next world by the fulfillment of a single commandment; (5) resurrection; (6) coming of the Messiah (1:23).

ELIJAH DELMEDIGO. Elijah Delmedigo's *Behinat ha-Dat* (written in 1496, ed. by I.S. Reggio, 1833) is the last of the medieval works on Jewish dogmatics with a strong philosophic orientation. It reflects the doctrine of the "double truth" propounded by the Christian Averroists. Delmedigo distinguishes between the basic dogmas *(shorashim)* which have to be accepted without interpretation *(perush; be'ur)* by masses and philosophers alike, and ramifications *(anafim)* which the masses must accept literally, while the philosophers are required to search for their deeper meaning. For Delmedigo Maimonides' 13 articles belong to the category of basic dogmas. Some of them he holds to be verifiable by reason (existence, unity and incorporeality of God), while the rest have to be taken on trust. The 13 articles are reducible to three: (1) existence of God; (2) prophecy; and (3) reward and punishment. Such topics as the "reasons of the commandments" belong to the category of ramifications as does the whole field of rabbinic *aggadah*. Here the philosopher must exercise great caution in publicizing his interpretations in areas where allegorizing may do harm to the unsophisticated.

ISAAC ARAMA. Isaac Arama in his *Akedat Yizhak* criticizes Crescas and Albo who saw as the criterion for a "fundamental" of Judaism whether a certain belief was basic to the general concept of revelation, an approach which had tacitly equated Torah with revealed religion in a universal rational sense. According to Arama the Torah reveals principles above and supplementary to reason. Hence a belief in the existence, unity, eternity, and simplicity of God cannot rank as a principle of the Torah (Maimonides and his followers) nor can free will and purpose (Crescas). The principles *(ikkarim)* of the Torah have to be discovered in the Torah itself. They are embedded in the commandments *(mitzvot),* particularly in the laws relating to the Sabbath and the festivals. Arama counts six "principles of the faith" *(ikkarei ha-emunah):* (1) the createdness of the world (Sabbath); (2) God's omnipotence (Passover); (3) prophecy and divine revelation (Feast of Weeks); (4) providence (New Year); (5) repentance (Day of Atonement); (6) the world to come (Tabernacles; ch. 67; in ch. 55 the Sabbath is described as implying all the six principles). Arama lays particular stress on the dogma of creation as the essential dogma of the Torah (ch. 67).

JOSEPH JABEẒ. Akin in spirit to Arama are his two contemporaries Joseph Jabeẓ and Isaac Abrabanel. Jabeẓ wrote two small treatises on dogmatics, called *Ma'amar ha-Ahdut* and *Yesod ha-Emunah* (first published together with his *Or ha-Hayyim* in Ferrara, 1554). In the first he rejects Maimonides', Crescas', and Albo's formulations of principles, substituting three of his own, all of which are explications of divine unity: (1) God alone is the Creator; (2) God alone is wondrously active in exercising providence; and (3) God alone will be worshiped in the messianic future. In the second he maintains that Maimonides' 13 principles are traceable to these three, but he now formulates them as: (1) createdness of the world *(hiddush ha-olam)*; (2) providence; and (3) unity of God. The third dogma implies that God alone will be worshiped in the messianic future. In both treatises the belief in creation is considered the most fundamental principle.

ISAAC ABRABANEL. Isaac Abrabanel's *Rosh Amanah* (written from 1499 to 1502) is a closely argued treatise on the "roots and principles" of the Jewish faith. Twenty-two of the work's 24 chapters are devoted to an analysis of Maimonides', Crescas', and Albo's respective positions. Abrabanel raises 28 "doubts" or objections to Maimonides' formulation of the creed, but, resolving these questions, he arrives at a complete vindication of Maimonides' views, while those of Crescas and Albo are found wanting. Abrabanel's own attitude, however, is close to Isaac Arama's. The search for "fundamental principles" has its place only in the human sciences which operate with "fundamental principles" that are either self-evident or borrowed from other, more fundamental, sciences. In the case of the Torah, divinely revealed, there is no exterior frame of reference that could furnish the fundamental principles of its laws and beliefs; everything contained therein has to be believed and there is no sense in trying to establish principles of Jewish belief. Were he to single out one principle of the divine Torah, Abrabanel states, he would select that of the createdness of the world (ch. 22).

Spinoza. The medieval Jewish philosophical tradition is still reflected in Spinoza who in his *Tractatus Theologico-Politicus* (publ. 1670) formulates seven "dogmas of universal faith" or "fundamental principles which Scripture as a whole aims to convey": (1) God's existence; (2) unity; (3) omnipresence; (4) supreme authority and power; (5) man's worship of Him in obedience, (6) the felicity of the obedient; (7) forgiveness of penitent sinners (ch. 14). Spinoza's scriptural religion stands between the "universal religion" of the philospher and the "religion of the masses" (Introd.; chs. 4, 7).

Modern Period. Moses Mendelssohn, the pioneer of the modern phase in Judaism, formulates the following principles of the Jewish religion: (1) God, the author and ruler of all things, is one and simple; (2) God knows all things, rewards the good and punishes evil by natural and, sometimes, supernatural means; (3) God has made known His laws in the Scriptures given through Moses to the children of Israel. Mendelssohn rejects the Christian dogmas of the trinity, original sin, etc. as incompatible with reason, and stresses the harmony between religion and reason within Judaism (*Betrachtungen ueber Bonnets Palingenesie*, in *Gesammelte Schriften*, 3 (1843), 159–66). The truths to be recognized by the Jew are identical with the eternal verities of reason, and they do not depend on a divine revelation. Only the laws of Judaism are revealed. Hence the Jewish religion does not prescribe belief nor does it lay down dogmas (symbols, articles of faith). The Hebrew term *emunah* means "trust" in the divine promises.

Nineteenth and Twentieth Centuries. Mendelssohn's distinction between the rational truths of Judaism and the revealed laws of the Torah did not appeal to the reformers of the 19th century, but it pervaded the catechisms and manuals of the Jewish religion written by the disciples of Mendelssohn in the early part of the century. It soon came up against opposition once the impact of Kant's critique of rational theology made itself felt. Moreover, Hegel's speculative interpretation of Christianity as the "absolute religion" was felt as a serious challenge. Solomon Formstecher's *Religion des Geistes* (1841) and Samuel Hirsch's *Religionsphilosophie der Juden* (1842) presented in their turn Judaism as the "absolute religion." In this changed climate of opinion Manuel Joel (*Zur Orientierung in der Cultusfrage*, 1869) spoke of dogmas in Judaism as the essential prerequisite of its cult and ritual. Abraham Geiger agreed with his repudiation of Mendelssohn and stressed the wealth of "ideas" with which Judaism entered history. He denied, however, the validity of the term "dogma" as applied to the Jewish religion, since the absence of ultimately fixed formulations of Jewish beliefs rendered the term "dogma" illegitimate. David Einhorn, on the other hand, had no objection to using this term (*Das Prinzip des Mosaismus* (1854), 11–13). The same view was strongly expressed by Leopold Loew (*Juedische Dogmen* (1871), 138–49). The formulations of the Jewish creed by a number of Jewish theologians of the latter part of the 19th century manifest the strongly felt desire to offer some clear guidance on the essential affirmations of Judaism. To these belong Samuel Hirsch's *Systematischer Katechismus der israelitischen Religion* (1856); Solomon Formstecher's *Mosaische Religionslehre* (1860); and Joseph Aub's *Grundlage zu einem wissenschaftlichen Unterricht in der mosaischen Religion* (1865). The Orthodox creed found its powerful spokesman in Samson Raphael Hirsch who in his *Choreb, Versuche ueber Jissroels Pflichten in der Zerstreuung* (1837; *Horeb: a Philosophy of Jewish Laws and Observances*, 1962) sought to interpret Judaism from within *halakhah*, expressing the view that "The catechism of the Jew is his calendar." Samuel David Luzzatto's *Yesodei ha-Torah* appeared in 1880, and Michael Friedlaender's *The Jewish Religion* in 1896. It was followed by Morris Joseph's *Judaism as Creed and Life* in 1903. Julien Weil wrote *La Foi d'Israel* (1926). Mordecai M. Kaplan discussed "Creeds and Wants" in his *Judaism in Transition* (1941), 206–38. A later formulation of Jewish beliefs is given in the form of an epitome of Hermann Cohen's *Religion der Vernunft* in his *The Purpose and Meaning of Jewish Existence* (1964). A modification of Maimonides' creed in the light of modern biblical criticism is offered by Louis Jacobs in his *The Principles of Judaism* (1964).

3 TRADITION

The term tradition (Heb. מָסֹרֶת, "*masoret*") derives from the Latin *tradere,* which means "to transmit" or "to give over." Generally, it refers to beliefs, doctrines, customs, ethical and moral standards, and cultural values and attitudes which are transmitted orally or by personal example. Under this designation, the process of transmission itself is also included. Theologically, in Judaism, tradition is the name applied to the unwritten code of law given by God to Moses on Mount Sinai.

Terms. *Masoret* is the general name for tradition. It is found in Ezekiel 20:37 and means originally "bond" or "fetter." Tradition is the discipline which establishes the correct practice and interpretation of the Torah and was therefore regarded as a hedge or fetter about the Law (Avot 3:14). Since this knowledge was handed down by successive generations, it was also associated with the Hebrew word *masor,* denoting "to give over." In the talmudic literature, the term *masoret* is used to include all forms of tradition, both those which relate to the Bible and those which concern custom, law, historical events, folkways, and other subjects. Different kinds of traditions were given special names. Traditions which specified the vocalization, punctuation, spelling, and correct form of the biblical text were called *masorah.* Those legal traditions which were revealed to Moses at Mount Sinai and were later preserved in writing, were known as *Halakhah le-Moshe mi-Sinai* ("law given to Moses on Sinai"). A legal tradition which was handed down by word of mouth, but did not necessarily emanate from Sinai, was called *shemu'ah* ("a report"). Religious and general traditions which became binding as the result of observance by successive generations were termed *minhag* ("custom"). Prophetic traditions described in the books of the prophets and Hagiographa were known as *Divrei Kabbalah* ("words of tradition"). Esoteric and mystical traditions concerning God and the world transmitted to the elect and then passed down through the ages were called Kabbalah, from *kibbel* ("to receive").

Origin. Many statutes were committed to writing by Moses. However, the vast majority of laws were handed down orally by him i.e., the Written and the Oral Law. The Written Law did not always detail the manner and form of practice, giving rise of necessity to tradition. An instance of this kind is the law relating to fish which meet the biblical dietary requirements. Leviticus 11:9 states that a fish that has a fin and a scale in the water can be eaten. However, the minimum number of fins and scales that a fish must have to be ritually edible is not specified. The traditions relating to the Bible and Mishnah taught that a fish needs at least one fin and two scales to satisfy the biblical dietary requirements (see Arukh, s.v. *Akunos*). Similarly, the Bible commands that a paschal lamb be slaughtered on the 14th day of Nisan. There is no mention in the Bible as to whether it is permissible to perform this act if the 14th day of Nisan occurs on the Sabbath when the slaughtering of animals is forbidden. In the year 31 B.C.E., the 14th of Nisan fell on the Sabbath. The Sons of Bathyra, the heads of the high court, forgot the precedent previously established. Hillel, a then unknown Babylonian, volunteered the information that he had heard from Shemaiah and Avtalyon, the foremost teachers of the age, that it was permissible to slaughter the paschal lamb on the Sabbath. This reported tradition of Hillel's mentors was readily accepted (TJ, Pes. 6:1, 33a), and it is mentioned that because of this display of erudition with regard to tradition, Hillel was appointed *nasi.* Tradition was also the vehicle of transmission for the rules of interpretation of the Written Law, such as the laws of hermeneutics. Since it was impossible within the confines of writing to record all the laws and their applications in all situations, a medium was needed to preserve this information. Even today, with the availability of writing media, much of our culture is handed down orally. Tradition was the means whereby extant law was maintained and applied to life. Thus R. Joshua b. Levi declared that all teachings both of the Bible, Mishnah, Talmud, and *aggadah* and those that were initiated by veteran scholars were already given to Moses on Mount Sinai (see TJ, Pe'ah 2:6, 17a). Some traditions arose as a result of the common practice of the community. These practices were considered to emanate from eminent religious authorities and owed their binding character to having been handed down by previous generations, from father to son, a principle upheld by R. Johanan in the Talmud. The citizens of Beth-Shean complained to him that the custom of not going from Tyre to Sidon on the eve of the Sabbath was impossible for them to observe. R. Johanan replied, "Your fathers have already taken it (this custom) upon themselves" (Pes. 50b). As a result, this tradition could not be abrogated.

History. In rabbinic Judaism, tradition was binding and had the force of law. The divine revelation to Moses consisted of the Written Law and Oral Law with its implied exposition by the sages of Israel. *Berakhot* 5a tells that R. Levi b. Ḥama said in the name of R. Simeon b. Lakish: "What is the meaning of the verse, 'and I will give thee the tables of stone, and the law and the commandments, which I have written to teach them' [Ex. 24:12]. It means as follows: 'the tables of stone' are the Ten Commandments, 'the law' is the Pentateuch, 'the commandments' is the Mishnah, 'which I have written' are the prophets and the Hagiographa, 'to teach them' is the *Gemara*. This teaches us that all these things were given at Sinai." Originally, the Oral Law was handed down by word of mouth. When its transmission became difficult, it was set down in writing in the Mishnah and Talmud. The validity of the Oral Law was attacked by the Sadducees, one of the early sects in Judaism. Josephus records that the Sadducees held that "only those observances are obligatory which are in the written word but that those which derived from the tradition of the forefathers need not be kept" (Ant. 13:297).

Talmudic Times. After the destruction of the Temple, the Sadducees disappeared. The body of tradition continued to grow as rites were introduced to replace the Temple ritual. *Megillah* 31b pictures the patriarch Abraham as concerned with how Israel could obtain forgiveness, once the Temple ceased to exist. God assures Abraham, "I have already ordained for them the order of the sacrifices. Every time that they read them, it is considered as if they offer up a sacrifice and I forgive them all their sins." After the destruction of the Temple, the system of public prayer was instituted to substitute for the Temple service. The liturgical traditions were handed down verbally, through the centuries, until they were compiled in the prayer book of Amram Gaon.

Medieval Times. At the end of the eighth century, rabbinic Judaism was again challenged by a new sect, the Karaites. They accepted the authority of the Bible but denied rabbinical tradition and law, which had developed further as the Mishnah and Talmud were elucidated and applied to life. Through its great exponents, Saadiah and Maimonides, rabbinic Judaism triumphed over the Karaites. The latter wrote his code of law, *Mishneh Torah* ("The Second Torah"), and showed the direct connection between the Written Law and its explanation in the Oral Law (Introd. Maim. Yad). As new situations arose, the talmudic, geonic, and post-geonic traditions were further amplified. They in turn were set down in writing in the responsa and codes. In the 16th century R. Joseph Caro produced his definitive code, the Shulḥan Arukh. With the addition of the glosses of R. Moses Isserles and later commentaries, it became the most comprehensive compendium of Jewish law and tradition to this day.

Modern Times. At the end of the 18th century rabbinic Judaism, which had maintained an unbroken chain of tradition from the days of Moses was again challenged. A Reform movement began in Germany which sought to assimilate the Jews into the general culture by modifying Jewish traditions. Among the reforms instituted were sermons in the German vernacular, hymns and chorals in German, the use of the organ, and the confirmation of boys on the Feast of Pentecost instead of the traditional bar mitzvah. In the course of time, this movement established itself in America. Here it continued to propound its doctrine that Judaism was primarily a universalistic and moral religion. Only the moral law was binding. Ceremonial laws which could be adapted to the views of the modern environment were to be maintained. Other Mosaic and rabbinic laws which regulated diet, priestly purity, and dress could be discarded.

In reaction to the reformers' break with tradition, the Conservative movement was formed in America. At the founding meeting of its congregational organization in 1913, it declared itself "a union of congregations for the promotion of traditional Judaism." Other aims were the furtherance of Sabbath observance and dietary laws, and the maintenance of the traditional liturgy with Hebrew as the language of prayer. As the complexion of American Jewry changed, the Conservative movement incorporated some Reform externals of worship such as family pews and the use of the organ in many congregations. However, it accepted the authority of rabbinic tradition, instituting changes advocated by its scholars, with regard for the attitude of the people and the place of the observance in Jewish tradition.

Transmitters of the Tradition. In rabbinic literature the chain of tradition is given as follows: Moses received the Torah on Sinai and delivered it to Joshua, who in turn delivered it to the elders, the elders to the prophets, and the prophets to the Men of the Great Synagogue (Avot 1:1). According to rabbinic Judaism, the teaching of the great sages in every generation in keeping with the *halakhah* is binding (Deut. 17:88). Thus, the transmitters of tradition included the successors to the Men of the Great Synagogue down to modern times, namely: the scribes *(soferim),* the pairs *(zugot)*, the *tannaim*, the *amoraim*, the *savoraim*, the *geonim*, the codifiers, the world famous Torah authorities of every era, and the *rashei ha-yeshivah* ("heads of the academies").

Significance. Tradition has given Judaism a continuity with its past and preserved its character as a unique faith with a distinct way of life. As the successor of rabbinic Judaism, Orthodoxy representing tradition harks back to the Sinaitic divine revelation and can only be changed within the framework of rabbinic law. In Conservative Judaism, tradition is a vital force capable of modification according to the historical evolution of Jewish law. Reform Judaism has recently displayed a greater appreciation of traditional practices but tradition remains voluntary in character.

Part Two:

MONOTHEISM

1 MONOTHEISM

Monotheism, in its literal meaning, is the oneness of the godhead (i.e., one God). The concept of monotheism is embedded in the domain of religious discourse, and its full and relevant significance must be derived from the connotation which it carries within this domain. Monotheism is usually attributed to biblical faith as its unique and distinct contribution to the history of religious thought. The significance of the word monotheism in its biblical context is taken to lie in the "mono," in the godhead's being one: As such, it is contrasted with paganism, the fundamental religious alternative to biblical faith, whose distinctive religious concept is taken to be polytheism, i.e., the plurality of the godhead (many gods). The difference between the biblical and pagan orientation is thus constituted here as a mere arithmetical difference, a difference between one and many gods. On this basis, biblical monotheism is seen by modern biblical scholars as emerging gradually and in a continuous line from the polytheistic thought of paganism. The mediating stage in such a development is found in monolatry, where the godhead is reduced to one only as far as worship is concerned, while ontologically there is a plurality of gods. It is a mediating stage inasmuch as the arithmetical reduction to oneness is partial. The full reduction of the godhead in all its aspects to oneness emerges from monolatry only later in biblical classical prophecy, when God is claimed not only as the one God of Israel but as the one God of universal history. Here, by drawing the arithmetical reduction to oneness in all the aspects of the godhead, biblical faith achieves ultimately its distinctive, unique character. It is observed, however, that an ontological arithmetical unity of the godhead is achieved also in paganism, even with a remarkable degree of purity (e.g., Plotinus). It must be concluded, therefore, that paganism too has a monotheistic formulation. Yet it is generally felt that a fundamental difference between biblical faith and paganism does exist, and that this difference is expressed in the respective concepts of monotheism. This difference, however, cannot be accounted for on the basis of monotheism understood as the arithmetical oneness of the godhead.

Theistic Monotheism. Consequently, it has been suggested that the difference between biblical and pagan monotheism lies in the fact that the former is theistic while the latter is pantheistic. While it is true that biblical monotheism is exclusively theistic and that pagan monotheism has a definite tendency toward pantheism, to formulate the difference between biblical and pagan monotheism on this basis is to formulate the difference with regard to a totally different aspect of the godhead from that to which the concept of monotheism refers. Monotheism refers to the being of the godhead as such, while theism and pantheism refer to the relation subsisting between the godhead and the world. Thus, while this attempt locates a difference which may follow from the fundamental difference within the concept of monotheism, it does not locate that fundamental difference itself.

Ethical Monotheism. The same point can be made regarding yet another attempt to locate the difference between biblical and pagan monotheism, according to which biblical monotheism is ethical while pagan monotheism is purely philosophical-ontological. Correlated to this is the suggestion that, while paganism arrives at the oneness of its godhead through philosophical reasoning and because of ontological-metaphysical considerations, biblical faith arrives at the oneness of its godhead because of ethical considerations and through a direct insight into the absolute character of the moral law. Thus, biblical monotheism can be distinguished from pagan monotheism in that it alone is ethical monotheism. Here again, however, the distinction is located in an aspect to which the concept of monotheism as such does not refer; the concept of monotheism as such conveys no ethical connotation. It may be that this distinction follows from the proper understanding of the difference between the meaning of monotheism in the biblical context and its use in the context of paganism, but this distinction as such does not capture this difference. In attempting to define the difference it is interesting first to note that the two formulations above have already shifted the aspect where the difference is to be located from the "mono" to the "theos" part of the concept of monotheism; the theistic-pantheistic distinction refers to the relation of the "theos" to the world while the ethical-metaphysical distinction refers to what kind of a "theos" is involved. This means that the difference between biblical faith and paganism is no longer seen as a quantitative difference, i.e., how many gods are involved, but as a qualitative difference, i.e., what kind of a god is involved. This shift is essential to a proper understanding of the difference and must form the basis of the attempted formulation.

Ultimate Being. On this basis it can be asserted that the minimal necessary connotation of the term "theos" in the concept of monotheism is that of ultimate being. As such, the arithmetical comparison between biblical monotheism and pagan polytheism is clearly seen to be illegitimate. The "theos" in pagan polytheism is not ultimate. It is superhuman, or "man writ large," but still it remains finite and non-absolute. In polytheism a plurality of ultimate beings is untenable and self-contradictory. Consequently, the "theos" in biblical monotheism and the "theos" in pagan polytheism connote two different kinds of being, for the difference between ultimate and non-ultimate being is not merely quantitative but qualitative. It is not legitimate, however, to compare quantitatively entities which belong to different orders of being. In order to locate the difference meaningfully it must be determined with reference to the 48   same kind of entity, i.e., to the ultimate being which is connoted by the concept of monotheism. As such, however, it is not correct to speak of the development of the concept of monotheism in paganism. Paganism always had a conception of ultimate being transcending its gods and, as indicated above, ultimate being necessitates oneness. There can be no development from many to one with regard to ultimate being. Thus, if the "theos" in monotheism signifies ultimate being, paganism always had a conception of monotheism. The only development that can be pointed to is a development in its articulation, i.e., a development from the cultic-mythological to the speculative-philosophical expression. If the "theos" in monotheism, however, signifies only ultimate being, then it would not be possible to locate any difference between biblical and pagan monotheism, for then the "mono" conveys no additional information which is not already conveyed by the "theos" in itself. In order for the concept of monotheism to have a distinct meaning, the "theos" has to stand for something more than ultimate being. It is here that the real, fundamental difference between pagan and biblical monotheism becomes evident.

Personal Monotheism. In biblical monotheism the "theos" stands for a god who is personal. The "mono" connotes essentially not arithmetical oneness but oneness in the sense of uniqueness. Ultimate being is uniquely one in that it excludes the existence of any other qualitatively similar being. Thus, the authentic meaning of biblical monotheism is the assertion that the "mono," i.e., the unique, the ultimate, is "theos," i.e., a personal being, and this is the distinctive and unique feature of biblical faith and its monotheistic formulation. Paganism, while it too always had a conception of ultimate being and thus a conception of a unitary being, never asserted that ultimate being is personal. It follows from this analysis that the development of biblical monotheism from paganism cannot be envisioned as a linear, continuous development, but must be seen as a "jump" from one orbit to another, for the change that biblical monotheism introduced is qualitative and not quantitative. There is no continuous line of development either from nonpersonal to personal being or from relative being to ultimate being. This development involves a shift in perspective. While the above articulates the distinctive and essential content of the monotheistic conception of Judaism, it does not preclude or invalidate the fact that the monotheistic conception in Judaism may convey also the arithmetical oneness and the ontological uniqueness of God. Indeed, in post-biblical Judaism (and even in some biblical instances) it is these notions that come to the fore and become the main expressions of the Jewish monotheistic conception. It would seem, however, that the notion of the arithmetical unity of God arises mainly as a reaction against pluralistic formulations found in other religions, such as the dualism of the Zoroastrian, Manichean, or Gnostic formulation and the trinitarianism of Christianity. The notion of the ontological uniqueness of the godhead arises mainly when Judaism conceives and expresses itself in the philosophical-metaphysical domain, i.e., when its God becomes the god of the philosophers.

Monotheism in Jewish Sources. Thus, Deutero-Isaiah, in response to Persian dualism, stresses the oneness of God in the sense that He alone is God, the one and only creator and ultimate cause of all phenomena: "I form light and create darkness; I make peace and create evil" (Isa. 45:7). This assertion is repeated frequently in rabbinic literature: "He who brought all things into being and who is their first cause is one" (Maimonides, *Sefer ha-Mitzvot,* positive commandment 2); "I have created all things in pairs. Heaven and earth, man and woman, . . . but my glory is one and unique" (Deut. R. 2:31). Likewise, the specific use of this assertion polemically against dualism and trinitarianism is extensive: "'I am the first' for I have no father, 'and I am the last' for I have no son, 'and beside me there is no God' for I have no brother" (Ex. R. 29:5); "The Lord, both in His role as our God [who loves us and extends His providence to us, i.e., the second person of the trinity] and the Lord [as He is in Himself, i.e., the first person of the trinity] is one from every aspect" (Leon de Modena, *Magen va-Ḥerev*, 2:7, 31–32). Furthermore, a number of the basic tenets of Judaism follow logically from this assertion of the arithmetical oneness of God, and rabbinic literature derives them from it. Thus, all forms of idolatry are rejected: God's absolute sovereignty and glory is proclaimed; both love and judgment, mercy and justice are attributed to one and the same God; God's infinity in time as the one God in the past, present, and future is declared. Although the concept of arithmetical oneness is involved also in the assertion of God's unity, the latter is distinct in that God is here distinguished qualitatively rather than merely quantitatively. This assertion finds its expression mainly in philosophical speculation, where the uniqueness of God is understood as essentially conveying the non-composite, non-divisible nature of His being. This view is clearly and trenchantly expressed by Maimonides when he says that God is "not one of a genus nor of a species and not as one human being who is a compound divisible into many unities; not a unity like the ordinary material body which is one in number but takes on endless divisions and parts" (*Guide of the Perplexed*, 1:51ff.). This means that "God is one in perfect simplicity" (Ḥasdai Crescas, *Or Adonai*, 1:1, 1), that He is wholly other (Saadiah Gaon, *Book of Beliefs and Opinions*, 2:1), and unique (Baḥya ibn Paquda, *Ḥovot ha-Levavot*, "Sha'ar ha-Yihud"). Even in rabbinic Judaism, although the emphasis is clearly placed on the two aspects of the monotheistic idea, i.e., the arithmetical oneness and the ontological uniqueness of God, the fundamental underlying assertion is that God is first and foremost a personal being. Thus, though shifting the emphasis, rabbinic Judaism remains fully bound to that aspect of the monotheistic idea where Judaism makes its fundamental and distinctive contribution to the history of religions.

2 IDOLATRY

In order to obtain a clear view of the character of image worship in biblical literature one must distinguish between the worshiping of "strange gods" (idolatry) and the use of images in the cult of God (iconolatry).

IN THE BIBLE

History. IDOLATRY IN ISRAEL. Idolatry in Israel had strong popular support. It was also promoted by the royal house, especially by the foreign queens (Maacah, Jezebel, and her daughter Athaliah). The nature of the foreign cult is not always clear. It is not always possible to determine, with any degree of certainty, whether a particular cult was wholly "foreign," syncretistic, or just a corruption of the worship of God. The most popular idolatrous cults among the Hebrews were of Canaanitic origin, such as those of Baal, Asherah, and Ashtaroth. The Book of Judges (2:11ff.; 3:7; 8:33; 10:10) and I Samuel (12:10) attribute the downfall of Israel to the worship of Baal and Ashtaroth. The popularity of Baal worship is attested by the strong reaction of the people against Gideon (Judg. 6:29ff.) for destroying (at God's command) the altar of Baal (Judg. 6:25). Samuel had to exhort the people before facing the enemy in battle to cast away "the foreign gods," i.e., "the Baals" (I Sam. 7:3-4). At the end of Solomon's reign there were erected, for the first time in the history of Israel, altars to Chemosh, Moloch, and Ashtoreth (I Kings 11:5-7), for his foreign wives. Abijam, probably at the insistence of his mother Maacah (who was half pagan), continued the practice of foreign cults (I Kings 15:1-3). The cult of Baal, as well as other foreign cults, gained prominence in the

North during the reign of Ahab. At the insistence of his wife Jezebel, he built an altar to Baal and worshiped it in public (I Kings 16:31). Four hundred and fifty priests of Baal and 400 priests of Asherah were in the entourage of Queen Jezebel (I Kings 18:19). Her missionary work seems to have been very successful. According to the testimony of the Bible, 7,000 people had abstained from bowing down to Baal (I Kings 19:18). A strong attack against Baal worship, especially against its promotion by the royalty (i.e., foreign queens), was launched by Jehu. He put to death Queen Jezebel (II Kings 9:33), destroyed the sanctuaries that she had built, and killed the priests and followers of Baal (II Kings 10:18ff.). The cult of Baal in Judah (at least its promotion by the royalty) seems to have been introduced by Queen Athaliah (Jezebel's daughter). It came to an end with the uprising engineered by Jehoiada the priest (II Kings 11:17). The most thorough cultic purge in the history of Israel took place in Judah, during King Hezekiah's reign. King Hezekiah purged Judah not only of the pagan cults, such as the asherahs and the pillars, but even of the brazen serpent built by Moses, because it was used in the cult of God. A strong criticism against the cult of Baal is voiced by Hosea (1–3; 11:2; 13:1) and Jeremiah (2:4ff.; 9:13; 11:13, 17; 12:16; 19:5; 23:13, 17, 27; 32:29). A new movement favoring idolatry, this time of more far-reaching consequences, was launched by the son of Hezekiah, King Manasseh. The boldness of King Manasseh's reform can be measured by the fact that instead of building sanctuaries to the foreign deities outside the Temple, as Queens Jezebel and Athaliah had done, King Manasseh transformed the very Temple of Jerusalem into a pagan pantheon (II Kings 21). The idolatrous practices that were in vogue during King Manasseh's reign were described by Ezekiel (8–11; 16:17; 20; 23). Its corrupting influence upon later generations was pointed out by Jeremiah (11:9ff.; 15:4). Other idolatrous cults popular in Israel were child sacrifice to Moloch (see II Kings 16:3; 21:6; 23:10; Jer. 7:31; 19:5; 32:35), sacred prostitution (I Kings 14:24; II Kings 23:7;

Ezek. 16:17; 23:5ff.; Hos. 4:14c–15), and the cult of Tammuz (Ezek. 8:14). Astral worship seems to have been widespread. The sun and the moon, known as the "Queen of Heaven" (i.e., Ishtar), are referred to throughout biblical literature as objects of worship (cf. Amos 5:26). Ezekiel (8:10) mentions also the worship of animals.

ICONOLATRY IN ISRAEL. Iconolatry, or the use of images in the worship of God, may be divided into three groups.

Iconolatry that was Practiced in the Time of the Patriarchs and Later Proscribed. The erection of pillars, *maẓẓevot* (pl. of *maẓẓevah*), in the cult of God (not to be confused with the commemorative *maẓẓevot,* such as in Gen. 31:45–52; Ex. 24:4; Josh. 4:4–9) was considered legitimate by the Patriarchs. Jacob erected a *maẓẓevah* in Beth-El to be used in the service of God (Gen. 28:18, 22; 35:14). This mode of worship continued in later times, but eventually was proscribed by Deuteronomy (16:22) and the Prophets (Ezek. 26:11; Hos. 3:4; 10:1–3; Micah 5:12). Likewise the planting of a tree for the service of God was practiced by Abraham (Gen. 21:33). This form of worship was later proscribed by Deuteronomy (16:21). The use of *maẓẓevot* and the planting of trees for the cult of God was widely in use during the time of the Monarchy (I Kings 14:15, 23; II Kings 17:10; 23:14). The "brazen serpent" seems also to fall in this group (see II Kings 18:4).

Illegitimate Iconolatry. The classic, and most illustrative, example of this type of iconolatry is the golden calf worshiped at the foot of Mt. Sinai and in the sanctuaries of Dan and Beth-El (Ex. 32:1–8; I Kings 12:28; II Kings 10:29; Ps. 106:13–20; Neh. 9:18; II Chron. 13:8). The golden calf made by the people at the foot of Mt. Sinai (Ex. 32:1–8) conforms with the general pattern of idolatry in the Near East. The people of Israel wanted to "make" a god ("Make for us a god"), not a lifeless image. The calf was consecrated as a God ("This is your God, O Israel"). The Bible states: "And they made it a molten calf and they said 'This is your God, O Israel.'" The conjunction "and" underlines the relationship between the making of the idol and its consecration. The rabbis report that the golden calf was made as a replica of the bull in the divine throne. This tradition corresponds to the religious ideas current at that time in the Near East. Reference to the "heavenly bull" is found in very ancient Egyptian sources. The bull was considered to be the seat of different gods in Egypt, Babylonia, and Aram (Wainwright, in bibl.). In Israelite tradition the bull formed part of the divine throne. In order that God should make His glory dwell among them, they manufactured a bull, a replica of the divine throne or "heavenly bull," so that God would make His spirit dwell in the calf, His earthly throne, and thereby fully identify with it. They in turn, by having possession of the idol, would in fact have a God in their midst. According to this view, God became the idol, in the same fashion as all other gods became the idols which were consecrated to them. The Bible rejects this concept of religion. God would never manifest His glory or spirit upon these images. As the prophet says in His name: "And My glory I will give to no other, nor My praise to idols" (Isa. 42:8). From this point of view, the worship of God through images is indistinguishable from the worshiping of "wood and stone." This type of image worship was widespread in Israel and the most common form of idolatry mentioned in the Bible. Micaiah (Jud. 17–18) made an image of God (i.e., an image consecrated to God). Gideon made a golden ephod, probably an image, for the cult of God (Judg. 8:27). Likewise, "the calves of Samaria" (Hos. 8:6) and other images worshiped in the Northern sanctuaries were idols for the cult of God. This form of worship accounts for most of the denouncement of image worship in biblical literature (see Kaufmann, Religion, 133ff.).

Legitimate Iconolatry. Not all images were proscribed according to the biblical cult. The figures of the cherubim were embroidered in the curtains (Ex. 26:1; 36:8) and in the *parokhet,* "veil," of the Tabernacle (Ex. 26:31; 36:35) and the Temple (II Chron. 3:14); they were carved upon the walls (I Kings 6:29; II Chron. 3:7; cf. Ezek. 41:18, 20, 25) and doors (I Kings 6:32, 35) and in the *mekhonot*, "molten sea" (I Kings 7:29, 36) of the Temple. There were two golden cherubim in the Tabernacle (Ex. 25:18–22; 37:7–9) and in the Temple (I Kings 6:23–28; 8:6–7; II Chron. 3:10–13). The cherubim seem to represent the cherubim of the heavenly chariot (see Ezek. 1:5–14; 9–11; cf. II Sam. 22:11; Ps. 18:11). The Lord "sits on the cherubim" of the Sanctuary (I Sam. 4:4; II Sam. 6:2; II Kings 19:15; Isa. 37:16; Ps. 80:2; 99:1; I Chron. 13:6). In considering the biblical view of idolatry one must examine the ground upon which a distinction between permitted and illicit iconolatry is possible. U. Cassuto (*Perush al Sefer Shemot* (1952), 285) was of the opinion that the distinction between illicit images and the cherubim was based on the character of the images: illicit images represented actual beings, whereas the cherubim did not represent actual beings. This view is too vague and too subtle. The actual form of the cherubim of the Temple is unknown. According to rabbinic tradition (Suk. 5b; Ḥag. 13b) the cherubim were in the form of young children. Moreover, even if one concedes that the form of the cherubim did not correspond to any actual being, one can not help wondering whether this subtlety is at all relative to the religious values and criteria of the ancient Near East and the Bible. On the other hand, Jewish medieval authors, Karaites (Jacob al-Kirkisānī, *Kitāb al-Anwār,* ed. L. Nemoy (1938), 6) and Rabbanites (Judah Halevi, *The Kuzari,* 1:96) expressed the view that the distinction between permitted and illicit iconolatry is fundamentally arbitrary: certain images were prescribed by the Law and others were proscribed. This view involves standards of values that fully agree with the basic theology of the Bible: the one God must be worshiped only as prescribed by the Law. The difference between the biblical ceremonies and their counterparts is not intrinsic but simply the fact that the former are prescribed by the Law while the latter are not. In the Bible, to worship the only God with rites that are not prescribed by the Law is an act of idolatry (more precisely, *avodah zarah,* "nonprescribed cult," which is the Hebrew equivalent of "idolatry"). This conception of religion is grounded on the belief in the absolute omnipotence of God. Thus no cult can condition or influence God's relation with man unless it was explicitly commanded by Him (see Faur, in bibl., 47–48).

The Biblical Injunction Against Idolatry. The biblical injunction against idolatry comprises three more or less separate matters: the worship of idols, the worship of God with pagan rites, and the making of idols. The biblical injunction against idol worship includes: 1) idol worship conforming to the pagan rituals (Ex. 20:5; Deut. 12:30; cf. Sanh. 61b); 2) bowing down (Ex. 34:14); 3) offering a sacrifice to another god (i.e., to idols, Ex. 22:19), which, according to the rabbis, includes the performance of any of the rituals that form part of the cult prescribed for the service of the Lord (e.g., the actual slaughtering of the sacrifice, the offering of incense, the offering of libation), although that particular ritual is not generally used in the service of the idol (Sanh. 7:6; cf. Sanh. 60b); 4) paying homage to an idol (Ex. 20:5)—according to the rabbis this prohibition refers to the veneration of an image, even if there is no intention of worshiping, such as kissing the idol or caressing it (Sanh. 7:6; cf. Sanh. 63a). The actual worshiping of supernatural beings, such as angels, is not explicitly proscribed in the Bible (cf. Judg. 13:16). The rabbis, however, consider the worship of angels idolatry (Tosef., Ḥul. 2:18). This reflects the actual biblical view of idolatry. The Bible conceives idolatry not merely as the worshiping of images but as the worshiping of anything, real or imaginary, other than God Himself. This is implicit in the second commandment (Ex. 20:3).

The injunction against worshiping God with pagan rites (Deut. 12:31; cf. Naḥmanides ad loc.) reflects the biblical view that God should be worshiped according to His will (see below).

Making idols is explicitly prohibited (Ex. 20:4, 23 [20]). According to the rabbis this prohibition applies both to one who makes an idol to worship it himself or for others to worship (see Sifra 7:1 end). The biblical prohibition of making idols does not include all images but only those images that were considered "gods" (e.g., Lev. 26:1). This distinction between an image and an idol will become clear in the light of the pagan belief that an image was not to be worshiped unless it was properly consecrated to a god and transformed, through the prescribed cult, into an idol.

THE BIBLICAL POLEMIC AGAINST IDOLATRY. In the course of the biblical polemic against idolatry the Bible does not introduce the issue of the merits of the religious and mythological values of the pagan world (see below). The reason for this is that the Bible rejects the pagan claim that idolatry actually represents religious values. The Bible attacks idolatry on two independent grounds: it violates the Covenant, and it is useless. Since idolatry is specifically forbidden (cf. Ex. 20:4ff.), its practice constitutes a violation of the Covenant (Deut. 31:16, 20; Jer. 11:10). This is grounded on the belief that the worship of God is to be determined by Him alone. Accordingly, any form of worship not specifically prescribed by Him is an affront to His absolute sovereignty and omnipotence. The second argument can be properly understood in light of the pagan belief that natural phenomena such as fertility, rain, health, and so on may be controlled by idolatry. Since, according to the Bible, God is in control of all nature, idolatry is useless (cf. Isa. 41:23–24; 44:6–21; Jer. 10:1–5). Furthermore, as Maimonides observed (*Guide*, 3:30), the Bible emphasizes that since idolatry is a violation of the Covenant, it produces negative results; as a punishment God will turn nature against the idolaters (cf. Deut. 11:13–18; 28).

In the Talmud. Idolatry is considered by the rabbis as one of the three cardinal sins, which one is enjoined to suffer martyrdom rather than transgress (the other two are incest and murder ("the shedding of blood": Sanh. 74a)). A whole tractate, *Avodah Zarah*, is devoted to the details of idolatry. The abstention from it is "equivalent to the fulfillment of all the commandments of the Torah" (Hor.

8a), and Daniel 3:12, "There are certain Jews..." is interpreted to teach that "he who denies idols is called a Jew" (Meg. 13a). Contrariwise, "he who recognizes idols denies the whole Torah" (Sif. Deut. 54). Despite this fact, the possibility of Jews practicing idolatry is largely discounted by the rabbis.

That idolatry was regarded as a "theoretical" and not a practical danger is also borne out by the fact that it is almost a commonplace of the rabbis to stress the gravity of social and ethical failings by stating that he who is guilty of them is "as though he were guilty of idolatry," whether "saying one's prayers while intoxicated" (Ber. 31b), or giving way to excessive anger (Shab. 105b), or not practicing charity (Ket. 68a), succumbing to evil inclinations (TJ, Ned. 9:1, 41b), breaking a promise, or even leaving crumbs on the table (Sanh. 92a). The violent reaction of the Jews against the Roman legions displaying the Roman eagle on their standards, as well as their determined resistance to statues of the emperor being set up in Palestine, had, of course, definite political undertones.

In general it was forbidden to have any dealings with gentiles during their festivals and for three days prior to them and to sell them anything which was obviously part of their idolatrous worship (Av. Zar. 1:5). Included in the prohibition were a number of superstitious practices given the general name of "the ways of the Amorites" (Tosef. Shab. 6, 7). It was naturally forbidden to harbor in one's house any images which were worshiped. A special prohibition was the use of libation wine, and it was treated so seriously that the prohibition was extended as a precautionary measure to all gentile wine *(setam yayin)*. The regulations with regard to this extend over half of chapter 4 and the whole of chapter 5 of the tractate *Avodah Zarah*. It was forbidden to use concoctions prepared for idolatrous rites for purposes of healing (Pes. 25a; Ex. R. 16:2).

In the Tosefta (Av. Zar. 6:8) there is a reference to three places in Erez Israel where the worship of the Asherah was still practiced at that time. Although there are references to obscene rites connected with idolatry (Sif. Num. 131) there is in the talmudic literature no reference to the formulas of heathen rites. A special prayer, "Blessed be He Who hath uprooted idolatry from the land," had to be recited when seeing a place where idol worship had been formerly practiced (Ber. 9:1).

3 GOD

IN THE BIBLE

The One, Incomparable God. God is the hero of the Bible. Everything that is narrated, enjoined, or foretold in biblical literature is related to Him. Yet nowhere does the Bible offer any proof of the Deity's existence, or command belief in Him. The reason may be twofold: Hebrew thought is intuitive rather than speculative and systematic, and, furthermore, there were no atheists in antiquity. When the psalmist observed: "The fool hath said in his heart 'There is no God'" (Ps. 14:1), he was referring not to disbelief in God's existence, but to the denial of His moral governance. That a divine being or beings existed was universally accepted. There were those, it is true, who did not know YHWH (Ex. 5:2), but all acknowledged the reality of the Godhead. Completely new, however, was Israel's idea of God. Hence this idea is expounded in numerous, though not necessarily related, biblical passages, and, facet by facet, a cosmic, awe-inspiring spiritual portrait of infinite magnitude is built up. Paganism is challenged in all its aspects. God is One; there is no other (Deut. 6:4; Isa. 45:21; 46:9). Polytheism is rejected unequivocally and absolutely (Ex. 20:3–5). There is no pantheon; even the dualism of Ormuzd and Ahriman (of the Zoroastrian religion) is excluded (Isa. 45:21); apotheosis is condemned (Ezek. 28:2ff.). Syncretism, as distinct from identification (Gen. 14:18–22), which plays a historical as well as a theological role in paganism, is necessarily ruled out (Num. 25:2–3; Judg. 18). Verses like Exodus 15:11—"Who is like Thee, O Lord, among the gods?"—do not lend support to polytheism, but expose the unreality and futility of the pagan deities. The thought is: Beside the true God, how can these idol-imposters claim divinity? The term "sons of gods" in Psalms 29:1 and 89:7 refers to angels, the servants, and worshipers of the Lord; there is no thought of polytheism (see E. G. Briggs, *The Book of Psalms* (ICC), 1 (1906), 252ff.; 2 (1907), 253ff.). The one God is also unique in all His attributes. The prophet asks: "To whom then will ye liken God? Or what likeness will ye compare unto Him?" (Isa. 40:18). Though the question is rhetorical, the Bible in a given sense provides a series of answers, scattered over the entire range of its teaching, which elaborate in depth the incomparability of God. He has no likeness; no image can be made of Him (Ex. 20:4; Deut. 4:35). He is not even to be conceived as spirit; the spirit of God referred to in the Bible alludes to His energy (Isa. 40:13; Zech. 4:6). In Isaiah 31:3, "spirits" parallels "a god" ('*el,* a created force) not the God, who is called in the verse YHWH. Idolatry, though it lingered on for centuries, was doomed to extinction by this new conception of the Godhead. It is true that the Torah itself ordained that images like the cherubim should be set up in the Holy of Holies. They did not, however, represent the Deity but His throne (cf. Ps. 68:5[4]); its occupant no human eye could see. Yet the invisible God is not a philosophical abstraction; He manifests His presence. His theophanies are accompanied by thunder, earthquake, and lightning (Ex. 19:18; 20:15[18]; Hab. 3:4ff.). These fearful natural phenomena tell of His strength; He is the omnipotent God (Job 42:2). None can resist Him (41:2); hence He is the supreme warrior (Ps. 24:8). God's greatness, however, lies not primarily in His power. He is omniscient; wisdom is His alone (Job 28:23ff.). He knows no darkness; light ever dwells with Him (Dan. 2:22); and it is He, and He only, who envisions and reveals the future (Isa. 43:9). He is the source of human understanding (Ps. 36:10[9]), and it is He who endows man with his skills (Ex. 28:3; I Kings 3:12). The classical Prometheus and the Canaanite Kôthar-and-Ḥasis are but figments of man's imagination. The pagan pride of wisdom is sternly rebuked; it is deceptive (Ezek. 28:3ff.); but God's wisdom is infinite and unsearchable (Isa. 40:28). He is also the omnipresent God (Ps. 139:7–12), but not as *numen, mana,* or *orenda.* Pantheism is likewise negated. He transcends the world of nature, for it is He who brought the world into being, established its laws, and gave it its order (Jer. 33:25). He is outside of time as well as space; He is eternal. Everything must perish; He alone preceded the universe and will outlive it (Isa. 40:6–8; 44:6; Ps. 90:2). The ever-present God is also immutable; in a world of flux He alone does not change (Isa. 41:4; Mal. 3:6). He is the rock of all existence (II Sam. 22:32).

The Divine Creator. God's power and wisdom find their ultimate expression in the work of creation. The miracles serve to highlight the divine omnipotence; but the supreme miracle is the universe itself (Ps. 8:2, 4[1, 3]). There is no theogony, but there is a cosmogony, designed and executed by the divine fiat (Gen. 1). The opening verses of the Bible do not conclusively point to *creatio ex nihilo.* The primordial condition of chaos *(tohu* and *bohu)* mentioned in Genesis 1:2 could conceivably represent the *materia prima* out of which the world was fashioned; but Job 26:7 appears to express poetically the belief in a world created out of the void (see Y. Kaufmann, Religion, 68), and both prophets and psalmists seem to substantiate this doctrine (Isa. 42:5; 45:7–9; Jer. 10:12; Ps. 33:6–9; 102:26; 212:2). Maimonides, it is true, did not consider that the Bible provided incontrovertible proof of *creatio ex nihilo (Guide,* 2:25). The real criterion, however, is the overall climate of biblical thought, which would regard the existence of uncreated matter as a grave diminution of the divinity of the Godhead. God is the sole creator (Isa. 44:24). The celestial beings ("sons of God") referred to in Job 38:7, and the angels who, according to rabbinic *aggadah* and some modern exegetes, are addressed in Genesis 1:26 (cf. 3:22) were themselves created forms and not co-architects or co-builders of the cosmos. Angels are portrayed in the Bible 63 as constituting the heavenly court, and as taking part in celestial consultations (I Kings 22:19ff.; Job 1:6ff.; 2:1ff.). These heavenly creatures act as God's messengers (the Hebrew *mal'akh* and the Greek $\dot{\alpha}\gamma\gamma\epsilon\lambda o s$, from which the word "angel" is derived, both mean "messengers") or agents. They perform various tasks (cf. Satan, "the Accuser"), but except in the later books of the Bible they are not individualized and bear no names.

Nor are the angels God's only messengers: natural phenomena, like the wind (Ps. 104:4), or man himself, may act in that capacity (Num. 20:16). Some scholars think that since the Bible concentrated all divine powers in the one God, the old pagan deities, which represented various forces of nature, were demoted in Israel's religion to the position of angels. The term *shedim* (Deut. 32:17; Ps. 106:37), on the other hand, applied to the gods of the nations, does not, according to Y. Kaufmann, denote demons, but rather "no-gods," devoid of both divine and demonic powers. The fantastic proliferation of the angel population found in pseudepigraphical literature is still unknown in the Bible. It is fundamental, however, to biblical as well as post-biblical Jewish angelology that these celestial beings are God's creatures and servants. They fulfill the divine will and do not oppose it. The pagan notion of demonic forces that wage war against the deities is wholly alien and repugnant to biblical theology. Even Satan is no more than the heavenly prosecutor, serving the divine purpose. The cosmos is thus the work of God above, and all nature declares His glory (Ps. 19:2, 13ff.). All things belong to Him and He is the Lord of all (I Chron. 29:11–12). This creation theorem has a corollary of vast scientific and social significance: the universe, in all its measureless diversity, remains a homogeneous whole. Nature's processes are the same throughout the world, and underlying them is "One Power, which is of no beginning and no end; which has existed before all things were formed, and will remain in its integrity when all is gone—the Source and Origin of all, in Itself beyond any conception or image that man can form and set up before his eye or mind" (Haffkine). There is no cosmic strife between antagonistic forces, between darkness and light, between good and evil; and, by the same token, mankind constitutes a single brotherhood. The ideal is not that of the ant heap. Differentiation is an essential element of the Creator's design; hence the Tower of Babel is necessarily doomed to destruction. Although uniformity is rejected, the family unity of mankind, despite racial, cultural, and pigmentary differences, is clearly stressed in its origin (Adam is the human father of all men) and in its ultimate destiny at the end of days (Isa. 2:2–4). The course of creation is depicted in the opening chapter of the Bible as a graduated unfolding of the universe, and more particularly of the earth, from the lowest levels of life to man, the peak of the creative process. God, according to this account, completed the work in six days (that "days" here means an undefined period may be inferred from Gen. 1:14, where time divisions are mentioned for the first time; cf. also N. H. Tur-Sinai, in EM, 3(1958), 593). The biblical accounting of the days, however, is not intended to provide the reader with a science or history textbook but to describe the ways of God. Running like a golden thread through all the variegated contents of the Bible is the one unchanging theme—God and His moral law. Of far greater significance than the duration of creation is the fact that it was crowned by the Sabbath (Gen. 2:1–3), bringing rest and refreshment to the toiling world. The concept of the creative pause, sanctified by the divine example, is one of the greatest spiritual and social contributions to civilization made by the religion of Israel.

God in History. The Sabbath did not mark the retirement of the Deity from the world that He had called into being. God continued to care for His creatures (Ps. 104), and man—all men—remained the focal point of His loving interest (Ps. 8:5[4]ff.). The divine providence encompasses both nations (Deut. 32:8) and individuals (e.g., the Patriarchs). Cosmogony is followed by history, and God becomes the great architect of the world of events, even as

He was of the physical universe. He directs the historical movements *(ibid.),* and the peoples are in His hands as clay in the hands of the potter (Jer. 18:6). He is the King of the nations (Jer. 10:7; Ps. 22:29). There is a vital difference, however, between the two spheres of divine activity. Creation encountered no antagonism. The very monsters that in pagan mythology were the mortal enemies of the gods became in the Bible creatures formed in accordance with the divine will (Gen. 1:21). Nevertheless, the stuff of history is woven of endless strands of rebellion against the Creator. Man is not an automaton; he is endowed with free will. The first human beings already disobeyed their maker; they acquired knowledge at the price of sin, which reflects the discord between the will of God and the action of man. The perfect harmony between the Creator and His human creation that finds expression in the idyll of the Garden of Eden was disrupted, and never restored. The revolt continued with Cain, the generation of the Flood, and the Tower of Babel. There is a rhythm of rebellion and retribution, of oppression and redemption, of repentance and grace, and of merit and reward (Jer. 18:7–10). Israel was the first people to write history as teleology and discovered that it had a moral base. The Bible declares that God judges the world in righteousness (Ps. 96:13); that military power does not presuppose victory (Ps. 33:16); that the Lord saves the humble (Ps. 76:10) and dwells with them (Isa. 57:15). The moral factor determines the time as well as the course of events. The Israelites will return to Canaan only when the iniquity of the Amorite is complete (Gen. 15:16); for 40 years the children of Israel wandered in the wilderness for accepting the defeatist report of the ten spies (Num. 14:34); Jehu is rewarded with a dynasty of five generations for his punitive action against the house of Ahab; and to Daniel is revealed the timetable of redemption and restoration (Dan. 9:24). It is this moral element in the direction of history that makes God both Judge and Savior. God's punishment of the wicked and salvation of the righteous are laws of the divine governance of the world, comparable to the laws of nature: "As smoke is driven away, so drive them away; as wax melts before fire, let the wicked perish before God . . ." (Ps. 68:2–3; cf. M. D. Cassuto, in *Tarbiz,* 12 (1941), 1–27). Nature and history are related (Jer. 33:20–21, 25–26); the one God rules them both. The ultimate divine design of history, marked by universal peace, human brotherhood, and knowledge of God, will be accomplished in "the end of days" (Isa. 2:2–4; 11:6ff.), even as the cosmos was completed in conformity with the divine plan. Man's rebellions complicate the course of history, but cannot change the design. God's purpose shall be accomplished; there will be a new heaven and a new earth (Isa. 66:22), for ultimately man will have a new heart (Ezek. 36:26–27).

The Divine Lawgiver. The covenant that binds the children of Israel to their God is, in the ultimate analysis, the Torah in all its amplitude. God, not Moses, is the lawgiver; "Behold, I Moses say unto you" (cf. Gal. 5:2) is an inconceivable statement. It would not only be inconsistent with Moses' humility (Num. 12:3), but would completely contradict the God-given character of the Torah. However, notwithstanding its divine origin, the law is obligatory on Israel only. Even idolatry, the constant butt of prophetic irony, is not regarded as a gentile sin (Deut. 4:19). Yet the Bible assumes the existence of a universal moral code that all peoples must observe. The talmudic sages, with their genius for legal detail and codification, speak of the seven Noachian laws (Sanh. 56a). Although the Bible does not specify the ethical principles incumbent upon all mankind, it is clear from various passages that murder, robbery, cruelty, and adultery are major crimes recognized as such by all human beings (Gen. 6:12, 13; 9:5; 20:3; 39:9; Amos 1:3ff.). It would thus appear that the Bible postulates an autonomous, basic human sense of wrongdoing, unless it is supposed that a divine revelation of law was vouchsafed to the early saints, such as assumed by the apocryphal and rabbinic literatures (and perhaps by Isa. 24:5.) The Torah—which properly means "instruction," not "law"—does not, in the strict sense of the term, contain a properly formulated code; nevertheless, detailed regulations appertaining to religious ritual, as well as to civil and criminal jurisprudence, form an essential part of pentateuchal teaching. The halakhic approach is reinforced by a number of the prophets. For instance, Isaiah (58:13), Jeremiah (34:8ff.), Ezekiel (40ff.), and Malachi (1:8; 2:10) lent their authority to the maintenance of various religious observances. Ezra and Nehemiah rebuilt the restored Jewish community on Torah foundations. Yet paradoxically the Bible also evinces a decidedly "anti-halakhic" trend. In Isaiah the Lord cries: "What to Me is the multitude of your sacrifices . . . I have had enough of burnt offerings of rams and the fat of fed beasts . . . who requires of you this trampling of My courts? . . . Your new moons and your appointed feasts My soul hates . . . When you spread forth your hands, I will hide My eyes from you; even though you make many prayers, I will not listen" (1:11–15). Jeremiah not only belittles the value of the sacrifices (7:22); he derides the people's faith in the Temple itself: "The temple of the Lord, the temple of the Lord, the temple of the Lord are these" (7:4). Even the Book of Psalms, though essentially devotional in character, makes an anti-ritual protest: "I do not reprove you for your sacrifices . . . I will accept no bull from your house . . . For every beast of the forest is Mine, the cattle on a thousand hills . . . If I were hungry, I would not tell you; for the world and all that is in it is Mine. Do I eat the flesh of bulls, or drink the blood of goats?" (50:8–13). These and similar passages represent a negative attitude towards established cultic practices. No less inconsonant with Torah law seems the positive prophetic summary of human duty formulated by Micah (6:8): "He has told you, O man, what is good; and what does the Lord require of you but to do justice, and to love lovingkindness, and to walk humbly with your God?" A similar note is sounded by Hosea (2:21–22 [19–20]): "I will espouse you with righteousness and with justice, with steadfast love, and with mercy. I will espouse you with faithfulness; and you shall be mindful of the Lord"; by Amos (5:14): "Seek good, and not evil, that you may live"; and by Isaiah (1:17): "Learn to do good; seek justice, correct oppression; defend the fatherless, plead for the widow." The emphasis here is on moral and spiritual conduct; the ceremonial and ritualistic aspects of religion are conspicuously left unmentioned. The paradox, however, is only one of appearance and phrasing. Inherently there is no contradiction. The ostensibly antinomian statements do not oppose the offering of sacrifices, prayer, or the observance of the Sabbath and festivals. It is not ritual but hypocrisy that they condemn. Isaiah (1:13) expresses the thought in a single phrase: "I cannot endure iniquity and solemn assembly." Organized religion must necessarily have cultic forms; but without inwardness and unqualified sincerity they are an affront to the Deity and fail of their purpose. The underlying motive of the precepts is to purify and elevate man (Ps. 119:29, 40, 68). The Torah (Wisdom) is a tree of life and its ways are ways of peace (Prov. 3:17, 18). Sin does not injure God (Job 7:20), but is a disaster to man (Deut. 28:15ff.). It is heartfelt devotion that saves the *mitzvah* from becoming a meaningless convention and an act of hypocrisy (Isa. 29:13). The specific commandments are in a sense pointers and aids to that larger identification with God's will that is conterminous with life as a whole: "In all your ways acknowledge Him" (Prov. 3:6). Just as the divine wonders and portents lead to a deeper understanding of the daily miracles of providence, so the precepts are guides to the whole duty of man. Biblical religion is thus seen to be an indivisible synthesis of moral and spiritual principles, on the one hand, and practical observances on the other.

The Biblical Theodicy. The moral basis of providence, reinforced by the ethic of the Torah, also raises another kind of problem. Can the biblical theodicy always be justified? The issue is raised already in the Bible itself. Abraham challenges the divine justice: "Shall not the Judge of all the earth do right?" (Gen. 18:25). Moses echoes the cry in another context: "O Lord, why hast Thou done evil to this people?" (Ex. 5:22). The prophets are no less perplexed: "Why does the way of the wicked prosper? Why do all who are treacherous thrive?" (Jer. 12:1). The psalmist speaks for the individual and the nation in many generations, when he cries: "My God, my God, why hast Thou forsaken me?" (22:2 [1]), and the Book of Job is, in its magnificent entirety, one great heroic struggle to solve the problem of unwarranted human suffering. The biblical answer appears to point to the limitations of man's experience and understanding. History is long, but individual life is short. Hence the human view is fragmentary; events justify themselves in the end, but the person concerned does not always live to see the denouement. In the words of the psalmist: "Though the wicked sprout like grass and all evildoers flourish, they are doomed to destruction forever" (92:8–10; cf. 37:35–39). The brevity of man's years is further complicated by his lack of insight. God's purpose is beyond his comprehension: "For as the heavens are higher than the earth, so are My ways higher than your ways and My thoughts than your thoughts" (Isa. 55:9). In the final analysis, biblical theodicy calls for faith: "But the righteous shall live by his faith" (Hab. 2:4); "they who wait for the Lord shall renew their strength" (Isa. 40:31). It is not an irrational faith:—Certum est quia impossibile est (Tertullian, De Carne Christi, 5), but is necessitated by innate human intellectual limitations. In another direction the problem is even more formidable. God, the Bible states categorically, hardened Pharaoh's heart; nevertheless the Egyptian ruler was punished for this. Indeed his obduracy was induced in order to provide the occasion for his punishment (Ex. 7:3). Here the fundamental norms of justice by any standards are flagrantly violated. The explanation in this sphere of biblical theodicy is not theological but semantic. Scripture ascribes to God phenomena and events with which He is only indirectly concerned. However, since God is the author of all natural law and the designer of history, everything that occurs is, in a deep sense, His doing. Even in human affairs the king or the government is said to "do" everything that is performed under its aegis. Thus God declares in Amos 4:7: "And I caused it to rain upon one city, and I caused it not to rain upon another city," although the next clause uses passive and impersonal verbal forms to describe the same occurrences. The processes of nature need not be mentioned, since the laws of the universe are dictates of God. Similarly Exodus states indiscriminately that "Pharaoh hardened his heart" (8:28), that "the heart of Pharaoh was hardened" (9:7), and that "the Lord hardened the heart of Pharaoh" (9:12). In the end it is all one; what God permits He does. This interpretation does not, however, fit another area of divine conduct. Uzzah, the Bible states, was struck dead for an innocent act that was motivated by concern for the safety of "the ark of God" (II Sam. 6:6–7). Wherein lay the iniquity? Here the reason appears to be of a different character. Even innocent actions may in certain circumstances be disastrous. Uzzah's attempt to save the ark from falling was well meant, but it was conducive to irreverence. Man needs God's help; God does not require the help of man (Sot. 35a; for a similar thought cf. Ps. 50:12; another explanation is given by Kimḥi, II Sam. 6:6). In one thoughtless moment Uzzah could have reduced the sacred ark in the eyes of the people to the impotent level of the idols, which the prophets depicted with such scathing mockery. The same principle operated in the tragedy of Nadab and Abihu, and Moses explained the underlying principle in the words: "I will show Myself holy among those who are near Me" (Lev. 10:1–3).

The Limitation of the Infinite God. Is the Godhead subject to restriction? The irresistible conclusion to be drawn from biblical teaching is that such a limitation exists. Man's freedom to resist or obey the will of God is a restriction of the Deity's power that is totally unknown in the physical universe. It must be added, however, that this restriction is an act of divine self-limitation. In His love for man God has, so to speak, set aside an area of freedom in which man can elect to do right or wrong (Deut. 5:26; 30:17). In rabbinic language: "Everything is in the power of Heaven except the reverence of Heaven" (Ber. 33b). Man is thereby saved from being an automaton. It adds a new dimension to the relationship between God and man. Man may defect, but when, on the other hand, he chooses the path of loyalty, he does so from choice, from true love. Needless to say, without such freedom there could be neither sin nor punishment, neither merit nor reward. The divine humility, which permits human dissent, is also the grace to which the dissenter succumbs in the end. Man is a faithful rebel, who is reconciled with his Maker in the crowning period of history. God's self-limitation is thus seen as an extension of His creative power. Other biblical concepts that might be construed as restrictions of God's infinitude are, on closer scrutiny, seen not to be real limitations. The association of the Lord with holy places like the Tent of Meeting, the Temple, Zion, or Sinai does not imply that He is not omnipresent. In prophetic vision Isaiah saw the divine train fill the Temple, and at the same time he heard the seraphim declare: "the whole earth is full of His glory" (6:1–3). God's geographical association, or His theophany at a given place, signifies consecration of the site, which thus becomes a source of inspiration to man; but no part of the universe exists at any time outside God's presence. Sometimes God is depicted as asking man for information (Gen. 3:9; 4:9). On other occasions He is stated to repent His actions and to be grieved (Gen. 6:6). These are mere anthropomorphisms. The Lord knows all (Jer. 11:20; 16:17; Ps. 7:10), and unlike human beings He does not repent (Num. 23:19). Genesis 6:6 is not a contradiction of this thesis; its "human" terminology does not imply a diminution of God's omniscience, but emphasizes the moral freedom granted to man. In addition to spiritual option, the Creator, as has been stated, gave man knowledge. This finds expression, inter alia, in magical powers, which, in as much as they are "supernatural," constitute a challenge to God's will. In Moses' protracted struggle with Pharaoh, the Egyptians actually pit their magical powers against the Almighty's miracles. In the end they acknowledge their relative weakness and admit that they cannot rival "the finger of God" (Ex. 8:15). This is to be expected, for the divine wisdom is unbounded (Job 11:7), whereas human understanding is finite. Nevertheless the use of all forms of sorcery, even by non-Israelites, is strongly denounced (Isa. 44:25); to the Israelite, witchcraft is totally forbidden (Deut. 18:10–11). The differentiation between magic and miracles had deep roots in Hebrew monotheism. To the pagan mind magical powers were independent forces to which even the gods had to have recourse. The miracle, on the other hand, is regarded in the Bible as a manifestation of God's power and purpose. It is an attestation of the prophet's mission (Isa. 7:11); whereas divination and sorcery are either forms of deception (Isa. 44:25) or, where magic is effective, as in the episode of the witch of Endor (I Sam. 28:7ff.), it represents an abuse of man's God-given knowledge. There is no independent realm of witchcraft, however; all power, natural and supernatural, emanates from the one God. To the Israelite all that happens is wrought by God.

The Divine Personality. Though inconceivable, God is portrayed throughout the Bible as a person. In contradistinction to the idols, who are dead, He is called the living God (II Kings 19:4, 16). He is neither inanimate nor a philosophical abstraction; He is the living source of all life. Anthropomorphisms abound in the Bible, but it is not by these that the divine personality, so to speak, is depicted. Anthropomorphic figures were intended to help early man to grasp ideas that in philosophical terms transcended the human intellect. God's essential personality is primarily reflected in His attributes, which motivate His acts. He is King, Judge, Father, Shepherd, Mentor, Healer, and Redeemer—to mention only a few of His aspects in His relationship to man. Different biblical teachers conceived God's character from different historical angles. Amos was conscious of God's justice. Hosea underscored the Lord's love, and made forgiveness and compassion the coefficient, as it were, of divinity: "I will not execute My fierce anger . . . for I am God and not man" (11:9). Ezekiel stresses that God does not desire the destruction of the wicked but that through repentance they may live (18:23). The heart of the matter is clearly stated in the Torah: "The Lord passed before him (Moses), and proclaimed, 'The Lord, the Lord, a God merciful and gracious, slow to anger, and abounding in steadfast love and faithfulness, keeping steadfast love for thousands, forgiving iniquity and transgression and sin, but who will by no means clear the guilty . . ." (Ex. 34:6–7). Maimonides was philosophically justified in insisting that God has no attributes and that the epithets applied to Him in the Bible really represent human emotions evoked by His actions (*Guide*, 2:54). The Bible, however, which is little interested in the speculative approach to the Deity, but teaches practical wisdom and religion as life, without the help of catechism or formulated dogmas, prefers to endow God with personality to which it gives the warmth and beauty of positive characterization. In sum, the divine nature is composed of both justice and love. The Bible recognizes that without justice love itself becomes a form of injustice; but in itself justice is not enough. It can only serve as a foundation; the superstructure—the bridge between God and man—is grace.

Between Man and God. Grace is the divine end of the bridge; the human side is existential devotion. Otherwise, what M. Buber felicitously called the "I—Thou" relationship cannot come into being. Hence, underlying all the commandments is the supreme precept: "And you shall love the Lord your God with all your heart, and with all your soul, and with all your might" (Deut. 6:5). This love is unqualified: "You shall be whole-hearted with the Lord your God" (Deut. 18:13). It calls for complete surrender; but this is not conceived as a narrow, if intense, religious attitude. It is broad-based enough to allow for deep-rooted spiritual communion. Man pours out his heart in prayer to God; it is to Him that he uplifts his soul in thanksgiving and praise; and it is also to Him that he addresses his most searching questions and most incisive criticism of life and providence. Sincere criticism of God is never rebuked. God reproaches Job's friends, who were on His side; but Job is rewarded despite his searing indictment of God's actions. The God–man relationship flowers in an evolutionary process of education: Man is gradually weaned from his own inhumanity, from atrocities, like human sacrifice (Gen. 22:2–14), from bestial conduct, and from wronging his fellowman. The goal again is love: "You shall love your neighbor as yourself" (Lev. 19:18). It is a corollary of the love of God: "I am the Lord." Reward and retribution play a role in the divine educational procedures; but their functions are limited—they are not ultimates. The eternal fires of hell are never used as a deterrent, though punishment of the wicked after death is obscurely mentioned (Isa. 66:24; Dan. 12:2), nor is paradise used as an inducement. The Torah-covenant is an unquenchable spiritual light (Prov. 6:23); but the "I—Thou" relationship does not end with the written word. God communes with man directly. The prophet hears the heavenly voice and echoes it; the psalmist knows, with unfaltering conviction, that his prayer has been answered and that salvation has been wrought before he actually experiences it. At one with God, man finds ultimate happiness: "In Thy presence is fullness of joy, in Thy right hand bliss for evermore" (Ps. 16:11).

The Hebrew term for the love that binds man to God (as well as to his fellowman) is *'ahavah;* but sometimes the Bible uses another word, *yir'ah* (literally: "fear"), which seems to turn the "I—Thou" nexus into an "It" relationship. The psalmist declares: "The fear of the Lord is the beginning of wisdom" (111:10), and Ecclesiastes comes to the conclusion: "The end of the matter; all has been heard. Fear God, and keep His commandments, for this is the whole duty of man" (12:13). The picture is thus completely changed. The heavenly Father suddenly becomes a divine tyrant, before whom man cowers in terror, as does the unenlightened pagan before the demonic force that he seeks to appease. This might be consonant with the notion of "the jealous God" (Ex. 34:14), but it would appear to be irreconcilable with the concept of the God of *ḥesed* ("lovingkindness," "grace"). Here, too, this is not a theological but a semantic problem. *Yir'ah* does not signify "fear"; it is best rendered by "reverence." "Love" and "reverence" are not antithetic but complementary terms. They are two aspects of a single idea. *'Ahavah* expresses God's nearness: *yir'ah* is the sublime expression of the measureless distance between the remote Deity and man. God spoke to Moses "mouth to mouth" (Num. 12:8), yet in his human frailty the Hebrew leader could not "see" his divine interlocutor (Ex. 33:20). The inner identity of "love" and "reverence" is reflected in the Torah's religious summary: "And now, Israel, what does the Lord your God require of you but to revere the Lord your God, to walk in all His ways and to love Him, and to serve the Lord your God with all your heart and with all your soul" (Deut. 10:12). Talmudic Judaism (Shab. 120a) drew a distinction between *ḥasidut* (steadfast love of God) and *yir'at shamayim* ("reverence of Heaven"), but this represents a later development. In the Bible this bifurcation does not exist; "reverence of God" is by and large the biblical equivalent of "religion."

Likewise there is no spiritual contradiction between the "gracious" and the "jealous" God. "Jealousy" is an anthropomorphic term used to define God's absolute character, which excludes all other concepts of the Godhead. It does not detract from the divine love and compassion; it serves only to protect them. The sum of all the divine attributes finds expression in the epithet "holy." It is the highest praise that prophet and psalmist can give to the Lord (Isa. 6:3; Ps. 22:4 [3]), and since man is created in the image of God (Gen. 1:26), the attribute of holiness becomes the basis of the concept of "the imitation of God": "You shall be holy; for I the Lord your God am holy" (Lev. 19:2). The Bible makes it clear, however, that, in seeking to model himself on the divine example, it is primarily God's moral attributes that man must copy. Even as God befriends the sojourner and acts as the father of the fatherless and as the judge of the widow, so must man, on his human scale, endeavor to do (Deut. 10:18–19; cf. Sot. 14a). Indeed all that uplifts man, including the Sabbath and abstention from impurity, is comprised in the concept of the imitation of God. At the highest level Israel's ethic and theology are indissolubly linked.

To sum up: the biblical conception of God was revolutionary both in its theological and its moral implications. The pagan world may occasionally have glimpsed, in primitive form, some of the higher truths inherent in Israel's ethical monotheism. Egypt for a brief span attained to monolatry (Akhenaton's heresy); Babylon had a glimmering of a unified cosmic process; Marduk, Shamash, and Aton punished evildoers; and some Greek philosophers commended the imitation of the godhead. Yet no cult in antiquity even remotely approached the elevated conceptions associated with the one God of the Bible. This spiritual revolution not only eventually brought paganism to an end, but its inner dynamic gave birth, in time, to two daughter religions, Christianity and Islam, which, despite their essential differences from Judaism, are deeply rooted in biblical thought.

IN TALMUDIC LITERATURE

Abstract philosophical concepts, such as are found in Philo, are foreign to the thought system of the rabbis of the Talmud and Midrash. However, a marked tendency is discernible among them to present an exalted picture of God, as well as to avoid expressions that could throw the slightest shadow on the conception of His absolute Oneness. In the Targums, the early Aramaic translations of Scripture, the name God is frequently rendered "*memra* ('word') of God." It is certain that no connection whatsoever is intended between this word and the "logos," or with the idea of an intermediary between God and the world. Were this the intention, the word *"memra"* would have been used in the Targum to such verses as:"The Lord sent a word unto Jacob" (Isa. 9:7); "so shall My word be that goeth forth out of My mouth" (*ibid.* 55:11); "He sent His word and healed them" (Ps. 107:20). It is precisely in these verses that the Targum employs the word *pitgam* ("word") or *nevu'ah* ("prophecy"). Even in the verse "By the word of the Lord were the heavens made" (Ps. 33:6) "word" is rendered by the Targums as *milta* ("word") of God. Nor is there any mention of the expression *"memra"* in the Targums of the account of creation. It is therefore certain that this word, which occurs only in the Targums, but not in the Talmud and the Midrash, was used only to guard against any idea which (in the minds of the common people for whom the Targum was intended) might militate against the exalted conception of the Divinity or tend to diminish the pure concept of God. For the same reason one finds many euphemisms employed as substitutes for the names of God, such as *Ha-Gevurah* ("Might"), *Raḥmana* ("the Merciful"), *Ha-Kadosh Barukh Hu* ("The Holy One, blessed be He"), or such terms as *Shamayim* ("Heaven"), *Ha-Makom* ("Omnipresent"), *Ribbono shel Olam* ("Lord of the Universe"), *Mi-she-Amar ve-Hayah ha-Olam* ("He who spoke, and the Universe came into being"), *Avinu she-ba-Shamayim* ("Our Father in heaven"), *Mi she-Shikken Shemo ba-Bayit ha-Zeh* ("He who caused His name to dwell in this house"). A special significance was given by the rabbis to the tetragrammaton, and to *Elohim,* the tetragrammaton denoting the attribute of mercy, and *Elohim,* that of judgment (Gen. R. 33:3). That this was a time-honored distinction is evident from its occurrence in Philo where, however, in conformity with the tradition of the Septuagint to translate the tetragrammaton by the Greek word κύριος, which corresponds more closely to the concepts of rule and judgment, the name is regarded as the symbol of the attribute of judgment, and the name *Elohim* (translated in the Septuagint by Θεός) as a symbol of the attribute of mercy. The idea of the unity of God, which was widely discussed in non-Jewish circles at the time, receives strong emphasis in the *aggadah*. The concept of the unity of God is based upon the premise that the cosmos, with all its activities, is inconceivable without the existence of a single power which determines and directs it in accordance with a preordained plan and in conformity with a definite purpose. In order to give concrete expression to this idea, the rabbis of the *aggadah* utilized various parables, whose prototypes are found in Philo. They were particularly fond of the parable of "the ship and the captain," or of "the building and its owner," or of "the building and its director" (Sif. Deut. 341; Gen. R. 12:12; Mid. Ps. 23 to 24:1ff.; Gen. R. 39:1). Just as it is impossible for the ship, for example, to reach its destination without a captain, so administration of the cosmos and of individuals is impossible without a directing and supervising force. Other parables frequently found in the *aggadah* were intended to bring about reverence for the might of God, whose awesomeness is rendered even greater for the very reason that it defies man's powers of comprehension. If the brilliance of the sun blinds the human eye, how much more so the light of God (Ḥul. 59b). Man is unable to observe more than a particle of His grandeur and sublimity. The rabbis of the *aggadah* also use the soul as an example in teaching this doctrine. If a man's own soul, the source of his life, is beyond his intellectual comprehension, how much less can he comprehend the Creator of the universe and the source of its life (Mid. Ps. to 103:1; Lev. R. 4:3).

The recognition of the oneness of God is regarded by the scholars of the Talmud as a cardinal principle of religion, concerning which mankind as a whole was commanded, the seven precepts binding upon Noachides including idolatry.

If there is any difference between the biblical concept of God and that of the Talmud it lies in the fact that the God of the Talmud is more "homey," so to speak, than the God of the Bible. He is nearer to the masses, to the broken-hearted, to the ordinary person in need of His help. Only in this sense, does He at times appear to be an even greater epitomization of ethical virtues than the God of Scripture.

The nearness of God is the predominating idea of the Talmud and Midrash. God mourns because of the evil decrees He has pronounced upon Israel; He goes into exile with His children; He studies Torah and gives His view on halakhic topics, and is overjoyed if the scholars triumph over him in *halakhah*. Every generation of Israel has been witness to the nearness of God. God revealed Himself at the Red Sea as a warrior; at Sinai as a sage filled with mercy; after the incident of the golden calf, as a congregational reader draped in a *tallit* ("prayer shawl"), instructing the people how to pray and repent. These metaphors are not intended anthropomorphically, but are rather devices for driving home the idea of God's nearness to his people, by the use of striking and daring images. The sages see no difference between God's closeness to Israel in the past and in the present. The idea of the selection of Israel and the greatness of its destiny stands, both in the past and in the present, at the very center of the relationship between God and His people, and complete confidence therefore exists that God will answer His people whenever they seek Him. The concept of God's nearness to man is also enshrined in the ethical teaching of the time, the rabbis enjoining man to imitate the attributes of God: "Just as He is merciful and compassionate, be thou too merciful and compassionate (Mekh., be-Shallaḥ 14:2; Sifra 19:1).

IN KABBALAH

The kabbalistic view of God is in principle a derivation from the desire to abolish the contradiction between the two concepts: God's unity and God's existence. The emphasis of God's unity leads the philosopher to reject anything that could undermine that absolute unity—any attribute, determination, or quality that can be interpreted as an addition to His unity and as evidence for plurality. On the other hand, the emphasis on God's life which is characteristic of religious faith endangers His unity, since life is variegated by its very nature: it is a process and not a state. In the opinion of many kabbalists the divinity should be conceived of in the following two fundamental aspects: (1) God in Himself who is hidden in the depths of His being; (2) the revealed God who creates and preserves his creation. For kabbalists these two aspects are not contradictory but complement one another. Regarding God Himself the first aspect suffices, and in the opinion of some (Moses Cordovero, and the Ḥabad Ḥasidism), one could doubt whether from this point of view anything at all exists apart from God. It is precisely the second view, however, that is required by religious faith: namely, a revealed God who can be recognized by His action and revelation.

In terms of God Himself, He has neither a name nor an attribute and nothing can be said of Him except that He is. This absolute divinity is usually called in Kabbalah *Ein-Sof* ("the Infinite"). *Ein-Sof* lacks any attributes, even more than, if one may say so, does the God of Maimonides. From the sayings of some early kabbalists, it is apparent that they are careful not even to ascribe personality to God. Since He is beyond everything—beyond even imagination, thought, or will—nothing can be said of Him that is within the grasp of our thought. He "conceals Himself in the recesses of mystery"; He is "the supreme cause" or "the great existent" (in *Berit Menuḥah,* Amsterdam, 1648), appellations which contain a negation of the personal nature of God. There were also kabbalists, however, who wished to give a personality to *Ein-Sof,* though in their opinion too this personality was indefinable: according to them the *Ein-Sof* is *ba'al ha-raẓon,* "the possessor of will" (Menaḥem Azariah da Fano) hence it is possible to say of Him, as do faithful pious Jews, "Blessed be He"; "May He be blessed and exalted," etc. Both these conceptions are met with in the pages of the Zohar. In favor of the personal character of *Ein-Sof* weighed the argument that even without the existence of emanations, the *Sefirot,* and the worlds, His perfection would not lack anything, hence one should not think that God acquired personality through the emanation of the "attributes" or the *Sefirot,* which determine for us the personal character of God. It should be said that, in the opinion of all kabbalists the *Ein-Sof* is divinity itself, but some kabbalists doubt whether it is also "God." For the life of the *Ein-Sof* is concealed within itself and is not revealed, while the religious man seeks the revelation of this concealed life. This revelation comes through the emanation of the *Sefirot,* which are the domain of the life of the revealed God. This emanation is not a necessity, according to the nature of the *Ein-Sof;* it is a voluntary activity of the emanator.

The special difficulty in connection with this view is that according to kabbalistic doctrine the ten *Sefirot* or worlds of heavenly *Parẓufim* ("configurations," in the Lurianic Kabbalah) are not created regions distinct from the *Ein-Sof,* like all the other creations, but are in fact included within the divine unity itself. The *Sefirot* are also attributes (and some kabbalists explicitly identify them with the "attributes of action" of the philosophers) but in actual fact they are more than attributes: they are the various stages at which God reveals Himself at the time of creation; they are His powers and His names. Each quality is one facet of his revelation. Hence every name applied to the divine is merely one of these qualities: *Eheyeh, Yah, El, Elohim, Ẓeva'ot, Adonai*—each points to a special aspect in the revealed God, and only the totality of all these qualities exhausts the active life of God. It is this totality, its order, and its laws, in which the theology of the Kabbalah is fundamentally interested. Here the personality of God is manifested even if it is not developed: God revealed himself not only at Mt. Sinai; He revealed Himself in everything since the beginning of the creation, and will continue to reveal Himself until the end of time; His act in creation is His main revelation. From this position stems a certain dualism in the realm of the revelation of the divine: on the one hand there is *Ein-Sof* which is transcendental and its traces are not discernable in the creatures; yet on the other hand the traces of the living God, who is embodied in the world of the *Sefirot,* are found in everything and

82

discernable in everything—at least to the mystic who knows how to interpret the symbolic language of outer reality. God is in His creation, just as He is outside of it. And if the *Sefirot*, active in the creation, are the "souls" and the inwardness of everything, then the *Ein-Sof* is the "soul of the souls." By the mere fact of being a creature, no creature is divine, though nevertheless something of the divine is revealed in it. The world of *Sefirot* then is the region of divine revelation per se, for the flow of divine life rises and descends in the stages of the *Sefirot*. The divine revelation emanates also upon the region of creation, through the "clothing" of the *Sefirot* in the mundane world.

In critical literature on Kabbalah opinions vary on the question to what extent the formulations of this fundamental standpoint are pantheistic. At various times a pantheistic view of God had been attributed in particular to the Zohar, to Moses Cordovero, and to Abraham Herrera. Important in the theology of the Kabbalah is the new view of the Divine Presence. *Shekhinah*, no longer a synonym for God Himself, but a name for the last *Sefirah* which is the passive and receptive element in God, although it is simultaneously active and emanating upon the creatures. The unity of God in the *Sefirot* is dynamic and not static and all explanations by kabbalists of the *Shema* ("Hear O Israel") testify to this: this is the unity of the stream of life flowing from the *Ein-Sof*, or, according to some opinions, from the will which is the first *Sefirah*.

IN MODERN JEWISH PHILOSOPHY

Moses Mendelssohn. Moses Mendelssohn, the first modern Jewish philosopher, believed that, "Judaism knows nothing of a revealed religion in the sense in which Christians define this term." The truths of religion, particularly those that have to do with the existence and nature of God, are principles of reason and, as such, are available to all men. Through rational reflection we know that God exists, that He is a necessary and perfect being, creator of the world, omnipotent, omniscient, and absolutely good. These truths, which constitute the essential grounds of salvation, are the elements of a natural religion shared by all men. What is peculiarly Jewish is not religion at all, but only divine legislation, God's revealed law, which binds and obligates the Jewish people alone and is the necessary condition of their salvation. True religion, on the other hand, is universal. God has made known to all men, through reason, the essential and eternal truths about His nature and the world He created.

Solomon Formstecher. Solomon Formstecher was especially indebted to the idealist philosopher Schelling for the metaphysical foundations of his theology. He conceived God as the "world-soul," which is the ultimate ground of the unity of all reality. While nature is the open manifestation of God in the world of our experience, it is only as spirit that God can truly be conceived. His essence is beyond all human knowledge, and to restrict God to the necessarily anthropomorphic conceptions of man borders on paganism. Formstecher believed that the world-soul is not in the world, but is prior to and independent of it. God is an absolutely free spirit, whose freedom is most clearly evident in His activity as creator of the world. Because of His absolute freedom, God is understood as the ultimate ethical being and as the ideal that man should strive to imitate and realize in his own ethical life.

Samuel Hirsch. Samuel Hirsch taught a doctrine similar to that of Formstecher, although he was more dependent on the philosophy of Hegel. He emphasized the centrality of the ethical even more than Formstecher did. Man discovers his freedom in his own self-consciousness. He knows himself, not as part of nature, but as an "I" who stands in freedom over against the world. God is conceived, on this human model, as a being who is absolutely free and supreme in power over all that exists. Through the miracles that He performs, God exhibits to man His absolute power and freedom. For Hirsch, Judaism is, above all, the religion of the spirit. Its highest purpose is the actualization of human freedom in the ethical life, because only in free and moral acts does man truly serve God.

Solomon Ludwig Steinheim. Unlike most of his contemporaries, Solomon Ludwig Steinheim thought that philosophy and religion are radically opposed. He held that the true knowledge of God can be acquired only through revelation, and that scriptural revelation contradicts the canons of human reason. If God is conceived in purely rational terms, then His freedom must necessarily be denied, because rationality entails causal necessity. The God of reason is subject to causal rules, since, even as first cause, He is limited to that which reason finds possible. Such a God is not absolutely free. Neither is He a true creator, for according to the principle that nothing comes from nothing, He could not have created the world freely and *ex nihilo.* Steinheim rejected reason in favor of revelation, denied the principle of causality, and represented God as the true and free creator who stands above the limitations of rational necessity. Only through such a theology does man become free. Freedom is possible for man only if he subordinates his reason to the God of revelation, whose creative freedom provides the sole ground of genuinely human existence.

Nachman Krochmal. Nachman Krochmal, although living in Eastern Europe, was more fully Hegelian than his Western Jewish contemporaries. They modified the prevailing philosophy to accommodate the personal God of traditional Judaism, but Krochmal developed a doctrine which borders on pantheism. He conceived God as Absolute Spirit, containing in itself all reality. Absolute Spirit has none of the characteristics of a personal God. Even as cause, He is impersonal: He causes the world only in the sense that He is its totality. The world is derived from God through emanation, which Krochmal understood as a form of divine self-limitation. In this Krochmal was affected by kabbalistic doctrines, which he combined with Hegelianism.

Hermann Cohen. Three figures of major importance appeared in the late 19th and early 20th centuries, Hermann

Cohen, Franz Rosenzweig, and Martin Buber. In his early years Cohen thought of God as a philosophical construct that served as the guarantor of morality and moral progress. The existence of God, according to this conception, cannot be proved. He is beyond all positive descriptions, and is thought of only as an "idea" in the technical Kantian sense. Though His nature is absolutely unknown to us, God as idea is the one absolutely necessary ground of morality. His reality is affirmed because the alternative of denying morality cannot be accepted. In his later years Cohen adopted more traditional language as he became more deeply concerned for Judaism. He then spoke of God as the Creator, the God of love, and the source of all being, who is absolutely one and unique.

Franz Rosenzweig. In Rosenzweig's view, God is not known through philosophic inquiry or rational demonstration. He is met in direct existential encounter, which is true revelation. In the anguished consciousness of his own creaturely contingency, man encounters God, who is the creator of the world, and above all he encounters dependence. This meeting reveals God as an all-powerful and loving father. His love for man results in commandments that bind every individual for whom the divine-human encounter is a reality.

Martin Buber. Like Rosenzweig, Buber stressed, above all, the personal quality of God. He is the Eternal Thou, whom one meets as the supreme partner in dialogue. This is not the depersonalized God of the philosopher-theologian, whose nature is expressed in a set of formal propositions. Man knows Him only as the Ever-Present, who meets him in true encounter. No effort to give a consistent definition of God succeeds. "Of course God is the 'wholly Other'; but He is also the wholly Same, the wholly Present. Of course He is the *Mysterium Tremendum* that appears and overthrows; but He is also the mystery of the self-evident, nearer to me than my I" (*I and Thou* (1937), 79).

Mordecai Kaplan. In the United States Mordecai Kaplan developed a naturalistic view of God in conscious opposition to the traditional, supernatural views. Convinced that modern science makes it impossible to believe in a transcendent, personal God, Kaplan nevertheless saw value in retaining the idea and the name "God." He conceived God simply as that power in nature which makes possible the fulfillment of man's legitimate aspirations. Despite his commitment to scientific naturalism, Kaplan believed that the world is so constituted that valid human ideals are supported and helped toward realization by the cosmic process. It is this force making for human salvation that Kaplan called God.

JUSTICE AND MERCY OF GOD

Central among the biblical affirmations about God are those that emphasize His justice *(mishpat)* and righteousness *(zedakah)* on the one hand, and His mercy *(rahamim)* and loving-kindness *(hesed)* on the other. God's justice and mercy are both affirmed in God's proclamation to Moses at Sinai before the giving of the Decalogue: "The Lord, the Lord, a God compassionate and gracious, slow to anger, abounding in kindness and faithfulness, extending kindness to the thousandth generation, forgiving iniquity, transgression, and sin; yet He does not remit all punishment, but visits the iniquity of the fathers upon children and children's children, upon the third and fourth generations" (Ex. 34:6–7). Justice and mercy are the bases of the covenant between God and the Israelites. God's mercy is revealed in the fact that he redeemed the people of Israel from slavery in Egypt to make them His people and contract a covenant with them: "When Israel was a child, I loved him, out of Egypt I called my son" (Hos. 11:1). His justice is revealed in the fact that He punishes the Israelites if they sin and do not uphold their side of the covenant: "You only have I known of all the families of the earth; therefore I will punish you all your iniquities"(Amos 3:2). Both the justice and mercy of God are evident in the biblical portrayal of God's relationship with Israel; "I will betroth you to me in righteousness and in justice, in steadfast love and in mercy" (Hos. 2:19). In exercising justice and punishing the people of Israel when they sin God reveals His power and lordship not only to Israel but to the world as a whole. God's justice is often tempered by His mercy: "My heart recoils within me, My compassion grows warm and tender. I will not execute My fierce anger, I will not again destroy Ephraim; for I am God and not man . . ." (Hos. 11:8–9). By exercising His mercy God hopes to encourage the people of Israel to uphold their side of the covenant and fulfill His demands as expressed in the Torah. The relationship between justice and mercy in God's attitude toward the people of Israel is intricate and varied, and while some biblical verses emphasize His justice and others, His mercy, it is impossible to say that one or the other is predominant.

In Post-biblical Judaism. This same intermingling of justice and mercy is to be discerned in the works of Philo and other post-biblical writings (see G. F. Moore, *Judaism in the First Centuries of the Christian Era,* 1(1927), 386–400). In rabbinic Judaism a vivid expression of this intermingling is found in a parable in Genesis Rabbah (12:15) comparing God to a king who in order to prevent a fragile goblet from shattering must mix hot and cold water when filling it. Thus the world exists because of the admixture of the attributes of mercy and justice (*middat ha-raḥamim* and *middat ha-din*). Behind this parable lies a complex development of biblical ideas in which the two divine appellations, the Tetragrammaton (YHWH) and *Elohim,* were understood to refer to the two main manifestations of God's providence: the first, to express the attribute of mercy; the second, that of justice (see A. Marmorstein, *The Old Rabbinic Doctrine of God,* pt. 1 (1927), 43–53, 181–208). The presence of both names in Genesis 2:4 signifies that mercy and justice were both necessary in order to make creation possible. Genesis Rabbah 39:6 expresses a similar notion: "If thou desirest the world to endure, there can be no absolute justice, while if thou desirest absolute justice the world cannot endure . . ." Insofar as God's justice and mercy are necessary for creation it is not only the community of Israel that is the major object of these divine activities but the world as a whole. Nonetheless, it must be recognized that rabbinic Judaism was more concerned with the divine activities of mercy and justice as they were directed toward the community of Israel. The fate of the Jewish people in the Roman period was a tragic impetus to this discussion. Faced, too, with the problem of the suffering of the righteous and the prosperity of the wicked, the rabbis examined the concept of divine justice and advanced a number of new interpretations of it in an effort to justify the apparent imbalance of suffering and prosperity in the world. It was suggested that ultimate reward and punishment would take place in the afterlife, that suffering was a process of purification *(yissurin shel ahavah)*, and that the individual often suffered for the sins of his ancestors or of the community at large.

While various trends in medieval Jewish philosophy and mysticism interpreted the divine attributes of justice and mercy differently, they all affirmed that these were qualities of God. In the face of the holocaust in the 20th century, some thinkers, for example, R. Rubenstein, have seriously questioned the concept of divine justice and mercy, while others, for example, Emil Fackenheim, maintain that it is a major obligation of Jewish religious thought to rediscover the meaning of the concept in the face of the contemporary situation.

CONCEPTIONS OF GOD

Monotheism. The normative Jewish conception of God is theism, or more exactly, monotheism. It conceives of God as the creator and sustainer of the universe, whose will and purposes are supreme. He is the only being whose existence is necessary, uncaused, and eternal, and all other beings are dependent on Him. God as conceived by Judaism transcends the world, yet He is also present in the world, and "the whole earth is full of His glory" (Isa. 6:3). He is a personal God, whom man can love with the highest and most complete love, while confronting Him as father, king, and master. He loves man and commands him, and his commandments are the criterion of the good. He is absolutely one, admitting no plurality in his nature, and absolutely unique, so that no other existing thing can in any way be compared to Him. This is essentially the picture of the biblical God as it was developed and understood in classical Jewish thought.

This conception of God contrasts sharply with the mythological gods, who have parents and children, eat and drink, have desires and passions. Judaism categorically rejected the mythological gods. However, a variety of more sophisticated conceptions of God confronted Judaism, presenting challenges and evoking responses.

Atheism. It might be supposed that the greatest threat to monotheism would be atheism, but throughout most of Jewish history this was not the case. In the Bible there is no awareness of genuine atheism. The biblical authors attacked idolatry and other mistaken conceptions of God. Frequently, they attacked those who deny that God is concerned with man and the world, but seemed unaware of men who did not believe in a superior power.

Atheism was known in the Middle Ages, and was countered by the various proofs for the existence of God that were common to all medieval philosophical theology. Yet, since the dominant medieval culture was overwhelmingly religious, atheism constituted only a minor threat. In modern times atheism became a significant and widely held doctrine, based on and reinforced by naturalistic scientific ideas and scientifically oriented philosophy. The classical proofs for God's existence have been largely discredited and no longer provide a satisfactory ground for theism. Modern theists usually offer arguments for the existence of God, but do not claim that they have proofs. These arguments, though not decisive, provide a justification for the theistic option, since it is claimed that these are matters about which no demonstrative certainty is possible. In the 20th century theistic belief usually rests on a combination of admittedly incomplete intellectual evidence and personal faith and commitment.

Polytheism and Dualism. Polytheism, the belief that there are many gods, was never a serious threat to normative Judaism, because it is a form of idolatry which could not be readily confused with biblical doctrine. Wherever polytheism appeared among Jews, recognized authorities rejected it vigorously.

Dualism was the only version of polytheism which made serious inroads into the cultural world of the Jews. Dualism teaches that there are two cosmic powers, each of which has dominion over one portion of the universe. The Zoroastrian version has a god of light and a god of darkness, while the Gnostics taught that there is a hidden god who is beyond all knowledge and the evident god who created and formed the world. Dualism is soundly rejected in a classical biblical passage which says, "I am the Lord, and there is none else, beside me there is no God . . . I form the light and create the darkness; I make peace and create evil; I am the Lord that doeth all these things" (Isa. 45:5,7). This forceful denial of dualism is repeated in a slightly modified form in the daily liturgy. The Talmud challenges the heresy of dualism explicitly with strong prohibitions against any deviations from standard liturgy that might have dualistic implications. Rabbinic rulings proscribe any form of prayer that suggests that there are *shetei reshuyot*, two independent powers controlling the world (Ber. 33b).

The medieval philosophers also argued against dualism. Saadiah Gaon dealt with the problem explicitly, offering three arguments against the dualistic position. He first showed that if the doctrine of one God is abandoned, there is no reason to restrict the cosmic powers to two. Arguments can then be made for almost any number one chooses. A second objection is that dualism makes unintelligible the fact that there is an ordered world, since, presumably, each power could frustrate the designs of the other. Finally, he argued that we cannot conceive of such powers as gods at all, since each would limit the other (*Beliefs and Opinions*, 2:2). Other medieval philosophers attacked dualism indirectly through their arguments for the necessary unity of God.

Though there are similarities between Kabbalah and Gnosticism, the kabbalists did not succumb to the temptations of dualism. "On the contrary," says Gershom Scholem "all the energy of 'orthodox' Kabbalistic speculation is bent to the task of escaping from dualistic consequences; otherwise they would not have been able to maintain themselves within the Jewish community" (Scholem, Mysticism, 13).

Trinity. The Trinitarian conception of God is associated especially with Christianity. Though Christian theologians normally intepret the Trinity as a doctrine of one God in three persons, Jewish thinkers rejected it categorically as a denial of the divine unity. Since only heretical Jewish sects could even entertain the possibility of a Trinitarian God, most Jewish anti-Trinitarian polemics were directed specifically against Christianity. Occasionally, kabbalistic doctrines seem to have a Trinitarian cast, as is the case in the thought of Abraham Abulafia (*ibid.*, 123ff.). However, these Trinitarian formulations are always interpreted in such ways that they clearly do not refer to a triune God. Some Shabbateans developed a trinity consisting of the unknown God, the God of Israel, and the *Shekhinah* ("Divine Presence": *ibid.*, 287ff.). Their heresy was vigorously attacked by official Jewish spokesmen.

Pantheism. A far more complex problem is posed by Jewish attitudes toward pantheism. This doctrine teaches that God is the whole of reality and that all reality is God. Because it does not involve any polytheistic notions and seems, therefore, compatible with standard Jewish doctrines about God's unity, pantheism found occasional followers among even highly respected Jewish thinkers. It also evoked great opposition, because it denies some of the fundamentals of Jewish monotheism. The pantheistic God

is not a separate being who transcends the world, nor is he

even a being who is immanent in the world. He is identical with the totality of the world. He is not a personal God; he neither commands men nor seeks their obedience. Consequently, there are almost no instances of pure pantheism within the normative Jewish tradition, though pantheistic tendencies have appeared at various times. They derive from an overemphasis on the immanence of God or an excessive stress on the nothingness of the world. They must be considered in any account of Jewish conceptions of God. Hermann Cohen expressed the extreme view of many thinkers when he stated categorically "Pantheism is not religion" (see *Ethik des reinen Willens* (1921²), 456–66.). Nevertheless, one can find various traces of pantheistic thought, if not actual pantheism, in many deeply pious Jewish thinkers. Some scholars attempted to put a pantheistic interpretation on the rabbinic use of *Makom* ("Place") as a name for God because "He is the place of the world, but the world is not His place" (Gen. R. 68). (The original significance of *Makom* as a divine name has no pantheistic connotations.) Philo also spoke of God as "Place" and for this reason is considered by some interpreters to have a pantheistic doctrine. H. A. Wolfson however, argues that for Philo the doctrine that God is the place of the world means that "God is everywhere in the corporeal world, thereby exercising His individual providence, but He is no part of the corporeal world and is unlike anything in it" (see his *Philo* (1947), 245ff.). The elements of pantheism which appeared periodically in the history of Jewish thought were almost always tempered by the use of theistic language and adjustments to theistic claims. Solomon ibn Gabirol conceived of reality as a graded continuum, moving from the Godhead through a series of levels of being down to the corporeal world (*Mekor Ḥayyim,* passim). His system seems pantheistic, because it treats all reality as one continuous emanation of the divine substance. Nevertheless, in his general religious orientation he returns to standard conceptions of a personal God who is the creator of the world. The thought of Abraham ibn Ezra exhibits a similar ambiguity. He used purely pantheistic language when he said that "God is the One. He is the creator of all, and He is all ... God is all and all comes from Him" (Commentary to Genesis, 1:26; to Exodus, 23:21). Yet, there are countless places in his writings where he also uses strictly conventional theistic terminology. Wherever there is strong neoplatonic influence on Jewish thought a suggestion of pantheism is usually present. Pantheism also appears in mystical doctrines that stress the immanence of God. In the Kabbalah there is an ongoing struggle between pantheistic and theistic tendencies. The former often provide the doctrinal base of a kabbalistic system, while the latter determine the language in which the system is expressed. Scholem states, "In the history of Kabbalism, theistic and pantheistic trends have frequently contended for mastery. This fact is sometimes obscured because the representatives of pantheism have generally endeavored to speak the language of theism; cases of writers who openly put forward pantheistic views are rare. ..The author of the Zohar inclines toward pantheism ... On the whole, his language is that of the theist, and some penetration is needed to lift its hidden and lambent pantheistic core to the light" (Mysticism, 222). The same tendency can observed in Ḥasidism. In a key passage R. Shneur Zalman of Lyady asserted that "there is truly nothing besides Him" (*Tanya, Sha'ar ha-Yiḥud ve-ha-Emunah*, ch. 3); yet, he can hardly be called a pure pantheist when we consider the many conventional theistic formulations in his writings. Only in the case of Nachman Krochmal does there seem to be an instance of genuine Jewish pantheism. Krochmal ascribed true existence only to God, who is Absolute Spirit. In his thought only the Absolute Spirit truly exists, and he denies any other mode of existence. Krochmal was far less inclined than earlier Jewish thinkers to adopt language appropriate to a doctrine of a personal, theistic God.

Deism. Deism was still another conception of God that confronted Jewish theology. Deistic doctrine contains two main elements. First is the view that God, having created the world, withdrew himself from it completely. This eliminates all claims of divine providence, miracles, and any form of intervention by God in history. Second, deism holds that all the essential truths about God are knowable by unaided natural reason without any dependence on revelation. The vast bulk of Jewish tradition rejected both deistic claims. It is hardly possible to accept the biblical God and still affirm the deistic view that he is not related to the world. Numerous rabbinic texts are attacks on the Greek philosophers who taught such a doctrine. Similar attacks continued throughout the history of Jewish philosophy. Of the medieval philosophers, only Levi ben Gershom seems to have had deistic tendencies.

Among modern Jewish thinkers, Moses Mendelssohn is sometimes classified as a deist because he held that there is a universal natural religion, whose doctrines are known by reason alone. It does not seem correct, however, to identify Mendelssohn's God with the deistic God, because he ascribes to God qualities of personality and involvement with the world that are hardly in accord with standard deism (see Guttmann, Philosophies, 291ff.). However, Mendelssohn is open to varying interpretations, and Leo Baeck was not alone when he propounded the view that for Mendelssohn "Judaism had become merely a combination of law and deistic natural religion." Over the centuries of its history Judaism has been exposed to a variety of conceptions of God, but none has ever been strong enough to overcome the basic Jewish commitment to monotheism. Other doctrines have influenced Jewish thought and have left their traces, yet, the monotheistic faith has consistently emerged as the normative expression of Jewish religion.

4 TORAH

Origin and Preexistence. "Moses received the Torah from Sinai" (Avot 1:1). Yet there is an ancient tradition that the Torah existed in heaven not only before God revealed it to Moses, but even before the world was created. The apocryphal book of the The Wisdom of Ben Sira identified the Torah with preexistent personified wisdom (1:1-5, 26; 15:1; 24:1ff.; 34:8; cf. Prov. 8:22-31). In rabbinic literature, it was taught that the Torah was one of the six or seven things created prior to the creation of the world (Gen. R. 1:4; Pes. 54a, et al.). Of these preexistent things, it was said that only the Torah and the throne of glory were actually created, while the others were only conceived, and that the Torah preceded the throne of glory (Gen. R. 1:4). According to Eliezer ben Yose the Galilean, for 974 generations before the creation of the world, the Torah lay in God's bosom and joined the ministering angels in song (ARN[1] 31, p. 91, cf. Gen. R. 28:4, et al.). Simeon ben Lakish taught that the Torah preceded the world by 2,000 years (Lev. R. 19:1, et al.) and was written in black fire upon white fire (TJ, Shek. 6:1, 49d, et al.). Akiva called the Torah, "the precious instrument by which the world was created" (Avot 3:14). Rav Hoshaiah, explicitly identifying the Torah with the preexistent wisdom of Proverbs, said that God created the world by looking into the Torah as an architect builds a palace by looking into blueprints. He also took the first word of Genesis not in the sense of "In the beginning," but in that of "By means of the beginning," and he taught that "beginning" (probably in the philosophic sense of the Greek *archē*) designates Torah, since it is written of wisdom (=Torah), "The Lord made

Moses receiving the Tablets of the Law at Mount Sinai while the Israelites stand behind a fenced mountain. A marginal illustration to the mishnaic tractate *Avot.* Florence, Italy, 1492. New York, Jewish Theological Seminary, *Rothschild Siddur,* fol. 139.

me the beginning of His way" (Prov. 8:22; Gen. R. 1:1). It was also taught that God took council with the Torah before He created the world (Tanḥ. B. 2, et al.). The concept **97**

Moses on Mount Sinai hands the Law down to one of the Children of Israel. *Leipzig Maḥzor*, S. Germany, c. 1320. Leipzig University Library, Ms. V. 1102, vol. 1, fol. 130v.

of the preexistence of the Torah is perhaps implicit in the philosophy of Philo, who wrote of the preexistence and role in creation of the Word of God (*logos*; e.g., Op. 20, 25, 36; Cher. 127) and identified the Word of God with the Torah (Mig. 130; cf. Op. and II Mos.).

Saadiah Gaon rejected the literal belief in preexistent things on the grounds that it contradicts the principle of creation *ex nihilo*. In his view, Proverbs 8:22, the verse cited by Rav Hoshaiah, means no more than that God created the world in a wise manner (*Beliefs and Opinions* 1:3; cf. Saadiah's commentary on Proverbs, ad loc.).

Judah b. Barzillai of Barcelona raised the problem of place. Where could God have kept a preexistent Torah? While allowing that God could conceivably have provided an ante-mundane place for a corporeal Torah, he preferred the interpretation that the Torah preexisted only as a thought in the divine mind. Ultimately, however, he expressed the opinion that the Torah's preexistence is a rabbinic metaphor, spoken out of love for the Torah and those who study it, and teaching that the Torah is worthy to have been created before the world (commentary on *Sefer Yeẓirah*, pp. 88–89; cf. Solomon b. Abraham Adret, *Perushei Aggadot*).

Abraham ibn Ezra raised the problem of time. He wrote that it is impossible for the Torah to have preceded the world by 2,000 years or even by one moment, since time is an accident of motion, and there was no motion before God created the celestial spheres; rather, he concluded, the teaching about the Torah's preexistence must be a metaphoric riddle (cf. Commentary on the Torah, introd., "the fourth method" (both versions); cf. also Judah Hadassi, *Eshkol ha-Kofer*, 25b–26a; and cf. Abraham Shalom, *Neveh Shalom*, 10:8).

Judah Halevi explained that the Torah precedes the world in terms of teleology; God created the world for the purpose of revealing the Torah; therefore, since, as the philosophers say, "the first of thought is the end of the work," the Torah is said to have existed before the world (*Kuzari* 3:73).

Maimonides discussed the origin of the Torah from the standpoint of the epistemology of the unique prophecy of Moses (*Guide of the Perplexed* 2:35; 3:51; et al.; cf. Yad, introd.). The tradition of the preexistence of the Torah was not discussed in the *Guide of the Perplexed;* however, the closely related tradition of the preexistence of the throne of glory was (2:26, 30, et al.). The discussions of Moses' prophecy and of the throne of glory are esoteric and each reader will interpret them according to his own views, perhaps inferring Maimonides' position on the Torah. 99

Within the framework of his Neoplatonic ontology, Isaac ibn Latif suggested that the Torah precedes the world not in time, but in rank. He cited the aggadic statements that the Torah and the throne of glory preceded the world, and that the Torah preceded the throne of glory, and he was of the view that the Torah is the upper world (wisdom or intellect) which ontologically precedes the middle world (the celestial spheres, the throne of glory) which, in turn, ontologically precedes the lower world (our world of changing elements; *Sha'ar ha-Shamayim*).

While the tradition of the preexistence of the Torah was being ignored or explained away by most philosophers, it became fundamental in the Kabbalah. Like Ibn Latif, the kabbalists of Spain held that the Torah precedes the world ontologically. Some kabbalists identified the primordial Torah with *Hokhmah* (God's wisdom), the second of the ten *Sefirot* in emanation. Others identified the Written Torah with the sixth *Sefirah, Tiferet* (God's beauty), and the Oral Torah with the tenth *Sefirah, Malkhut* (God's kingdom). Emanational precedence signifies creative power; and it was with the Torah that God created the angels and the worlds, and with the Torah He sustains all (Zohar 3, 152a; Num. 9:1).

Ḥasdai Crescas, who in the course of his revolutionary critique of Aristotelian physics had rejected the dependence of time on motion, was able to take preexistence literally as chronological. He interpreted the proposition about the preexistence of the Torah as a metonymy, referring actually to the purpose of the Torah. Since, according to him, the purpose of the Torah and the purpose of the world are the same, namely, love, and since the purpose or final cause of an object chronologically precedes it, it follows that the purpose of the Torah (i.e., love) chronologically preceded the world. As its final cause, love (=the purpose of the Torah) is a necessary condition of the world; and this is the meaning of the talmudic statement, "Were it not for the Torah [i.e., the purpose of the Torah, or love], heaven and earth would not have come into existence" (Pes. 68b; *Or Adonai* 2:6, 4; cf. Nissim b. Reuben Gerondi, Commentary on Ned. 39b).

Joseph Albo also interpreted the preexistence of the Torah in terms of final causality, but his position was essentially that of Judah Halevi, and not that of his teacher, Crescas. He reasoned that man exists for the sake of the Torah; everything in the world of generation and corruption exists for the sake of man; therefore, the Torah preceded the world in the Aristotelian sense that the final cause in (the mind of) the agent necessarily precedes the other three causes (*Sefer ha-Ikkarim* 3:12; cf. Jacob b. Solomon ibn Ḥabib, *Ein Ya'akov,* introd.; Joseph Solomon Delmedigo, *Novelot Ḥokhmah,* 1).

The theory, based on the statement of Rav Hoshaiah, that the Torah was the preexistent blueprint of creation was elaborated by Isaac Arama, Isaac Abrabanel, Moses Alshekh, Judah Loew b. Bezalel, and others.

In modern Jewish philosophical literature, Nachman Krochmal analyzed the interpretation of the author of *Sha'ar ha-Shamayim* (Ibn Latif and not, as Krochmal supposed, Ibn Ezra) of the Torah's preexistence, and his analysis bears implications for his own idealistic concept of the metaphysical and epistemological precedence of the spiritual (*Moreh Nevukhei ha-Zeman,* 17; cf. 12, 16).

Franz Rosenzweig, in his existentalist reaction to the intellectualist interpretation of the Torah by German rabbis, appealed to the *aggadah* of the preexistence of the Torah in an attempt to show the absurdity of trying to base the claim of the Torah merely on a juridical or historical reason: "No doubt the Torah, both Written and Oral, was given Moses on Sinai, but was it not created before the creation of the world? Written against a background of shining fire in letters of somber flame? And was not the world created for its sake?" ("The Builders," in: N. Glatzer (ed.), *On Jewish Learning* (1955), 78).

Nature and Purpose. In the Bible, the Torah is referred to as the Torah of the Lord (Ex. 13:9, et al.) and of Moses (Josh. 8:31, et al.), and said to be given as an inheritance to the congregation of Jacob (Deut. 33:4). Its purpose seems to be to make Israel "a kingdom of priests and a holy nation" (Ex. 19:6). It was said that "the commandment is a lamp and the Torah is light" (Prov. 6:23). The Torah was called "perfect," its ordinances "sweeter than honey and the flow of honeycombs" (Ps. 19:8, 11; cf. 119: 103; Prov. 16:24). Psalm 119, containing 176 verses, is a song of love for the Torah whose precepts give peace and understanding.

In the apocryphal book The Wisdom of Ben Sira, the Torah is identified with wisdom (see above). In another apocryphal work, the laws of the Torah are said to be drawn up "with a view to truth and the indication of right reason" (Arist. 161). The Septuagint rendered the Hebrew *torah* by the Greek *nomos* ("law") probably in the sense of a living network of traditions and customs of a people. The designation of the Torah by *nomos,* and by its Latin successor *lex* (whence, "the Law"), has historically given rise to the sad misunderstanding that Torah means legalism.

It was one of the very few real dogmas of rabbinic theology that the Torah is from heaven (Heb. *Torah min ha-shamayim;* Sanh. 10:1, et al.; cf. Ex. 20:22 [19]; Deut. 4:36); i.e., the Torah in its entirety was revealed by God. According to the *aggadah,* Moses ascended into heaven to capture the Torah from the angels (Shab. 89a, et al.). In one of the oldest mishnaic statements, Simeon the Just taught that (the study of the) Torah is one of the three things by which the world is sustained (Avot 1:2). Eleazar ben Shammua said: "Were it not for the Torah, heaven and earth would not continue to exist" (Pes. 68b; Ned. 32a; cf. Crescas' interpretation above). It was calculated that "the whole world in its entirety is only 1/3200 of the Torah" (Er. 21a; cf. TJ, Pe'ah 1:1, 15d). God Himself was said to study the Torah daily (Av. Zar. 3b, et al.).

The Torah was often compared to fire, water, wine, oil, milk, honey, drugs, manna, the tree of life, and many other things; it was considered the source of freedom, goodness, and life (e.g., Avot 6:2, 3, 7); it was identified both with wisdom and with love (e.g., Mid. Ps. to 1:18). Hillel summarized the entire Torah in one sentence: "What is hateful to you, do not to your fellow" (Shab. 31a). Akiva said: "The fundamental principle of the Torah is the commandment, 'Love thy neighbor as thyself'" (Lev. 19:18). His disciple Simeon ben Azzai said that its fundamental principle is the verse (Gen. 5:1) which teaches that all human beings are descended from the same man, and created by God in His image (Sifra, Kedoshim 4:12; TJ, Ned. 9:3, 41c; Gen. R. 24:7).

Often the Torah was personified. Not only did God take council with the Torah before He created the world (see above), but according to one interpretation, the plural in "Let us make man" (Gen. 1:26) refers to God and the Torah (Tanḥ. Pekudei, 3). The Torah appears as the daughter of God and the bride of Israel (PR 20; 95a, et al.). On occasion, the Torah is obliged to plead the case of Israel before God (e.g., Ex. R. 29:4).

The message of the Torah is for all mankind. Before giving the Torah to Israel, God offered it to the other nations, but they refused it; and when He did give the Torah to Israel, He revealed it in the extraterritorial desert and simultaneously in all the 70 languages, so that men of all nations would have a right to it (Mekh., Yitro, 5; Sif. Deut. 343; Shab. 88b; Ex. R. 5:9; 27:9; cf. Av. Zar. 3a: "a pagan who studies the Torah is like a high priest"). Alongside this universalism, the rabbis taught the inseparability of Israel and the Torah. One rabbi held that the concept of Israel existed in God's mind even before He created the Torah (Gen. R. 1:4). Yet, were it not for its accepting the Torah, Israel would not be "chosen," nor would it be different from all the idolatrous nations (Num. 14:10; Ex. R. 47:3, et al.).

In the Hellenistic literature contemporaneous with the early rabbinic teachings, Philo considered the Torah the ideal law of the philosophers, and Moses the perfect lawgiver and prophet and the philosopher-ruler of Plato's *Republic* (II Mos. 2). His concept of the relationship of the

Torah to nature and man was Stoic: "The world is in harmony with the Torah and the Torah with the world, and the man who observes the Torah is constituted thereby a loyal citizen of the world" (Op. 3). He wrote that the laws of the Torah are "stamped with the seals of nature," and are "the most perfect picture of the cosmic polity" (II Mos. 14, 51). Josephus, in his *Against Apion*, discoursed on the moral and universalistic nature of the Torah, emphasizing that it promotes piety, friendship, humanity toward the world at large, justice, charity, and endurance under persecution. Both Philo and Josephus wrote that principles of the Torah, e.g., the Sabbath, have been imitated by all nations.

Saadiah Gaon expounded a rationalist theory according to which the ethical and religious-intellectual beliefs imparted by the Torah are all attainable by human reason. He held that the Torah is divisible into (1) commandments which, in addition to being revealed, are demanded by reason (e.g., prohibitions of murder, fornication, theft, lying); and (2) commandments whose authority is revelation alone (e.g., Sabbath and dietary laws), but which generally are understandable in terms of some personal or social benefit attained by their performance. Revelation of the Torah was needed because while reason makes general demands, it does not dictate particular laws; and while the matters of religious belief revealed in the Torah are attainable by philosophy, they are only attained by it after some time or, in the case of many, not at all. He taught that the purpose of the Torah is the bestowal of eternal bliss (*Beliefs and Opinions,* introd. 6, ch. 3). He held that Israel is a nation only by virtue of the Torah (see below).

In the period between Saadiah and Maimonides, most Jewish writers who speculated on the nature of the Torah continued in the rationalist tradition established by Saadiah. These included Baḥya ibn Paquda, Joseph ibn Ẓaddik, Abraham ibn Ezra, and Abraham ibn Daud. Judah Halevi, however, opposed the rationalist interpretation. He allowed that the Torah contains rational and political laws, but considered them preliminary to the specifically divine laws and teachings which cannot be comprehended by reason, e.g., the laws of the Sabbath which teach the omnipotence of God and the creation of the world (*Kuzari* 2:48, 50). The Torah makes it possible to approach God by awe, love, and joy (2:50). It is the essence of wisdom, and the outcome of the will of God to reveal His kingdom on earth as it is in heaven (3:17). While Judah Halevi held that Israel was created to fulfill the Torah, he wrote that there would be no Torah were there no Israel (2:56; 3:73).

Maimonides emphasized that the Torah is the product of the unique prophecy of Moses. He maintained that the Torah has two purposes; first, the welfare of the body and, ultimately, the welfare of the soul (intellect). The first purpose, which is a prerequisite of the ultimate purpose, is political, and "consists in the governance of the city and the well-being of the state of all its people according to their capacity." The ultimate purpose consists in the true perfection of man, his acquisition of immortality through intellection of the highest things. The Torah is similar to other laws in its concern with the welfare of the body; but its divine nature is reflected in its concern for the welfare of the soul (*Guide of the Perplexed,* 3:27). Maimonides saw the Torah as a rationalizing force, warring against superstition, imagination, appetite, and idolatry. He cited the rabbinic dictum, "Everyone who disbelieves in idolatry professes the Torah in its entirety" (Sif. Num. 110; Guide 3:29; Yad, Ovedei Kokhavim, 2:4), and taught that the foundation of the Torah and the pivot around which it turns consists in the effacement of idolatry. He held that the Torah must be interpreted in the light of reason.

Of the Jewish philosophers who flourished in the 13th and early 14th centuries, most endorsed Maimonides' position that the Torah has as its purpose both political and spiritual welfare. Some, like Samuel ibn Tibbon and Isaac Albalag, argued that its purpose consists only or chiefly in political welfare. Others emphasized its spiritual purpose, like Levi b. Gershom, who taught that the purpose of the

Torah is to guide man—the masses as well as the intellectual elite—toward human perfection, that is, the acquisition of true knowledge and, thereby, an immortal intellect.

While Maimonides and the Maimonideans generally restricted their analyses of the nature of the Torah to questions of its educational, moral, or political value, the Spanish kabbalists engaged in bold metaphysical speculation concerning its essence. The kabbalists taught that the Torah is a living organism. Some said the entire Torah consists of the names of God set in succession (cf. Naḥmanides, *Perushei ha-Torah,* Preface) or interwoven into a fabric (cf. Joseph Gikatilla, *Sha'arei Orah*). Others said that the Torah is itself the name of God. The Torah was identified with various *Sefirot* in the divine body (see above). Ultimately, it was said that the Torah is God (Menahem Recanati, *Ta'amei ha-Mitzvot,* 3a; Zohar 2, 60a [Ex. 15:22]). This identification of the Torah and God was understood to refer to the Torah in its true primordial essence, and not to its manifestation in the world of creation.

The first Jewish philosopher to construct a metaphysics in which the Torah plays an integral role was Ḥasdai Crescas, who, notwithstanding his distinguished work in natural science, was more sympathetic to the Kabbalah than to Aristotle. He taught that the purpose of the Torah is to effect the purpose of the universe. By guiding man toward corporeal happiness, moral and intellectual excellence, and felicity of soul, the Torah leads him to the love of neighbor and, finally, the eternal love of God *(devekut),* which is the purpose of all creation (*Or Adonai,* 2:6). Like Judah Halevi, he took an ultimately anti-intellectualist position, and maintained, in opposition to the Maimonideans, that the very definition of the Torah as the communication of God to man implies beliefs about the nature of God and His relation to man which cannot, and need not, be proved by philosophy.

Joseph Albo, developing some Maimonidean ideas, taught that the Torah, as divine law, is superior to natural law and conventional-positive law in that it not only promotes political security and good behavior, but also guides man toward eternal spiritual happiness (*Sefer ha-Ikkarim,* 1:7).

In the writings of Isaac Arama, Isaac Abrabanel, Moses Alshekh, Judah Loew b. Beẓalel, and other late medievals, the conflicting approaches to the Torah of Maimonideanism and the Kabbalah converged to give expression to the theme, already adumbrated in Philo, that the Torah exists in the mind of God as the plan and order of the universe (Arama, *Akedat Yiẓḥak;* Abrabanel, *Mifalot Elohim,* 1:2; Alshekh, *Torat Moshe* to Genesis 1:1; Judah Loew, *Netivot Olam,* 1:1; *Tiferet Yisrael,* 25; cf. above). In Italy, Judah b. Jehiel (Messer Leon), influenced by the Renaissance emphasis on the art of rhetoric, composed the *Nofet Ẓufim,* in which he analyzed the language of the Bible and, in effect, presented the first aesthetic interpretation of the Torah (cf. Judah Abrabanel, *Dialoghi di Amore*).

Influenced by Maimonides, Baruch Spinoza took the position taken by some early Maimonideans that the Torah is an exclusively political law. However, he broke radically with those Maimonideans and with all rabbinic tradition by denying its divine nature, by making it an object of historical-critical investigation, and by maintaining that it was not written by Moses alone but by various authors living at different times. Moreover, he considered the Torah primitive, unscientific, and particularistic, and thus subversive to progress, reason, and universal morality. By portraying the Torah as a product of the Jewish people, he reversed the traditional opinion (but cf. Judah Halevi) according to which the Jewish people are a product of the Torah.

Like Spinoza, Moses Mendelssohn considered the Torah a political law, but he affirmed its divine nature. Taking a position similar to Saadiah's, he explained that the Torah does not intend to reveal new ideas about deism and morality, but rather, through its laws and institutions, to arouse men to be mindful of the true ideas attainable by all men through reason. By identifying the beliefs of the Torah with the truths of reason, Mendelssohn affirmed both its scientific respectability and its universalistic nature. By defining the Torah as a political law given to Israel by God, he preserved the traditional view that Israel is a product of the Torah, and not, as Spinoza claimed, vice versa.

With the rise of the science of Judaism (*Wissenschaft des Judentums*) in the 19th century, and the advance of the historical-critical approach to the Torah, many Jewish intellectuals, including ideologists of Reform like Abraham Geiger, followed Spinoza in seeing the Torah, at least in part, as a product of the primitive history of the Jewish nation. Nachman Krochmal, in his rationalist-idealist philosophy, attempted to synthesize the historical-critical thesis that the Torah is a product of Jewish history, with the traditional thesis that the entire Torah is divinely revealed. He maintained that, from the days of Abraham and Isaac, the Hebrew nation has contained the Absolute Spiritual, and this Absolute Spiritual was the source of the laws given to Moses on Mt. Sinai, whose purpose is to perfect the individual and the group, and to prevent the nation's extinction. The Oral Torah, which is, in effect, the history of the evolution of the Jewish spirit, is inseparable from the Written Torah, and is its clarification and conceptual refinement; the true science of the Torah, is the vocation of the Jewish spirit, is the conceptualization of the Absolute Spiritual (*Moreh Nevukhei ha-Zeman*, esp. 6–8, 13).

The increasing intellectualization of the Torah was opposed by Samuel David Luzzatto and Salomon Ludwig Steinheim, two men who had little in common but their fideism. They contended—as Crescas had against the Maimonideans—that the belief that God revealed the Torah is the starting point of Judaism, and that this belief, with its momentous implications concerning the nature of God and His relation to man, cannot be attained by philosophy. Luzzatto held that the foundation of the whole Torah is compassion. Steinheim, profoundly opposing Mendelssohn, held that the Torah comes to reveal truths about God and His work.

While Spinoza and Mendelssohn had emphasized the political nature of the Torah, many rationalists of the late 19th and early 20th centuries emphasized its moral nature. Moritz Lazarus identified the Torah with the moral law, and interpreted the rabbinical statement, "Were it not for the Torah, heaven and earth would not continue to exist" (see above), as corresponding to the Kantian teaching that it is the moral law that gives value to existence. Hermann Cohen condemned Spinoza as a willful falsifier and a traitor to the Jewish people for his claim that the Torah is subversive to universalistic morality. He held that the Torah, with its monotheistic ethics, far from being subversive to universalism, prepares a Jew to participate fully and excellently in general culture (in this connection, he opposed Zionism and developed his controversial theory of "Germanism and Judaism"). He maintained that in its promulgation of commandments affecting all realms of human action, the Torah moves toward overcoming the distinction between holy and profane through teaching all men to become holy by always performing holy actions, i.e., by always acting in accordance with the moral law.

In their German translation of the Bible, Martin Buber and Franz Rosenzweig translated *torah* as *Weisung* or *Unterweisung* ("Instruction") and not as *Gesetz* ("Law"). In general, they agreed on the purpose of the Torah: to convert the universe and God from It to Thou. Yet they differed on several points concerning its nature. Buber saw the Torah as the past dialogue between Israel and God, and the present dialogue between the individual reader, the I, and God, the Thou. He concluded that while one must open himself to the entire teaching of the Torah, he need only accept a particular law of the Torah if he feels that it is being spoken now to him. Rosenzweig objected to this personalist and antinomian position of Buber's. Taking an existentialist position, he maintained that the laws of the Torah are commandments to do, and as such become comprehensible only in the experience of doing, and, therefore, a Jew must not, as Buber did, reject a law of the

Torah that "does not speak to me," but must always open himself to the new experience which may make it comprehensible. Like Cohen—and also like the Ḥasidim, he marveled that the law of the Torah is universal in range. He contended that it erases the barrier between this world and the world to come by encompassing, vitalizing, and thereby redeeming everything in this world.

The secular Zionism of the late 19th and early 20th centuries gave religious thinkers new cause to define the relationship between the Torah and the Jewish nation. Some defined the Torah in terms of the nation. Thus, Mordecai Kaplan translated Aḥad Ha-Am's sociological theory of the evolution of Jewish civilization into a religious, though naturalistic, theory of the Torah as the "religious civilization of the Jews." Others, like Buber and Rosenzweig, considering secular nationalism dangerous, tried to "interdefine" the Torah and the nation. Whereas Buber saw the Torah as the product of a dialogue between the nation and God, he held that the spirit of the nation was transfigured by that dialogue. Rosenzweig, whose position here resembles Judah Halevi's, stated both that the nation's chosenness is prior to the Torah, and that the acceptance of the Torah is an experiential precondition of its chosenness. Other thinkers defined the nation in terms of the Torah. Thus, Abraham Isaac Kook, whose thought was influenced by the Kabbalah, taught that the purpose of the Torah is to reveal the living light of the universe, the suprarational spiritual, to Israel and, through Israel, to all mankind. While the Written Torah, which reveals the light in the highest channel of our soul, is the product of God alone, the Oral Torah, which is inseparable from the Written Torah, and which reveals the light in a second channel of our soul, proximate to the life of deeds, derives its personality from the spirit of the nation. The Oral Torah can live in its fullness only when Israel lives in its fullness—in peace and independence in the Land of Israel. Thus, according to Kook, modern Zionism, whatever the intent of its secular ideologists, has universalistic religious significance, for it is acting in service of the Torah (see esp. *Orot ha-Torah*).

In the State of Israel, most writers and educators have maintained the secularist position of the early Zionists, namely, that the Torah was not revealed by God, in the traditional sense, but is the product of the national life of ancient Israel. Those who have discussed the Torah and its relation to the state from a religious point of view have mostly followed Kook or Buber and Rosenzweig. However, a radically rationalist approach to the nature of the Torah has been taught by Yeshayahu Leibowitz who, in the Maimonidean tradition, emphasizes that the Torah is a law for the worship of God and for the consequent obliteration of the worship of men and things; in this connection, he condemns the subordination of the Torah to nationalism or to religious sentimentalism or to any ideology or institution. Outside the State of Israel, a similarly iconoclastic position has been taken by the French phenomenologist Emmanuel Levinas, who has gone further and written that the love for the Torah should take precedence even over the love for God Himself, for only through the Torah—that knowledge of the Other which is the condition of all ethics—can man relate to a personal God against Whom he can rebel and for Whom he can die.

ETERNITY (or NON-ABROGABILITY). In the Bible there is no text unanimously understood to affirm explicitly the eternity or non-abrogability of the Torah; however, many laws of the Torah are accompanied by phrases such as, "an everlasting injunction through your generations" (Lev. 3:17, et al.).

The doctrine that the Torah is eternal appears several times in the pre-tannaitic apocryphal literature; e.g., Ben Sira 24:9 ("the memorial of me shall never cease") and Jubilees 33:16 ("an everlasting law for everlasting generations").

Whereas the rabbis understood the preexistence of the Torah in terms of its pre-revelation existence in heaven, they understood the eternity or non-abrogability of the

Torah in terms of its post-revelation existence not in heaven; i.e., the whole Torah was given to Moses and no part of it remained in heaven (Deut. 8:6, et al.). When Eliezer ben Hyrcanus and Joshua ben Hananiah were debating a point of Torah and a voice from heaven dramatically announced that Eliezer's position was correct, Joshua refused to recognize its testimony, for the Torah "is not in heaven" (Deut. 30:12), and must be interpreted by men, unaided by the supernatural (BM 59b). It was a principle that "A prophet is henceforth not permitted to innovate a thing" (Sifra, Be-Ḥukkotai 13:7; Tem. 16a; but he was permitted to suspend a law temporarily (Sif. Deut. 175)). The rabbis taught that the Torah would continue to exist in the world to come (e.g., Eccles. R. 2:1), although some of them were of the opinion that innovations would be made in the messianic era (e.g., Gen. R. 98:9; Lev. R. 9:7).

Philo saw the eternity of the Torah as a metaphysical principle, following from the Torah's accord with nature. He believed that the laws and enactments of the Torah "will remain for all future ages as though immortal, so long as the sun and the moon and the whole heaven and universe exist" (II Mos. 14; cf. Jer. 31:32–35). The belief in the eternity of the Torah appears also in the later apocryphal works (e.g., I Bar. 4:1; Ps. of Sol. 10:5) and in Josephus (Apion 2:277).

With the rise to political power of Christianity and Islam, two religions which sought to convert Jews and which argued that particular injunctions of the Torah had been abrogated, the question of the eternity or "non-abrogatability" of the Torah became urgent.

Saadiah Gaon stated that the children of Israel have a clear tradition from the prophets that the laws of the Torah are not subject to abrogation. Presenting scriptural corroboration for this tradition, he appealed to phrases appended to certain commandments, e.g., "throughout their generations, for a perpetual covenant" (Ex. 31:16).

According to one novel argument of his: the Jewish nation

is a nation only by virtue of its laws, namely, the Torah; God has stated that the Jewish nation will endure as long as the heaven and earth (Jer. 31:35–36); therefore, the Torah will last as long as heaven and earth (cf. Philo, above). He interpreted the verses, "Remember ye the Torah of Moses . . . Behold, I will send you Elijah . . ." (Mal. 3:22–23), as teaching that the Torah will hold valid until the prophet Elijah returns to herald the resurrection (*Beliefs and Opinions* 3:7).

Maimonides listed the belief in the eternity of the Torah as the ninth of his 13 principles of Judaism, and connected it with the belief that no prophet will surpass Moses, the only man to give people laws through prophecy. He contended that the eternity of the Torah is stated clearly in the Bible, particularly in Deuteronomy 13:1 ("thou shalt not add thereto, nor diminish from it") and Deuteronomy 29:28 ("the things that are revealed belong unto us and to our children for ever, that we may do all the words of this Torah"). He also cited the rabbinic principle: "a prophet is henceforth not permitted to innovate a thing" (see above). He offered the following explanation of the Torah's eternity, based on its perfection and on the theory of the mean: "The Torah of the Lord is perfect" (Ps. 19:8) in that its statutes are just, i.e., that they are equibalanced between the burdensome and the indulgent; and "when a thing is perfect as it is possible to be within its species, it is impossible that within that species there should found another thing that does not fall short of the perfection either because of excess or deficiency." Also, he mentioned the argument that the prophesied eternity of the name of Israel ("For as the new heavens and the new earth, which I will make, shall remain before Me . . . so shall your seed and your name"; Isa. 66:22) entails the eternity of the Torah (cf. Saadiah above). He held that there will be no change in the Torah after the coming of the Messiah (commentary on Mishnah, Sanh. 10; Yad, Yesodei ha-Torah, 9; cf. *Sefer ha-Mitzvot; Guide of the Perplexed* 2:29, 39; Abraham ibn Daud, *Emunah Ramah*).

Ḥasdai Crescas listed the eternity of the Torah as a nonfundamental true belief; i.e., required by Judaism, but not essential to the concept of Torah. Unlike Saadiah and Maimonides, he did not try to found this belief directly on a biblical text (but cf. his *Bittul Ikkarei ha-Noẓerim,* 9), but solely on the rabbinic dictum: "A prophet is henceforth not permitted to innovate a thing" (see above). To elucidate the belief from the point of view of speculation, he presented an argument from the perfection of the Torah, which differed markedly from its Maimonidean precursor. The argument proceeds as follows: The Torah is perfect for it perfectly guides men toward the ultimate human happiness, love. If God were to abrogate the Torah, He would surely replace it, for it is impossible that He would forsake His purpose to maximize love. Since the Torah is perfect, it could be replaced only by an equal or an inferior; but if inferior, God would not be achieving His purpose of maximizing love; and if equal, He would be acting futilely. Therefore, He will not abrogate the Torah. Against the argument that replacement of the Torah by an equal but different law would make sense if there was an appreciable change—for better or worse—in the people who received it, he retorted characteristically that the Torah is the excellent guide for all, including both the intellectuals and the backward (*Or Adonai,* 3, pt. 1, 5:1–2).

Joseph Albo criticized Maimonides for listing the belief in the eternity of the Torah as an independent fundamental belief of Judaism. In a long discussion, which in many places constitutes an elaboration of arguments found in Crescas, he contended that non-abrogation is not a fundamental principle of the Torah, and that moreover, no text can be found in the Bible to establish it. Ironically, his ultimate position turned out to be closer to Maimonides' than to Crescas'; for he concluded that the belief in the non-abrogation of the Torah is a branch of the doctrine that no prophet will surpass the excellence of Moses (*Sefer ha-Ikkarim,* 3:13–23).

After Albo, the question of the eternity of the Torah

became routine in Jewish philosophical literature (e.g., Abraham Shalom, *Neveh Shalom* 10:3–4; Isaac Abrabanel, *Rosh Amanah,* 13). However, in the Kabbalah it was never routine. In the 13th century *Sefer ha-Temunah* a doctrine of cosmic cycles or *shemittot* (cf. Deut. 15) was expounded according to which creation is renewed every 7,000 years, at which times the letters of the Torah reassemble, and the Torah enters the new cycle bearing different words and meanings. Thus, while eternal in its unrevealed state, the Torah, in its manifestation in creation, is destined to be abrogated. This doctrine became popular in later kabbalistic and ḥasidic literature, and was exploited by the heretic Shabbetai Ẓevi and his followers, who claimed that a new cycle had begun, and in consequence he was able to teach that, "the abrogation of the Torah is its fulfillment!"

Like his contemporary Shabbetai Ẓevi, but for much different reasons (see above), Spinoza committed the heresy of advocating the abrogation of the Torah. Subsequently, in the 19th century, Reform ideologists held that the abrogation of parts of the traditional Torah was not a heresy at all but was necessary for the progress of the Jewish religion. Similarly, many intellectuals and nationalists held that it was necessary for the progress of the Jewish nation. Aḥad Ha-Am called for the Torah in the Heart to replace the Torah of Moses and of the rabbis, which having been written down, had, in his opinion, become rigid and ossified in the process of time.

Jewish philosophers of modern times have not concentrated on the question of the eternity or non-abrogability of the Torah. Nevertheless, it is not entirely untenable that the main distinction between Orthodox Judaism and non-Orthodox Judaism is that the latter rejects the literal interpretation of the ninth principle of Maimonides' Creed that there will be no change in the Torah.

5 HOLINESS

The term most generally used in the Bible for holiness is *kodesh;* mishnaic Hebrew, *kedushah,* and that which is regarded as holy is called *kadosh.* Jewish exegetes, following early rabbinic interpretation *(Sifra)* of Leviticus 19:2: "You shall be holy, for I the Lord your God am holy," have consistently taken the verb *kadesh* to mean "distinguished, set apart." The *Sifra* paraphrases the command with the words "You shall be set apart" (Heb. *perushim*). The traditional interpretation coincides with the findings of modern phenomenologists of religion who describe the holy as "the wholly other" and as that which is suffused with a numinous quality. The latter is both majestic and fearsome (*The Idea of the Holy,* Rudolph Otto, 1923, ch. 8) or to use the term Otto popularized, "the mysterium tremendum."

General Considerations. The concept of holiness, because of its centrality in the Bible, affords an excellent illustration of how the biblical authors, under the dominance of the monotheistic idea, radically refashioned, in whole or part, notions of the sacred in the religions of the Near East. In primitive Semitic religions, as in primitive religions generally, the holy is considered an intrinsic, impersonal, neutral quality inherent in objects, persons, rites, and sites, a power charged with contagious efficacy and, therefore, taboo. Seldom is the quality of holiness ascribed to the deity. In biblical religion, on the contrary, holiness expresses the very nature of God and it is He who is its ultimate source and is denominated the Holy One. Objects, persons, sites, and activities that are employed in the service of God derive their sacred character from that relationship. The extrinsic character of the holy is reflected in the fact that by consecrating objects, sites, and persons to God, man renders them holy. Further, since holiness is conceived as the very essence of God, biblical religion, in both the priestly and prophetic writings, incorporates moral perfection as an essential aspect of holiness, though by no means its total content. Therefore, unlike contemporary ancient Near East religions, biblical Judaism does not confine the sacred to the sphere of the cult. God's moral perfection and purpose is not in static terms alone but in its redemptive acts in history. Indeed, holiness, since it is derived from God, is related to the realm of nature, history, human experience and conduct as well as to the election of Israel and the covenant. "The energy with which from the time of Moses onward the person of the divine Lord concentrates all religious thought and activity upon himself gives even the statements about holiness an essentially different background from that which they possess in the rest of the Near East" (*Theology of the Old Testament*, Walther Eichrodt, 1961, vol. 1, p. 271). Finally, since pagan religions regard holiness as a mysterious intrinsic power with which certain things, persons, locales, and acts are charged, the division between the realms of the holy and the profane are permanently, unalterably fixed. In fact, the latter represents an ever-present danger to the former. By contrast, biblical religion looks forward to the universal extension of the realm of the holy in the end of days so as to embrace the totality of things and persons.

While biblical religion recognizes an area of the profane ("impure") as capable of defiling and polluting the sacred, nowhere does it regard the former as possessing a threatening dangerous potency. The following elements of the concept of holiness are, however, held by the Bible in common with other ancient Near Eastern religions: (1) the concept of the mortal danger involved in unauthorized approach to or contact with the sacred; (2) the notion of various degrees of holiness; and (3) the contagious, communicable character of the sacred. In the words of Eichrodt: "The whole system of taboo is pressed into the service of a loftier idea of God" (*ibid.*, p. 274).

The following sections offer specific and varied biblical illustrations of the general considerations set forth above.

The Holiness of God. Seeking to express the ineffab holiness of God, an ultimate category, the biblical authors drew on a vast and varied series of predicates. With the single exception of God's moral perfection and action, they all fall within the scope of the "mysterium tremendum." The most frequent is "fearsome," "awesome," (Heb. *nora*; Ps. 89:7, 8; 99:3; 111:9). A site at which a theophany has been experienced is described as "awesome" and induces in the visioner a state of fear (Gen. 28:17). God's works are called "fearful" (Ex. 15:11; 34:10; Ps. 66:3, 5). This aspect of the divine holiness and man's attitude toward it are perhaps best summed up in the verse (I Sam. 6:20), "Who is able to stand before the Lord, the Holy God?" In several passages, e.g., Joshua 24:19, God's fearful, unapproachable holiness is equated with His jealousy, His unrelenting demand for exclusive virtue.

The fearful aspect of the divine holiness is reflected in the warning to keep one's distance from the outward manifestation of the divine presence (Ex. 3:5; 19:12, 13, 23; Num. 18:3; Josh. 5:15). To gaze directly upon the divine manifestation or even upon the sacred vessels when the latter are not in actual use may cause death (Ex. 33:20; Num. 4:20; 18:13; Judg. 13:22; I Kings 19:13). God is "glorious in holiness" (Ex. 15:11); His holiness is unique (I Sam. 2:2); His "way" is that of holiness (Ps. 77:14).

Preeminently, it is the divine name which is characterized as holy since the name of God expresses His essence (Lev. 20:3; 22:2, 32; Ps. 103:1; 105:3; 145:21; I Chron. 16:10). Noteworthy is Ezekiel's repeated use of the phrase "My Holy Name." To Isaiah, we owe the appellation of God as the "Holy One of Israel" (Isa. 1:4; 5:19, 24; 10:20; 12:6; 17:7; 29:23; 30:12, 15; 31:1; 37:23). The term is employed even more consistently by Deutero-Isaiah (Isa. 41:14; 43:3, 14; 45:11; 47:4; 48:15; 49:7; 54:5; 60:14). It appears once in Jeremiah (50:29) and in Psalms (71:22).

Isaiah's tendency to characterize God as the "Holy One of Israel" may be assumed to derive from the divine call to the prophet (ch. 6) in which he hears the dramatic thrice-repeated proclamation of the seraphim (the trisagion) of "Holy, holy, holy, the Lord of Hosts, the whole earth is full of his glory" (6:3). In this encounter, in the presence of the absolute holiness of God—the apparent intention of the dramatic repetition— the prophet is overcome by an acute sense of his own sinfulness and that of the people among whom he dwells (v. 5). The passage clearly implies, and indeed emphasizes, the moral aspect of God's holiness.

However, it is erroneous to assert, as is frequently done, that the interpretation of the divine holiness as essentially an expression of God's moral perfection is the unique contribution of the prophets. Distinctly priestly writers associate God's holiness with moral qualities. This is to be seen in the so-called Holiness Code (Lev. 17–26). In priestly law (Lev. 19) the purely ritualistic aspects of holiness are combined with distinctly moral injunctions. Priestly liturgy (Ps. 15; 24:3–6) stresses that only he who "has clean hands and a pure heart" can stand on God's holy mountain (Ps. 24:3, 4). The prophets deepen and broaden the moral dimension of the divine holiness. For Amos (2:7) oppression of the poor and sexual profligacy are tantamount to the profanation of God's holy name. For Hosea, divine compassion constitutes a basic element in God's holiness (Hos. 11:8f.), and the prophet insists on purity of heart and a radical break with moral offense as preconditions for any intimacy with the holy God. For Isaiah, it is righteousness that sanctifies the holy God (5:16). Deutero-Isaiah conceives of God's holiness as active in the realm of history as a redemptive power. The "Holy One of Israel" is the redeemer of Israel (Isa. 41:14; 43:3, 14; 47:4; 48:17; 49:7; 54:15). Divine holiness is thus conceived less as a state of being than as an expression of the fulfillment of divine purpose. It manifests itself in divine judgment and destruction (Isa. 1:4–9; 5:13, 16; 30:8–14; Ezek. 28:22; 36:20–32) as well as in divine mercy and salvation (Isa.

10:20–23; 12:6; 17:7–9; 29:19–21). For Ezekiel, God manifests His holiness in the sight of the nations (20:31; 28:25; 36:23; 38:23), when He vindicates himself as supreme Lord of the world.

Fire as Symbol of God's Holiness. Perhaps the ambivalent effects of fire, at once warming and creative yet consuming and destructive, suggested it as an apt symbol of the divine holiness, itself conceived as essentially polar in effect (see below). Whatever the origin of fire as a symbol for the sacred, its employment in the Bible is as vast as it is varied. Only some of the passages in which it is associated with holiness can be cited here (Ex. 3:2, 3; 19:18; 24:17; Deut. 4:12, 24; 5:22–27; 9:3; Ezek. 1:4–28; Hab. 3:3, 4). Repeatedly in the laws and practices of the cult, fire imagery is used in those passages that emphasize holiness (Lev. 2:3, 9, 10; 6:16–18; 7:3–5).

The Transitive Effects of God's Holiness. As stated above, whatever or whoever is engaged in the service of God and therefore stands in intimate relationship with Him becomes endowed with holiness. Essentially, that which brings man or things or locales into the realm of the holy is God's own activity or express command. The nation is sanctified and commanded to be holy since it has entered into a covenant relationship with the holy God (Ex. 19:6; Lev. 11:44ff.; 19:2; 20:7; Deut. 7:6; 26:19). The Ark of the Covenant is holy since it is regarded as the throne of the invisible God. Though the phrase "Holy Ark" (Heb. *Aron Kodesh*) is not found in the Bible, numerous contexts indicate that it was regarded as sacred as were all the vessels employed in the tabernacle, as well, of course, as the sanctuary itself. The prophet, having been summoned and consecrated to God's service, is looked upon as a holy man (II Kings 4:9). Initially, it is God who ordains the holy seasons and places—"And God blessed the seventh day and declared it holy" (Gen. 2:3). But the Sabbath, having been declared holy, must be sanctified by Israel (Ex. 20:8; Deut. 5:12; Jer. 17:22; Neh. 13:22). In the case of the festivals, the divine declaration is joined with the injunction that they should be proclaimed: "These are my fixed times, the fixed time of the Lord, which you shall proclaim as sacred occasions" (Lev. 23:21). Likewise, it is God who sanctifies the Tent of Meeting, the altar, Aaron and his sons (Ex. 29:43) but each of these undergoes rites of consecration performed by humans (see Ex. 29 for the description of the elaborate rites of consecration of Aaron and his sons).

War, since it is carried out under the aegis of God as "Man of War" (Ex. 13:3), is service rendered to Him. In His martial activity, the warrior enters the sphere of the holy and becomes subject to the particular prohibitions incumbent upon those directly involved in that sphere (I Sam. 21:5–7; II Sam. 11:11). This concept serves as the basis for the verbal usage "to consecrate war" (Heb. *kiddesh milḥamah;* Micah 3:5; Jer. 6:4). Frequently, the enemy's goods and chattels are declared banned (Heb. *ḥerem*); that is to say, banned from human use. For the priestly biblical authors, the concept of holiness, as might be expected, finds its focus in the realm of the cult and everything involved in it. Accordingly, there is mention of "holy garments" (Ex. 28:2, 4; 29:21; 31:10); "holy offerings" (Ex. 28:36; Lev. 19:8); the "holy priestly crown" (Ex. 29:6; 39:30); "holy flesh" (Ex. 29:37); "holy anointing oil" (Ex. 30:31–37); the "holy tabernacle" and its furnishings (Ex. 40:9); "holy fruit" (Lev. 19:24); and "holy food" (Lev. 22:14).

The Polarity of Holiness. As has been noted, the concept of God's holiness is rooted in a basic polarity; the quality of holiness is majestic and hence attractive, and yet it remains fearsome. It is, therefore, no cause for wonder that this polarity finds expression in both the rituals and objects of holiness. In the law of the "red heifer," whereby the ashes of the sacrificial victim are used in a rite to purify one who has become defiled through contact with a corpse, the priest who ministers the rite becomes defiled (Num. 19:8–10; Lev. 16:26–28). This polarity is to be discerned in several biblical episodes describing an improper entrance into the inner precincts of the sanctuary. Here, in the holy of holies, the ritual of expiation is carried out. Yet, when Nadab and

Abihu, the sons of Aaron, bring "strange fire" into the inner sanctuary, they are consumed by divine fire (Lev. 10:1–11; cf. Num. 16–17; II Sam. 6:6; cf. the warning in Ex. 19:10ff.).

The idea that holiness can be conveyed by mere touch or intimate approach is illustrated in various biblical passages. Those, for instance, who come in physical contact with the altar automatically become holy (Ex. 29:37; 30:29; Lev. 6:11, 20). The notion is likewise reflected in the divine command that the vessels used by Korah and his company were to be added to the altar as an outer covering because, once having been brought "into God's presence," they had become holy (Num. 17:2).

Holiness and Glory. Glory (Heb. *kavod*) is intimately associated with God's holiness and signifies the self-manifesting presence of God, whereas holiness (Heb. *kodesh*) is expressive of God's transcendence (Ex. 14:4f.; Lev. 10:3; Num. 20:13; Ezek. 20:41), though the polar concepts of holiness and glory are strikingly joined by Isaiah—"Holy, holy, holy, the Lord of Hosts, His glory fills the whole earth" (6:3). The hope that the divine glory will fill the whole earth takes on a messianic tinge in Numbers 14:21. The latter is conceptually linked with Zechariah 14:20, 21. There, in a messianic prophecy, Zechariah anticipates the day when even the bells of the horses will be engraved with the legend "Holy unto the Lord" as well as every pot in Jerusalem and Judah. The ultimate extension of the sphere of the holy so that it will embrace even the mundane and profane underscores the biblical concept of holiness not as a natural, inherent quality, but rather as a quality conferred both by God and man. This aspect of holiness in the messianic age is reflected in the prophet Joel's promise that prophecy—an endowment of holiness—will become a gift possessed by young and old, by servants and handmaids (3:1, 2).

In Rabbinic Literature. In rabbinic theology, holiness is repeatedly defined as separateness. The Sifra (Lev. 19:2) paraphrases the verse (Lev. 19:2) "Ye shall be holy" by

"You shall be separated." While separation (Heb. *perishut*) is frequently equated with abstinence from illegitimate sexual relations as well as from lewdness generally and he who abstains from such practices is called holy (TJ, Yev. 2:4, 3; cf. Lev. R. 24:6; Ber. 10b), the concept of holiness is by no means restricted to the connotation of sexual purity despite the emphasis placed on the latter meaning. An examination of a variety of contexts in which "separate-ness" (equated with holiness) appears yields the following distinct meanings: (1) Strict abstention from all practices even remotely related to idolatry, e.g., attending circuses or cutting one's hair in the heathen fashion (Sifra, Kedoshim, Perek 9:2, Aḥarei, Perek 13:9; Sif. Deut. 85). Separation from the nations and their "abominations" (idolatrous practices) is tantamount to holiness. Accordingly, R. Nahum b. Simai is called a holy man because he never looked at the figure of the emperor engraved on a coin (TJ, Av. Zar. 3:1, 42c). (Presumably, his refusal to do so was based on emperor worship prevalent in his time.) (2) Separation from everything that is impure and thus defiling. This is suggested by the context of the verse (Lev. 11:44), one among several, on the basis of which the Sifra equates separateness with holiness. (3) Abstention from meat and wine (BB 60b; Tosef. Sot. 15:11. See also Ta'an. 11a where the biblical designation of the Nazirite as holy is attributed to the latter's abstention from wine). (4) Moderation or complete abstention from marital intercourse (Sot. 3:4; Shab. 87a; Gen. R. 35:1). The connotation of sexual modesty and restraint is reflected in the reason given (Shab. 118b) for the appellation of R. Judah ha-Nasi as "Our Holy Master" (Heb. *Rabbenu ha-Kadosh*). It is probably the latter meaning of holiness that R. Phinehas b. Jair had in mind when he described some of the rungs of the ladder of virtue as "separateness leads to purity, purity leads to holiness" (Mid. Tannaim to Deut. 23:15; Av. Zar. 20b; TJ, Shek. 3:4, 47c). However, in the case of other *tannaim* who earned the epithet holy (R. Meir-TJ, Ber. 2:75b; Gen. R. 100:7 and R. Ḥiyya Gen. R. 33:3), the respective contexts indicate that the epithet bears no particular or especial reference to sexual matters. In this connection, it may be noted that in keeping with rabbinic thought, the human body too could be regarded as holy since sin defiles the body as well the soul. The rabbis state (Gen. R. 45:3) that Sarah declared to Hagar: "Happy art thou, that thou clingest to a holy body" (i.e., that of Abraham).

Holiness is considered God's very essence and the "Holy One, Blessed be He" (Heb. *Ha-Kadosh Barukh Hu*) is the most frequent name of God found in rabbinic literature. God's holiness is incommensurate with that of man and is permanently beyond human attainment (Gen. R. 90:2). "For God is holy in all manner of holiness" (Tanḥ. B. Kedoshim 3). Even though the divine holiness is absolute, Israel sanctifies God (Ex. R. 15:24) just as God sanctifies Israel (*ibid.*). "As much as to say, if you make yourselves holy, I impute it to you as though you hallowed Me; and if you do not make yourselves holy, I impute it to you as though you did not hallow Me. Can the meaning be, if you make Me holy, I am holy, and if not, I am not made holy? Scripture, however, teaches: 'For I am holy.' I abide in My holiness whether you hallow Me or not." (Sifra Kedoshim Parashah 1:1.) Unlike God's holiness, that of Israel is not inherent. It is contingent upon its sanctification through the performance of the commandments. Their fulfillment lends holiness to Israel. The latter concept originated with the *tannaim*. Preeminent among the commandments whose observance sanctifies Israel are the Sabbath (Mekh. Shabbat 1) and the ritual fringes (Sif. Num. 115). This notion is expressed in the formula of the traditional benediction "... who has sanctified us by His commandments," the benediction recited on the performance of a commandment. It has been suggested that in this way rabbinic thought sought to strip the material objects involved in the performance of various commandments of any inherent holiness magico-mythical thought ascribed to them. Clearly implied is the notion that the observance of a commandment endows the observer with sanctity and that the object is merely a means thereto (Heb. *tashmish kedushah*). Material objects such as a Scroll of the Torah, phylacteries, and *mezuzah* possess sanctity only if they have been prepared by someone who is legally bound to perform the commandment involved and for the purpose for which they were originally intended (Git. 45b). The Mishnah (Kel. 1:6-9) enumerates ten ascending degrees of holiness beginning with the Land of Israel and concluding with the Holy of Holies. The notion of ascending degrees of holiness is reflected in the halakhic principle that sacred objects or, more precisely, objects that serve a sacred purpose should only be sold or exchanged for objects that possess a higher sanctity (Meg. 9b).

The epithet holy as applied to man is used sparingly in rabbinic literature. The angels, the Midrash declares, upon seeing Adam at the time of his creation wanted to sing and praise him as a holy being. But when God cast sleep upon him, they realized that he was a mere mortal and they refrained (Gen. R. 8:10). The Patriarchs, according to the Midrash (Yalkut Job 907), were not called holy until after their death. But here, as elsewhere in rabbinic thought, there is no dogmatic consistency. Thus, the Talmud declares (Yev. 20a) that he who fulfills the words of the sages is called holy. Man has it in his power to sanctify himself and, if he does so, even in small measure, he is greatly sanctified from above (Yoma 39a). Man is bidden to sanctify himself by voluntarily refraining from those things permitted to him by the Law (Yev. 20a). Nor is it abstemiousness alone that wins sanctity for man. When men fulfill the requirements of justice and thus exalt God, God causes His holiness to dwell among them (Deut. R: 5:6). The sanctity of man's deeds invokes God's aid (Lev. R. 24:4). An extraordinary act of charity is deemed a sanctification of the name of God (PdRK 146b). It is supremely hallowed when men are prepared to lay down their lives rather than abandon their religion or violate the law of God. Such an act is known as "sanctification of the Name" (Heb. *kiddush ha-Shem*). It may fairly be said to embody the highest ideal of rabbinic Judaism (Ber. 61b). Solomon Schechter wrote "Holiness is the highest achievement of the Law and its deepest experience as well as the realization of righteousness. It is a composite of various aspects not easily definable, and, at times, seemingly contradictory" (*Some Aspects of Rabbinic Theology,* 199).

In Jewish Philosophy. Medieval Jewish philosophers rarely use the term "holiness" as a technical term. When they do use this term, it appears, as a rule, in connection with quotations from Scripture or from the sages, and its explication derives from these sources. Thus, "holiness" describes the distinction between spirit and flesh, between the eternal and temporal, and between the absolute and changing. God is holy, for He has been "hallowed [distinguished] from any like Him" and He is "aloof and above all change." The people of Israel is holy, because it separated itself from worldly pursuits and turned to the worship of God. The Sabbath is holy, since it is devoted to spiritual matters rather than worldly affairs (Abraham b. Ḥiyya, *Meditation of the Sad Soul,* passim). There is, therefore, a close connection between the notions of "holiness" and "uniqueness" in the sphere of theology, and "holiness" and "separation" in the sphere of ethics, though the term "holiness," in its primary meaning refers to the realm of ritual.

Maimonides. Maimonides associates holiness with the idea of distinction and uniqueness, giving it an extreme intellectual interpretation. God is holy for He is absolutely different from creation. He is not similar to it in any of His attributes, and is independent from its being (Yad, Yesodei ha-Torah, 1:3). The angels are holy, for they are separate from any body (*ibid.,* 4:12), and the heavenly spheres are holy, for their body can neither be destroyed nor changed (*ibid.,* 3:9). Sanctification, therefore, means separation from the body. A place, name, or object are holy only insofar as they have been set aside from the outset to divine worship (*ibid.,* 6 passim). Sanctification through the precepts of the Torah also implies uniqueness and separation. There are three ways, according to Maimonides, of sanctification through the precepts (*Guide of the Perplexed*, 3:47): (1) sanctification by virtue, i.e., the restraint of physical desires and their satisfaction only up to the limits of necessity, in order to devote oneself wholly to God; (2) the fulfillment of those precepts which remove man from concern with this world and its errors, and prepare him for the attainment of truth; (3) the holiness of worship, which means observance of the laws of pollution and purity, which are not of primary importance in the doctrine of Maimonides. A man who has attained the highest degree of sanctification, as did the Patriarchs or Moses, is freed from his dependence upon his flesh, and thus he imitates God, for he too acts without being involved in creation (*ibid.*, 3:33).

Judah Halevi. Judah Halevi also states that God is holy because He is of the spirit, aloof from the defects which inhere in matter, and governs creation without being dependent on it (*Kuzari*, 4:3). Nevertheless, Halevi is far from the intellectual and distinctive conception of Maimonides. Holiness, according to Judah Halevi, is a power that engulfs the soul which unfolds toward it. This is a living spiritual power flowing from God and present in everybody who worships Him (*ibid.*; see also 1:103). The people of Israel is called holy, for such a power, manifested mainly in prophecy, inspires the people, the Hebrew language, in the Land of Israel, and the Temple. There is some notion of separation in Judah Halevi's conception of holiness. The prophet and the worshiper must purify themselves from sin, from negative emotions, from sorrow and weariness, exactly as they have to be pure from vice and wicked acts; but this does not mean separation from the world. Nor is the purpose of purification the attainment of truth; it is rather a preparation for the proper performance of the commandments and rituals prescribed by the Torah. The consecrating person has to separate himself from the polluted, but not from the living flesh; he has to overcome dullness, tiredness, frustration and stupidity, but not to remove himself from the life of the senses and emotions.

Nachman Krochmal. The discussion of the term "holiness" in modern Jewish philosophy is associated with medieval ideas, but has undergone changes under the influence of various secular systems. Nachman Krochmal, influenced by Hegel, defines the holy as a static and lasting spiritual attribute, whose opposite is profane, which is dynamic and variable (*Moreh Nevukhei ha-Zeman* (1824), ch. 6). The holy is a symbol of the spiritual, i.e., it arouses spiritual thoughts. The precepts sanctify, for their fulfillment reflects perception and enforces it. Objects are pure insofar as the idea embodied in them can be perceived clearly, i.e., they are capable of receiving holiness, while the polluted is the body which is impenetrable to reason, i.e., a barrier to holiness *(ibid.)*. This appears to be an integration of elements from both Maimonides and Judah Halevi, but actually, contrary to them, Krochmal conceived the spiritual as innate in nature and history, identifying it with reason. Sanctification, therefore, is not withdrawal from the world, but the self-realization of reason within existence itself.

Moritz Lazarus. Under the influence of neo-Kantianism, a change took place. Moritz Lazarus identified the holy with conduct, according to the pure moral postulates of reason, which is free from causal necessity existing in nature. According to this system, God is identified with the idea of moral conduct. He has no reality beyond this ideal and only in this respect is He holy. Divine worship is, therefore, identical with ethics (the ritual is only a symbol of pure ethics). Thus, one is holy through moral conduct, and society is sanctified by subordinating it to the categorical imperative (*Ethik des Judentums,* 1 (1904), 311ff.), although, according to Lazarus, this can never be achieved.

Hermann Cohen. Hermann Cohen, similarly, defines the holy as the sphere of ethical activity, the meeting place between human and divine reason. God is holy because the ideal of ethics is inherent in Him; but only man can accomplish this ideal, with God's help, thus consecrating himself and society by his conduct (*Religion der Vernunft*

(1929), 116–29). Thus, according to him, holiness is the sphere where the human and the divine meet to perfect each other.

Franz Rosenzweig. A diametrically opposite view is to be found in the existentialist doctrine of Franz Rozenzweig. He returns to the emphasis of the "otherness" or separation contained in holiness. God is placed opposite the world. He is holy, for He is eternal and, therefore, exists beyond the world. The world attains holiness only through revelation, which is the grace of God granted to man. Facing God, man is freed from the temporal and transient, and becomes associated with the eternal. This is the function of the biblical commandments, which consecrate the life of the Jew within the framework of his community (*Der Stern der Erloesung,* 3 (1954), passim). It should be pointed out that new trends have emerged, which derive directly from the Kabbalah philosophy of the Middle Ages. Outstanding among them is the doctrine of R. Abraham I. Kook, who interpreted holiness, in the spirit of the Kabbalah, as the all-embracing existence of the divine in its absolute unity.

Part Three:

SOCIAL JUSTICE

1 ETHICS

IN THE BIBLE

There is no abstract, comprehensive concept in the Bible which parallels the modern concept of "ethics." The term *musar* designates "ethics" in later Hebrew, but in the Bible it indicates merely the educational function fulfilled by the father (Prov. 1:8) and is close in meaning to "rebuke." In the Bible ethical demands are considered an essential part of the demands God places upon man. This close connection between the ethical and religious realms (although the two are not completely identified) is one of the principal characteristics of the Bible; hence, the central position of ethics throughout the Bible. Accordingly, the Bible had a decisive influence upon the molding of ethics in European culture in general, both directly and indirectly through the ethical teachings in apocryphal literature and the New Testament which are based on biblical ethics.

Social Ethics. The command to refrain from harming one's fellow man and to avoid doing evil to the weak is fundamental to biblical ethics. Most of the ethical commands specified in the Bible belong to this category: due justice (Ex. 23:1–2; Deut. 16:18–20); avoidance of bribery (e.g., Ex. 23:8), robbery, and oppression (Ex. 22:20; Deut. 24:14); defense of the widow and the orphan; compassionate behavior toward the slave; and the prohibition of gossip. Added to these were the commands to sustain the poor (Deut. 15:7–11), feed the hungry, and clothe the naked (Isa. 58:7; Ezek. 18:7). The radical but logical conclusion derived from this is that man is obliged to suppress his desires and feed even his enemy (Prov. 25:21), return his enemy's lost property, and help him raise his ass which is prostrate under its burden (Ex. 23:4–5). Biblical ethics, which cautions man to love and respect his fellow man, reaches its highest level in the commandment: "You shall not hate your kinsman in your heart, reprove your neighbor," which concludes with "Love your neighbor as yourself. I am the Lord" (Lev. 19:17–18). The principle aim of this commandment, as of others, is the avoidance of unfounded hatred which destroys the life of the society.

The general trend of social ethics was summed up by the prophets who said: "Hate evil and love good and establish justice in the gate" (Amos 5:15); and similarly: "He has told you, O man, what is good; and what does the Lord require of you but to do justice and love kindness, and to walk humbly with your God" (Micah 6:8). These passages and their like not only summarize the teaching of ethics, but also place it at the center of the Israelite faith. A summation of biblical ethical teachings is contained in the well-known saying of Hillel: "What is hateful to you do not do unto another" (Shab. 31a).

The Ethical Perfection of the Individual. Unlike the ethical system of Greek philosophy, which seeks to define the various virtues (who is courageous, generous, or just, etc.), the Bible demands of every human being that he perform the good deed, and behave virtuously toward his fellow man, and is not concerned with abstract definitions. This attitude is almost explicitly expressed in Jeremiah 9:22–23: "Let not the wise man glory in his wisdom, let not the strong man glory in his strength, let not the rich man glory in his riches. Only in this should one glory: in his earnest devotion to me. For I am the Lord who exercises kindness, justice, and equity in the world; for in these I delight—declares the Lord." From this it follows that doing what is right and just is the essence of biblical ethics. The personal ethical ideal is that of the *ẓaddik* (the good man). The prophet Ezekiel defines him in detail for the purpose of explaining the doctrine of reward and punishment, and his definition is nothing but an enumeration 133 of the deeds performed by the good man and of those from which he refrains (Ezek. 18:5–9). The essence of all of these acts is the proper relationship between man and man, except for one commandment, to shun idolatry, which is solely a duty of man to God. A similar definition of the good man appears in Isaiah 33:15 and in Psalm 15. Added to the ideal of the righteous man in Psalms is the God-fearing man who finds happiness in the teachings of God and in the worship of Him and who shuns the life devoid of ethical earnestness (e.g., Ps. 1). The personal ethical ideal received further expression in the character of Abraham, who was credited with several especially fine and noble qualities. He was complaisant in his relationship with Lot, hospitable, compassionate toward the evil inhabitants of Sodom, humble and generous in his dealings with the people of Heth, and he refused to profit from the booty of the war with Amraphel.

Distinguishing Feature of Social Ethics in the Bible. The lofty level of biblical ethics which is evident in the command to love one's neighbor, in the character of Abraham, and in the first Psalm, is peculiar to the Bible, and it is difficult to find its like in any other source; however, the general ethical commandments in the Bible, which are based on the principle of refraining from harming others, are a matter of general human concern and constitute the fundamentals of ethics. Some characteristic features of biblical ethics, such as due justice and the rights of the widow and the orphan, are prevalent in the ancient Near East (see below). Therefore the generalization that the Bible is unique among religious works in the content of its ethical teachings cannot be made. However, the Bible does differ from every other religious or ethical work in the importance which it assigns to the simple and fundamental ethical demand. The other nations of the ancient Near East reveal their ethical sense in compositions that are marginal to their culture: in a few proverbs dispersed throughout the wisdom literature, in prologues to collections of laws, in various specific laws, and in confessions (see below). The connection between ethical teachings and primary cultural creations—the images of the gods, the cult, the major corpus of law—is weak. The ethical aspirations of these cultures are sometimes, but not always, expressed in their religion and social organization, while the Bible places the ethical demand at the focus of the religion and the national culture. The ethical demand is of primary concern to the prophets, who state explicitly that this is the essence of their religious teaching. Basic sections of biblical law—the Ten Commandments, Leviticus 19, the blessings and curses of Mount Gezirim and Mount Ebal (Deut. 27:15–26)—contain many important ethical commandments. Biblical law itself testifies to its ethical aim: "Or what great nation has laws and norms as just *(ẓaddikim)* as all this Teaching . . ." (Deut. 4:8). While the wisdom literature of Israel is similar to that of the neighboring cultures, it is distinctive in the greater stress it places upon ethical education (see below). The assumption that God is—or should be—just, and the question of reward and punishment which follows from that assumption, are the bases of the religious experiences found in Psalms, Job, and some prophetic passages. The opinion of Hillel the Elder that the ethical demand is the essence of the Torah may be questioned, for it can hardly be said to be the only pillar of the biblical faith. However, there is certainly a clear tendency in the Bible to place the ethical demand at the focus of the faith, even if it does share it with other concerns such as monotheism.

Biblical ethics teachings, though clear and forceful, are not extraordinary in content, for the Bible requires nothing other than the proper behavior which is necessary for the existence of society. Biblical ethics does not demand, as do certain other systems of ethics (Christianity, Buddhism, and even some systems in later Judaism), that man withdraw completely or even partially from everyday life to attain perfection. Asceticism, which views the normal human situation as the root of evil, is foreign to the Bible and to the cultures of the Near East in general. The Bible approves of life as it is, and, accordingly, makes its ethical demand 135 compatible with social reality. However, the degree of justice which it is possible to achieve within the bounds of reality is demanded with a clear forcefulness which allows for no compromise. This makes the Bible more radical than most ethical systems. The ethical teachings of the Bible, like the Bible generally, are addressed first and foremost to Israel. But some biblical passages extend the ethical demand to encompass all mankind, such as the Noachian laws (Gen. 9:1–7), the story of Sodom (Gen. 19:20ff.), or the rebuke of Amos against the neighboring kingdoms for their cruelty (Amos 1:3–2:3). The setting of the Book of Job is also outside the Israelite realm.

Sexual Ethics. What has been said up to here applies only to social ethics, in view of the fact that in the realm of sexual morality the biblical outlook differs from that of neighboring cultures. The Bible abhors any sexual perversion such as homosexuality or copulation with animals, prescribing severe punishments for offenders (Lev. 18:22–23; 20:13, 15–16). The adulteress sins not only against her husband, but also against God (e.g., Ex. 20:14; Lev. 20:10; Mal. 3:5). Fornication is generally frowned upon, severely condemned by Hosea, and legally punishable by death in some cases (Lev. 21:9; Deut. 22:21). The other peoples of the ancient Near East did not treat these offenses with such severity. They regarded adultery as essentially an infringement upon the rights of the husband—damage done to his property, like robbery or theft—and not as an abominable act sinful to God. Society was reconciled to prostitution, although a certain stigma was attached to it. Therefore Babylonian law, for example, defines the legal status of the various types of prostitution and treats it as it treats other phenomena in society (e.g., Code of Hammurapi, 145, 181, in: Pritchard, Texts, 172, 174; Middle Assyrian Laws, 40, in: *ibid.*, 183). There is little opposition to sexual perversions: homosexuality is numbered among the sins in the Egyptian "Book of the Dead" (see below); Hittite law punishes copulation only with certain animals, and even these not very severely (see below). This opposition, which is occasionally expressed, does not declare these acts to be an outright abomination. Fornication and more serious sexual offenses are ascribed to the gods in mythology, and possibly played a role in the cult. Therefore, it is clear that the biblical stand on these matters is unique. The biblical sexual ethic was imposed by Christianity on most of the civilized world—in theory if not in practice—but in the ancient world it was unique to Israel.

Ethical Teaching in the Bible. MEANS OF INSTRUCTION. The orientation of biblical ethics is uniform in content, but is expressed in different ways, according to the viewpoint of the particular book of the Bible. The strongest and most radical expression of the goal of biblical ethics is found in the rebukes of the prophets, who chastise the people relentlessly for ethical transgressions and demand ethical perfection (especially in the realm of social ethics) without compromise. But their rebukes do not really constitute instruction, for they do not always teach one how to behave in particular situations.

Biblical law is concerned with providing ethical instruction in particular acts. The legal sections of the Torah explicitly and in detail forbid various offenses such as murder, robbery, and bribery, and explicitly demand support of the poor, love of one's neighbor, and the like (see below).

Both prophecy and law demand of man in the name of God that he behave properly. Their ethical outlook is a fundamental element in their demand that man do God's will, and therefore is not practical utilitarianism, even though they teach the doctrine of reward and punishment. This ethical attitude is given added depth in the Psalms, where it becomes a matter of religious feeling that throbs in the heart of the righteous man who seeks closeness with his God (see Ps. 1; 15, especially verses 2, 4, 24:4; 34:13–15). The Book of Job also stresses the commandment of righteousness to which the individual is subject, but from another aspect. Job is not content to protest that he did not commit transgressions of robbery, oppression, or bribery, but asserts that he actually observed positive ethical 137 commandments and was strict with himself beyond the requirements of the law. For example, he claims he did much to support those in need of his help: "Because I delivered the poor who cried, and the fatherless who had none to help him. The blessing of the destitutes came upon me, and I gladdened the heart of the widow" (Job 29:12–13). Job 31 contains a series of oaths concerning his righteousness, all beginning with 'im, "if," which is often equivalent to "I swear": "(I swear) I have not rejected the cause of my man servant . . ." (verse 13); "(I swear) I have not made gold my trust . . ." (verse 24). Job is careful to be above suspicion not only in social ethics, but also in sexual ethics, for he claims: "If I have been enticed by a woman, and have lain in wait at the door of another man, may my wife be used by another . . ." (31:9–10).

The ethical teachings in all the biblical books so far surveyed are considered an essential element of God's demands of man. In this respect, the attitude of Proverbs is different. Most of the proverbs aim at proving to man that it is worthwhile for him to follow the good path from the consideration of simple worldly wisdom. For example, Proverbs does not declare that adultery is prohibited but points out the dangers in it (6:24–35). In a similar vein are the following verses: "Do not slander a servant to his master, lest he curse you, and you be made to feel your guilt" (Prov. 30:10), and "If your enemy is hungry, give him bread to eat . . . for you will heap coals of fire on his head, and the Lord will reward you" (25:21–22). Although there is also a reference to God here, man is placed at the center of ethical instruction. This approach is more practical and utilitarian than the approach of the Bible in general, due to the practical educational orientation of the Book of Proverbs. While Proverbs belongs to the category of general wisdom literature which was prevalent in the ancient Near East, it nevertheless differs from other works of this type in the prominence it gives to ethical instruction; in Proverbs it is of prime importance, while in the wisdom 138 literature of the peoples of the ancient Near East, it is of secondary importance. There are two reasons for this: first, Proverbs aims at the education of the young citizen while the works of Ahikar and Egyptian didactic literature place more emphasis on the training of the official; second, Israelite wisdom literature identified the righteous man with the sage on the one hand, and the evil man with the fool on the other (e.g., Prov. 10:21, 23).

Ecclesiastes, in those sections that deviate from stereotyped wisdom literature, casts doubt on the benefit of widsom in general, and on the simple utilitarian ethical instruction contained in Proverbs. He knows that "there is not one good man on earth who does what is best (i.e., leads to the most desirable results, 6:12) and does not err" (7:20). In his despair he says: "don't overdo goodness . . ." (7:16–18).

ETHICAL INSTRUCTION IN THE BIBLICAL NARRATIVE. Narrative is the one literary form in the Bible which is not entirely infused with an ethical orientation. In biblical narratives ethical instruction is presented indirectly in the form of words of praise for noble deeds, and even this praise is, for the most part, not explicit. Deeds which are represented as noble include Joseph's fleeing from adultery (Gen. 39:7–18), the mercy shown by David in not killing Saul (I Sam. 24; 26:3–25), and the story of Rizpah, daughter of Aiah (II Sam. 21:10). Abraham is the only biblical character who can truly be described as an ethical model. The other heroes in biblical narrative (Judah, Joseph, Moses, Caleb, Joshua), although blessed with fine qualities, are not described as models of ethical perfection. The Bible portrays their shortcomings clearly (though implicitly; Isaac's weakness of character, Jacob's cunning, the sins of Saul and David) and does not make the slightest attempt to whitewash the ethical defects of its heroes. However, it is the rule in biblical narrative that appropriate punishment follows specific transgressions: Jacob, who bought the birthright by deception, is himself deceived by Laban; David is punished for his sin with Bath-Sheba, and so on. Yet these features are not especially emphasized and thus do not give biblical narrative a prominent ethical orientation. It has been said that biblical narrative takes no clear moral stance, but rather rejoices in the success of its heroes even when they act immorally (Jacob, when he bought the birthright; Rachel, when she stole the household idols; Jael, when she killed Sisera). It is true that the main intent of biblical narrative is to make known the greatness of God, whose acts are the only ones that are perfect. Thus the narrator can afford to see human beings as they are. He does not force himself to moralize overmuch, or to make his heroes model men, but introduces the ethical aspect only where it suits the story. Thus in the narrator's attitude to his heroes one observes a kind of tolerant, knowledgeable understanding of human nature: it is this which makes most biblical stories great.

LAW AND ETHICS. The Bible does not make a formal distinction between those commandments which could be classified as ethical, those which are concerned with ritual (circumcision, sacrifices, the prohibition against eating blood), and those which deal with common legal matters. Scholarship is obligated to differentiate between these categories and to see where the ethical aim appears. The ethical aim can be distinguished by recognizing the difference between the basic, general commandment "Thou shalt not murder" and the laws concerning the punishment of the murderer (e.g., Num. 35). Thus ethical commandments, in the strict sense, are laws without sanctions, to be obeyed but not enforced, e.g., the commandments of gleanings, the forgotten sheaf, and the corner of the field (Lev. 19:9–10, Hebrew: *Leket, Shikhḥah,* and *Pe'ah*): the prohibition against harming the orphan and the widow (e.g., Ex. 22:21–23); the prohibition against delaying payment of wages (Lev. 19:13). Aside from the clearly ethical commandments, there is a general tendency in biblical law to emphasize the aspiration for justice which is the basis for every law. To be sure, every law is based upon the ethical viewpoint of the legislator and attempts, 140 through the power of practical regulations, to enforce the ethics accepted by the existing society; however, biblical law aspires to this end clearly and consistently, as for example, "Justice, justice shall you pursue" (as the summary of practical regulations concerning the establishment of courts, Deut. 16:18–20), the laws of the Bible are defined explicitly as "just laws and statutes" (Deut. 4:8). Accordingly ethical and social reasons were attached to several laws, such as the commandment for the Sabbath: "So that your male and female slave may rest as you do. Remember that you were a slave..." (Deut. 5:14–15). This tendency is revealed in laws whose purpose was to defend the weak and to limit the power of the oppressor, such as the laws governing the Hebrew slave (Ex. 21:2; Deut. 15:12) or the relatively lenient punishment of the thief. Yet it must be remembered that law is based not only on the abstract viewpoint of the legislator, but also on the needs of the society according to its particular structure and customs. Therefore an evaluation of biblical law is incomplete if only the ethical aspect is considered; however, the discussion of the aim of law is not essential to the definition of biblical ethics.

IN LATER JEWISH THOUGHT

The Jewish religion has essentially an ethical character. From its biblical origins to its present stage of development, the ethical element has always been central to the Jewish religion, both as a principle and as a goal. However the intimate connection between religion and ethics was differently interpreted in different periods of Jewish thought. At least two principal trends can be distinguished, the first identifying Jewish ethics with moderation (the middle way), the second insisting on the extreme demands of an absolute ethic. Many thinkers emphasize that Judaism transcends the ethical framework of religion, thereby assuming a metaethical character. Examples of this trend are divine demands, made in prophetic revelations, which seem to conflict with moral norms, and the existence of human suffering.

In talmudic literature, legislative concerns are never the last word. Not only does the *aggadah,* by means of moral lessons, complete and temper the autonomy of the *halakhah,* and not only is the tractate *Avot* an anthology of moral thought; but, more obviously, in every conflict between the legal rigidity of the law and the criteria of ethics, the latter hold sway. Fear of God is superior to wisdom; actions surpass ideas; man is called upon to take a stand in favor not of reason but of the good. Ethics appear not as speculative principles but in terms of human experience; the talmudic sages are presented as moral exemplars and the ideal of holiness is identified with a scrupulously honest and pure life.

Medieval and modern literature testify to the dual tendency to formulate an ethic which is both theoretical and practical. Some medieval Jewish philosophers developed systematic formulations of Jewish ethical ideas, as for example Saadiah Gaon and Solomon ibn Gabirol, whose *Tikkun Middot ha-Nefesh* is unusual in that it expounds an autonomous ethic which has no connection with religious doctrine. Maimonides' *Shemonah Perakim* is a classical work of Jewish ethics which shows similarities to the *Ethics* of Aristotle. There is scarcely a Jewish philosopher or exegete of the Middle Ages who does not devote at least some portion of his work to showing that the body of Jewish thought and its biblical or talmudic sources revolved around ethics. This trend continues to modern times when Jewish philosophers, since Moses Mendelssohn, place ethics at the center of their description of the universe. For example, Moritz Lazarus and Elijah Benamozegh, in the 19th century, give this tendency a classical expression, one composing a standard work entitled *Die Ethik des Judentums* ("Ethics of Judaism"), the other by comparing Jewish and Christian ethics *(Morale juive et morale chrétienne).* It would be out of place to mention Spinoza in this connection, for while his *Tractatus Theologico-Politicus* shows Jewish influences, the same is not true of his *Ethics.*

In addition to the literature mentioned there are a number of works which are important for the development of medieval and modern Jewish ethics because they reflect an individual or collective experience. The Kabbalah and other mystical currents contributed greatly to the emergence of these works. Examples of this type of literature are Baḥya ibn Paquda's *Ḥovot ha-Levavot,* the *Sefer Ḥasidim* of the Ḥasidei Ashkenaz, and M. Ḥ. Luzzatto's *Mesillat Yesharim.* These works have become very popular and have been adopted by such opposing Jewish circles as the Ḥasidim and Mitnaggedim. In the 19th century, under the influence of R. Israel Lipkin (Salanter), the Musar movement reintroduced the primacy of ethics into the highly intellectual talmudic academies.

The Middle Way and the Absolute. The intimate connection between religion and ethics was interpreted differently in different periods of Jewish life and thought. At least two principal tendencies can be distinguished. In line with the ideal set down in Proverbs and various Psalms, and also in the Jewish Hellenistic writings and Palestinian teachings in the rabbinic period, Jewish ethics strives for moderation. It condemns excess, obviously in the sense of evil but also in the sense of good, and condemns equally greed and waste, debauchery and abstinence, pleasure and asceticism, impiety and bigotry. Maimonides developed this identification of Jewish ethics with the middle way (*Shemonah Perakim;* Yad, De'ot) though, at times, he tends toward a more ascetic position. The majority of medieval and modern Jewish philosophers follow Maimonides' general view and the theme of moderation in Jewish ethics. Consequently, they were opposed to ethical extremism such as that of Christianity, and this view became a commonplace in Jewish apologetics.

Nevertheless, the notion of moderation is not the only facet of Jewish ethics. The biblical books of Job and Ecclesiastes strongly criticize the middle way. In the Book of Job especially, where the middle way is recommended by the friends of Job this approach is ultimately rejected by

God. The Talmud goes further in its declaration that the attitude of moderation is the attitude of Sodom: "He that says, 'What is mine is mine and what is thine is thine'—this is the middle way, and some say that this is the way of Sodom" (Avot 5:13). It is not surprising, therefore, that the Talmud praises well-known sages who, going beyond the strict letter of the law *(li-fenim mi-shurat ha-din)*, gave their entire fortune to the poor (R. Yeshevav), practiced celibacy (Ben Azzai), spent many hours of the day and night in prayer (R. Ḥanina b. Dosa), and, altogether, seemed generally to conform to the monastic ideals of the Essenes. Asceticism is central to the works of Baḥya and Luzzatto, the *Sefer ha-Ḥasidism,* and, in a way even to 18th century Ḥasidism. It is true that in this mystical movement, whose influence is still being felt today, asceticism was transformed into joy, but the ethic of this joy was as extreme and absolute as was the ascetic ethic.

It would therefore be incorrect to associate Jewish ethics with a uniform and moderate attitude. This attitude, which is often presented as a contrast to Christian ethics, is actually only one aspect of Jewish ethics. The other aspect, with its extreme and absolute demands, is equally typical of Jewish thought.

The Ethical and the Metaethical. By the implications of certain of its teachings, Judaism goes beyond the limits of the ethical, and enters the domain of the metaethical, "beyond good and evil." Already in the Bible, the concept of holiness is affirmed much more often as a category which transcends ethical considerations, rather than as an ethical postulate. The transcendence of God elevates holiness above the moral equity guaranteed by the Covenant. The well-known verse of Isaiah, "For my thoughts are not your thoughts, neither are your ways My ways" (55:8), is often employed by medieval and modern Jewish thinkers as a key for interpreting certain problems which escaped all ethical definition, most notably the problems of freedom and suffering.

How should one accept, from the point of view of ethics,

the unusual conduct of certain prophets (Hosea's association with a prostitute; the nudity of Isaiah; the celibacy of Jeremiah)? Unless they resorted to allegorical exegesis, the biblical commentators were forced to admit, and they did so willingly, that there operated here a certain arbitrary divine will which transcended ethical categories. Maimonides expounded this theme in stating that God remains the supreme arbiter of the gift of prophecy. Prophecy is not intrinsically bound to ethical qualities. Of course, only an ethical person can become a prophet, but the man of the highest ethical qualities cannot become a prophet without God's charismatic and transcendent will.

Similarly, the midrashic interpretations of the sacrifice of Isaac, of the dramas of Saul or of Job, are much closer to the existentialist point of view of Kierkegaard or of Kafka than to the systems of Maimonides or of Kant. The conflict between Saul and David was not a matter of ethics but of good or bad fortune. Abraham, ultimately, should have disobeyed the divine command to sacrifice his son, which was inspired more by Satan than by God. Job was perfectly innocent, and his inexplicable sufferings could generate nothing but tears. These, and similar themes, which are scattered throughout talmudic and ḥasidic literature, were often taken up by the Jewish existentialists of the 20th century such as Martin Buber and Franz Rosenzweig. They culminate in the doctrine of radical insecurity, whose sources one may find in the Bible, but which finds a more cohesive expression in a talmudic formulation: Kulei hai ve-ulai ("All this and perhaps?"). Even while the most apparently perfect conditions can be gathered together to weigh the balance in favor of good or evil, there yet remains a coefficient of uncertainty which is beyond good and evil. It is possible that events will follow the ethical expectations. It is also possible, however, that these expectations will not be fulfilled. It is true that this disorder is interpreted as a voluntary (and temporary) weakness of God which permits man to exercise his will. Thus, this metaethical Jewish view remains ultimately ethical and never leads to a passive 145 pessimism. The divine transcendence does not disturb the ethical equilibrium except in order to call upon man to reestablish, together with God, an equilibrium which has been disrupted. The metaethical is the price for the inalienable moral essence of the Covenant.

2 REGARD FOR HUMAN LIFE

Pikku'aḥ Nefesh (Heb. פְּקוּחַ נֶפֶשׁ: "regard for human life") is the rabbinical term applied to the duty to save human life in a situation in which it is imperiled. The danger to life may be due to a grave state of illness or other direct peril *(sakkanat nefashot)*. or indirectly, to a condition of health which, though not serious, might deteriorate and consequently imperil life *(safek sakkanat nefashot)*. *Pikku'aḥ nefesh* is a biblical injunction derived from the verse "Neither shalt thou stand idly by the blood of thy neighbor" (Lev. 19:16), and according to the Talmud it supersedes even the Sabbath laws (*pikku'aḥ nefesh doheh et ha-Shabbat;* Yoma 85a). One should be more particular about matters concerning danger to health and life than about ritual observances (Ḥul 10a). The strict rules of hygiene codified in the Shulḥan Arukh center around the principle of *pikku'aḥ nefesh* (YD 116). The rabbis interpreted the verse "Ye shall therefore keep my statutes and my ordinances which if a man do he shall live by them" (Lev. 18:5), that man shall "live" by these commandments, and not die as a result of observing them (Yoma 85b; Sanh. 74a).

The Talmud (BM 62a) discusses the problem of an individual faced with the choice of saving his own life or that of his companion, and mentions the example of two men in a desert with a supply of water sufficient for one only. Although Ben Peturah advocated that neither should attempt to save his own life at the expense of the other but that both share the water, R. Akiva, whose opinion prevailed, ruled that one should save one's own life and not share the water. Only when faced with a choice between death and committing idolatry, unlawful sexual intercourse, or murder is martyrdom to be preferred (Sanh. 74a–b). One must also sacrifice one's life rather than submit to what may be taken for a renunciation of faith through the violation of any religious law in public (Sanh. 74a–b; Sh. Ar., YD 157). In all other cases, the rule of *pikku'aḥ nefesh* takes precedence (Sanh. 74a–b; Maim., *Iggerot ha-Shemad* 3).

The rule that one may profane one Sabbath in order to save the life of a person and enable him subsequently to observe many others (Yoma 85b) is inferred by the rabbis from the verse "The children of Israel shall keep the Sabbath to observe the Sabbath" (Ex. 31:16). Thus, on the Sabbath (or a festival), every type of medical treatment must be accorded to a dangerously ill person, to the extent of even putting out the light to help him sleep (Shab. 2:5; Sh. Ar., OḤ 278). Equal efforts must be made even where there is only a possibility of danger to life (*safek sakkanat nefashot*, Yoma 8:6; *ibid.* 84b). Only in cases of minor illnesses or physical discomforts should violations of the Sabbath be kept to the minimum; if possible a non-Jew should perform these duties (Sh. Ar., OḤ 328:17). In all other instances, the medical treatment should be administered by a Jew, and those who are assiduous in their help, comfort, and work for the sick on the Sabbath, are deemed worthy of the highest praise (*ibid.* 328:12–13). If a dangerously ill person is in need of food on the Sabbath, one should slaughter animals and prepare them according to the dietary laws, rather than feed him ritually forbidden food (*ibid.*, 328:14). If, however, it is deemed necessary for the recovery of the patient that he eat forbidden food he is allowed to do so (*ibid.* 328). A woman in confinement is considered dangerously ill for a period of three days after delivery. Should one of these days be a Sabbath, everything possible must be done to ease her pain and lessen her discomfort, including the kindling of a fire to warm her (Maim. Yad, Shabbat 2:13–14; Sh. Ar., OḤ 330:1, 4–6). A sick person is forbidden to fast on the Day of Atonement if it is thought that this would seriously endanger his recovery. Moreover, even a healthy person seized by a fit of "ravenous hunger" which causes faintness *(bulmos)*, must be fed on the Day of Atonement with whatever food is available (including ritually forbidden food (Sh. Ar., OḤ 618:9)) until he recovers (Yoma 8:6; Sh. Ar., OḤ 618).

3   ATTITUDE TO WOMEN

The classical writings of Judaism, which were almost exclusively written by men, and which encompass a period of over 2,000 years, naturally depict a variety of views on women. It is impossible, therefore, to speak of a single Jewish attitude to women. Opinions were affected by different cultural and social backgrounds, by the special patterns which obtained in a given age, and by the personal experiences and individual temperaments of the Jewish teachers.

While in biblical law polygamy is sanctioned (Deut. 21:15), the Adam and Eve narrative implies that monogamy is the ideal but that the wife is inferior to her husband who will "rule over her" (Gen. 3:16). The husband can divorce his wife but she, on the other hand, cannot divorce him (Deut. 24:1–4). Women attended the Sanctuary together with the men (I Sam. 1:1–19) and participated in the choral services of the Temple (Ezra 2:65). Some biblical scholars hold that there are differing attitudes to women in the two versions of the Decalogue (Ex. 20:14 and Deut. 5:21). In the latter the neighbor's wife is mentioned in a separate verse whereas in the former she is mentioned together with his other chattels. The oft-quoted last section of Proverbs (31:10–31) in praise of the virtuous woman is somewhat ambiguous in that it still depicts a situation in which the wife is definitely a subordinate. The prophetic comparisons of the love of God for Israel to the love of a husband for his wife can only have been made in a society in which women were respected and occupied an important place. Although the masculine pronoun is applied to God in the Bible and He is described as a Father, there is also a prophetic simile comparing God's comfort to those who mourn, to the comfort which a mother offers her son (Isa. 66:13).

A variety of attitudes is found in rabbinic literature. The wording of the benediction recited each day in which a man praises God for not having made him a woman (Men. 43b) should not be overinterpreted since from the context it is clear that the thanks are for the greater opportunities a man has for carrying out the precepts, women being exempt from those positive precepts which for their performance depend on a given time of the day or year (Kid. 1:7). C. G. Montefiore (*A Rabbinic Anthology* (1938), 507) uses the benediction to state: "No amount of modern Jewish apologetic, endlessly poured forth, can alter the fact that the Rabbinic attitude towards women was very different from our own. No amount of apologetics can get over the implications of the daily blessing, which orthodox Judaism has still lacked the courage to remove from its official prayer book. 'Blessed art thou, O Lord our God, who hast not made me a woman.' At the same time it must be readily admitted that the Rabbis seemed to have loved their wives, that they all, apparently, had only one wife each, and that the position of the wife was one of much influence and importance." That the rabbis did not themselves practice polygamy is fairly well established. Indeed, it has been convincingly argued that while polygamy was legally sanctioned in rabbinic times it was rarely practiced by Jews. The oriental Jews who, in the Middle Ages and later, had more than one wife, were influenced by Islamic practice rather than by talmudic legislation.

Women were exempt from the precept of studying the Torah. Although R. Eliezer's view that "whosoever teaches his daughter Torah teaches her lasciviousness" (Sot. 3:4) was a minority opinion, there was general agreement that a woman was not obliged to study the Torah. As a result few women were learned. The saying that women acquire merit by sending their sons to study and by encouraging their husbands to study is very revealing in this connection (Ber. 17a). The reason for God creating Eve from Adam's rib is

Niello key casket, probably given to a bride, Ferrara(?), Italy, c. 1470. The front is decorated with illustrations of the three commandments incumbent on a woman: setting aside a portion of the dough, ritual immersion, and blessing the Sabbath lights. On the lid are listed items of household linen with dials to indicate quantity. Height, 2½ in. (6.6 cm.), length, 5 in. (13 cm.), width, 2½ in. (6 cm.), depth, 1½ in. (4 cm.). Jerusalem, Israel Museum.

Photo R. M. Kneller, Jerusalem.

stated thus: "God said: I will not create her from the head that she should not hold up her head too proudly; nor from the eye that she should not be a coquette; nor from the ear that she should not be an eavesdropper; nor from the mouth that she should not be too talkative; nor from the heart that she should not be too jealous; nor from the hand that she should not be too acquisitive; nor from the foot that she should not be a gadabout; but from a part of the body which is hidden" that she should be modest (Gen. R. 18:2). It is said, however, that it was all to no effect and that four qualities in particular are ascribed to women: they are greedy, eavesdroppers, lazy, and jealous; they are also querulous and garrulous (Gen. R. 45:5). "Ten measures of speech descended to the world; women took nine" (Kid.

49b). Women are said to be "light-minded" (Shab. 33b), i.e., unreliable.

Women were feared as a source of temptation. In Babylon, possibly because of the greater laxity in sexual matters among the general population, it was said that a woman's voice is a sexual enticement as is her hair and her leg (Ber. 24a) and that one should under no circumstances be served at a table by a woman (Kid. 70a). In all probability this is the reason for the extremely harsh description of a woman, paralleled by the Church Fathers, as "a pitcher full of filth with its mouth full of blood, yet all run after her" (Shab. 152a).

On the other hand it is said that a man without a wife lives without joy, blessing, and good, and that a man should love his wife as himself and respect her more than himself (Yev. 62b). When R. Joseph heard his mother's footsteps he would say: "let me arise before the approach of the *Shekhinah*" (Kid. 31b). Israel was redeemed from Egypt by virtue of its righteous women (Sot. 11b). A man must be careful never to speak slightingly to his wife because women are prone to tears and sensitive to wrong (BM 59a). Women have greater faith than men (Sif. Num. 133) and greater powers of discernment (Nid. 45b) and they are especially tenderhearted (Meg. 14b). The Torah, the greatest joy of the rabbis, is frequently hypostatized as a woman (e.g., in Yev. 63b) and is represented as God's daughter and Israel's bride (Ex. R. 41:5).

POST-TALMUDIC ATTITUDES. In the Middle Ages thinkers like Maimonides followed rabbinic teachings on man's duty to care adequately for his wife and generally treat women with kindness and compassion, but the gates of learning were normally open only to males. The juxtaposition in Maimonides' works of "women and the ignorant" is frequent. According to Maimonides (Yad, Melakhim 1:6), a woman was not to be appointed to any communal office. Maimonides (Yad, Ishut 21:3 and 10) also rules that if a wife refuses to carry out such wifely duties as washing her husband's hands and feet, or serving him at table, she is to be chastised with rods. Maimonides' critic, Abraham b. David, objects however: "I have never heard that it is permitted to raise a rod to a woman." Maimonides was possibly influenced by contemporary Muslim practice. In France, Germany, and Poland it was unheard of that a husband should be allowed to beat his wife (see *Rema*, EH 154:3).

The attitude of the kabbalists to women stemmed from their views on the female element in the Godhead, as described in the doctrine of the *Sefirot* and especially in the doctrine of the *Shekhinah*. On the one hand this resulted in an increased respect for womanhood seen as the counterpart on earth of these supernal mysteries: "It is incumbent on a man to be ever 'male and female' in order that his faith may be firm, and that the *Shekhinah* may never depart from him. What, then, you will say, of a man who goes on a journey and, being absent from his wife, is no longer 'male and female'? His remedy is to pray to God before he starts his journey, while he is still 'male and female,' in order to draw to himself the presence of his Maker. When he has offered his prayer and thanksgiving and the *Shekhinah* rests on him, then he can depart, for through his union with the *Shekhinah* he has become 'male and female' in the country as he was 'male and female' in the town . . . . When he does return home again, it is his duty to give his wife some pleasure, because it was she who acquired for him his heavenly partner" (Zohar, Genesis, 49b–50a). Luria used to kiss the hands of his mother on the eve of the Sabbath. In his circle the custom arose of reciting Proverbs 31:10–31 in praise of the *Shekhinah*. Eventually the origin of the custom was forgotten and was adopted by Jews far removed from Kabbalism who understood the passage as referring to their wives. On the other hand, however, since the female element is passive and belongs to the "left side," the side of judgment and severity, and ultimately the source of the demonic, women were seen by the kabbalists as more cruel, less creative, and less capable of the higher reaches of
154 thought than men. G. Scholem (*Major Trends . . .* (1954[3]),

37f.) attributes this to the absence of female mystics in Judaism.

There is some truth in the contention that Ḥasidism gave women an honored position. Among the ḥasidic heroines are Adel (Odel), daughter of Israel b. Eliezer Ba'al Shem Tov; Aryeh Leib Sarahs' mother, after whom he is called; Feige, daughter of Adel and mother of Naḥman of Bratslav; and Frieda, daughter of Shneur Zalman of Lyady. Some women were ḥasidic "rabbis," e.g., Perele, daughter of Israel of Kozienice; Sarah, daughter of Joshua Heschel Teumim Frankel; "Malkele the Triskerin"; and Hannah Rachel the "Maid of Ludomir."

In modern times both the Jewish Haskalah in Russia and the Reform movement sought to improve the position of the Jewish woman, particularly in the area of the legal disabilities under which she suffered.

4 LABOR

In the Bible and Apocrypha. Directed to the common man, the Bible regards labor as man's destiny and an aspect of the cosmic order. According to Genesis 2:5, a condition of the creation of plant life was the presence of man to cultivate it; Adam's role was to till and keep the Garden of Eden (Gen. 2:15). Similarly, the utopian visions of the prophets take the continuation of man's labor for granted (cf. Isa. 2:4, "... into plowshares ... pruning hooks"), the blessedness of the times being manifest in the abundance of produce ("The plowman shall overtake the reaper, and the treader of grapes him who sows seed," Amos 9:13). The curse entailed by Adam's sin was not labor but the sweaty toil required henceforth to wrest bread from a thorny and thistly earth (Gen. 3:17ff.).

Labor was considered so much a part of the cosmic order that God Himself is depicted as a worker. He "founded" the earth, and the heavens are his "handi- (or "finger-") work" (Ps. 8:4; 102:26); He is the "fashioner" (*yozer*) of everything (Jer. 10:16); man is clay and God the potter (*yozer;* Isa. 64:7, based on Gen. 2:7). He worked six days at creating the world and rested (so Ex. 20:11; in Gen. 2:2–3 "ceased") on the seventh; wherefore the Israelites must do the same (Ex. 20:8ff.; cf. the lesson of the gathering of the manna, Ex. 16). It is not remarkable, therefore, that many of Israel's heroes were workers, or began as such: Moses (Ex. 3:1), Gideon (Judg. 6:11), Saul (I Sam. 11:5), David (17:34), Elisha (I Kings 19:19), and Amos (1:1; 7:14).

The sapiential literature lauds work and condemns sloth and idleness: "One who is slack in his work is brother to him who is a destroyer" (Prov. 18:9). The sluggard is sent to the provident for a lesson in industry (6:6ff.; cf. 20:4). Work is better than words (14:23), for "he that tills his ground shall have plenty of bread, but he who pursues vain things shall have plenty of poverty" (28:19; cf. 10:4; 12:24). The efficient, hardworking woman *('eshet ḥayil)* no less than her male counterpart *('ish mahir bi-melakhto)* is extolled (22:29; 31:10ff.). Contentment is the lot of the honest laborer:

> When you eat the fruit of your own labors
> You shall be happy and contented (Ps. 128:2);
> Sweet is the sleep of the laborer,
> Whether he eat little or much (Eccles. 5:11).

Success is not, however, an automatic outcome of work: "Unless the Lord builds the house, its builders will have toiled in vain" (Ps. 127:1); hence the customary felicitation with which one greeted workers, "The blessing of the Lord be upon you!" (Ps. 129:8; cf. Judg. 6:12; Ruth 2:4). Ecclesiastes, the late writer, concluded after long brooding and observation that even enjoyment of one's acquisitions was entirely a matter of luck—a gift of God to those who pleased him (for inscrutable reasons; Eccles. 2:18–26; 3:12–13; 5:12–6:2, etc.).

The Torah is solicitous of the wage earner. An employer must pay his day laborer "on the same day, before the sun sets, for he is needy and urgently depends on it; else he will cry to the Lord against you and you will incur guilt" (Deut. 24:15; cf. Lev. 19:13; on the length of the workday, from sunrise to sunset, cf. Ps. 104:23). This ruling applies equally to Israelite and foreign laborers (Deut. 24:14). Violations of this injunction are denounced by prophets (Jer. 22:13; Mal. 3:5). The laws concerning debts and debtors and the Jubilee had as their object the protection of laborers and farmers.

The Israelites did not take kindly to the conscription of labor for service to their kings (i.e., corvée). Samuel warned them of its hardships (I Sam. 8:11–12), perhaps on the basis of Canaanite royal practice, and under Solomon 157 its rigors were such (I Kings 5:27–28) that they led to the rebellion and secession of the North (I Kings 12). (By royal privilege a citizen or family might be exempt *(ḥofshi)* from such service; I Sam. 17:25.) A glimpse of life among such conscripts is afforded by a letter dating to the seventh century B.C.E. recovered from a fortress near Yavneh recording the complaint of a laborer against his superior for seizing his cloak (Pritchard, Texts³, 568).

For the most part, the literature that has been preserved from the Second Temple period expresses this plebeian outlook. "Hate not laborious work or husbandry," urges Ben Sira, "for it was ordained by God" (7:15). Issachar is the ideal figure of a God-fearing, chaste, industrious farmer in the Testament of the Twelve Patriarchs. Injunctions to treat hired labor kindly and not keep back their pay appear in Tobit 4:14; Ben Sira 7:20; 34:22. Horror of a beggar's life is expressed in Ben Sira 40:28ff.

A new note (anticipated in an Egyptian "Satire on the Trades" a millennium earlier (Pritchard, Texts, 43ff.)) is sounded in Ben Sira 38:24–34. Here the superiority of the learned scribe over the laborer and artisan is forcefully stated. The latter are, admittedly, necessary, but their horizons are bounded strictly by the requirements of their craft.

> Without them a city cannot be inhabited,
> And wherever they dwell they hunger not.
> But they shall not be inquired of for public council.
> And in the assembly they enjoy no precedence.
> On the seat of the judge they do not sit,
> And law and justice they understand not.
> They do not expound the instruction of wisdom,
> Nor understand the proverbs of the wise.
> They understand the work of the world,
> And their thought is on the practice of their craft (38:32–34).

A learned patrician speaks here, heralding a clash in values that would shortly ripen into sectarian conflict.

In the Talmud. Out of the many references to labor in the talmudic literature a clear picture emerges of the rabbinic attitude to labor. The need for having an occupation was raised to the level of a positive biblical commandment. The first half of Exodus 20:9, "six days shalt thou labor," was regarded as a separate injunction and not merely as an introduction to the prohibition of work on the Sabbath. Rabbi (Judah ha-Nasi) said, "these words constitute a separate commandment. In the same way as Israel was commanded concerning the Sabbath, so were they commanded concerning work" (Mekh. SbY to 20:9; cf. ARN[1] 11, 44 and Gen. R. 16:8). The virtue of work is continually extolled: "Man should love toil and not hate it." Adam did not partake of anything until he had worked, as it is said, "to dress it and to keep it"; the *Shekhinah* descended upon the children of Israel only after they had worked, as it is said, "and they shall make Me a sanctuary and I shall dwell in their midst" (ARN[1] loc. cit.).

Two reasons were given for the duty of being gainfully employed. One was the need for economic independence. No work was degrading if it achieved this: "Make thy Sabbath as a weekday (in respect to forgoing the added special meal) rather than be dependent on others" (Shab. 118a); "Flay a carcass in the street and earn a wage, and say not, 'I am a great man and degrading work is not for me'" (BB 110a); and "he who enjoys the work of his hands is greater than the man who fears heaven" (Ber. 8a). When R. Judah went to the *bet midrash* he would carry a pitcher on his shoulder, declaring, "great is labor for it honors the person who does it" (Ned. 49b). "Great is work. Even the high priest, if he were to enter the Holy of Holies on the Day of Atonement other than during the *Avodah,* is liable to death; yet for labor in it even those ritually unclean or blemished were permitted to enter" (Mekh. SbY to 20:9).

No less important, however, was the consideration of the social evil of idleness, irrespective of economic needs: "Idleness leads to unchastity" or "to degeneration" (Ket. 5:5) and "no man dies except from idleness" (ARN *ibid.*).

"If a man has no work to perform, what shall he do? If he has a neglected courtyard or field let him go and work in it" *(ibid)*. "He who does not teach his son a trade is as though he taught him to be a robber" (Kid. 29a). "Whosoever has a craft is like a vineyard surrounded with a protective hedge" (Tosef. Kid. 1:11). The therapeutic value of work is also stressed (Git. 67b). Nevertheless, one should, as far as possible, be selective in choosing one's occupation. There were "clean and easy trades" such as perfume-making and needlework, and there are mean occupations such as "ass drivers, wagoners, shepherds and shopkeepers." The trade of butcher was regarded as of an especially mean character, and people were enjoined to choose the former and avoid the latter. Similarly, trades which brought men into undesirable contact with women, such as jewelers, carders of wool, barbers, launderers, and bath attendants, should be avoided (Kid. 82a–b).

The dignity of labor was stressed: "Those engaged in work are not required to stand before a scholar while they are engaged in their tasks" (Kid. 33a), and it was emphasized that laborers also are "the children of Abraham, Isaac, and Jacob" (BM 7:1).

Nevertheless, this view of the supreme importance of labor per se is diminished by the consideration that the highest ideal is to be free from all worldly occupation in order to be able to devote oneself entirely to spiritual pursuits, to the study of Torah, or generally, "in order to serve one's Maker." According to this view, labor is a punishment inflicted upon man: "Simeon b. Eleazar said, 'Hast thou ever seen a wild animal or bird practicing a craft? Yet they find their sustenance without trouble, though they were created only to serve me. But I was created to serve my Maker; how much more so should I receive my sustenance without trouble? But I have wrought evil and so forfeited my right'" (Kid. 4:14). This view is emphasized by Simeon b. Yohai: "If a man has to plow in the plowing season, sow in the sowing season, reap . . .

thresh . . . and winnow, what will become of the Torah? But

Bezalel and Oholiab building the Tabernacle. Woodcut from the *Koberger Bible*, Nuremberg, 1483. Jerusalem, Israel Museum Archives.

when Israel fulfills the will of the Omnipresent their work is done for them by others and when they do not fulfill the will of the Omnipresent not only have they to carry out their work themselves, but they have to do the work of others" (Ber. 35b; cf. ARN[1] 11:44). Its highest expression is in the statement of Nehorai: "I would ignore all the crafts in the world and teach my son only Torah," since unlike manual toil it guards him both in old age and sickness and in the world to come (Kid. 4:14).

The compromise between these two extreme views is found in the ideal which was followed by most of the rabbis, in the combination of study with a worldly occupation. It is stated by Ishmael in explicit contradiction to the above-mentioned view of Simeon b. Yohai, and the maxim of Rabban Gamaliel in *Avot* (2:2) is "excellent is the study of the Torah combined with a worldly occupation for the toil involved in both makes sin to be forgotten. All study of the Torah without work is futile and is the cause of sin." This ideal is especially advocated by Meir, who, however, in addition to his many maxims extolling the value of manual labor urges that one should diminish one's worldly occupation as far as possible in order to be free for the study of the Torah (Avot 4:10). "The former generations made study their main concern and their work subsidiary to it, and they prospered in both; the later generations did the opposite and prospered in neither" (Ber. 35b).

Laborers and Employers. As mentioned, the dignity of labor and concern for the rights of laborers is emphasized. The biblical injunction to pay the laborer in time (Lev. 19:13) is expanded to the effect that "he who withholds an employee's wages is as though he had taken his life" (BM 112a), and in disputes between employees and workers the rights of the latter were given preference over those of the former (BM 77a). Especially significant is the rule laid down that the laborer has the right to withdraw his labor at any time, as an expression of his freedom from servitude to his fellowman (BK 116b; BM 10a). The extent to which the employer was liable for the laborer's food (BM 7:1) and the prerequisites to which the laborer was entitled are carefully laid down (BK 119, a–b).

A constant anxiety is nevertheless expressed at the tendency toward idleness and the exploitation of their employers on the part of laborers. "The laborers are sluggish," stated by Tarfon metaphorically about the service of God (Avot 2:15), seems to reflect actual conditions. "A laborer usually works faithfully for the first two or three hours of the day only, after which he becomes lazy" (Gen. R. 70:20). "He who has been left a large fortune by his father and wishes to squander it, let him hire workers and not work together with them" (BM 29b). The law that a laborer could recite the *Shema* while on a tree or on the scaffolding of a building (Ber. 2:4) or curtail the Grace After Meals (Ber. 46a) was designed not in the laborer's interests but in that of his employer's time. For reciting the *Amidah*, however, which is prayer proper, they had to descend to the ground.

labor and social justice was often stressed in rabbinic writings. Labor was considered a blessing in itself, and it was held that the Bible required the state to concern itself with its citizens during unemployment, old age, and illness. These benefits were to be granted as a matter of legal right and in a manner which was not offensive to the recipients' sense of dignity (Simon Federbush, *The Jewish Concept of Labor* (1956), 50–51, Z. Warhaftig (ed.), *Osef Piskei Din Rabbaniyyim*, 45). The workers' right to organize into unions was upheld by the rabbis, and it was viewed as an extension of the dictum that "townspeople may inflict penalties for breach of their regulations" (BB 8b; Rabbi Abraham Isaac Kook cited in Katriel Tchorsh, *Keter Efrayim* (1967), 160–171; cf. Moshe Feinstein, *Iggerot Moshe: Ḥoshen Mishpat*, 108–9). The workers' right to strike was justified (Shillem Warhaftig, bibl., 982, 984; *Iggerot Moshe* 110–111), although one opinion would not permit work-stoppages in the disputes of workers engaged in providing health services, electricity, and education (*Keter Efrayim*, 171). Another viewpoint was that all strikes were only permitted if the employers refused the workers' request to arbitrate their differences (Raphael Katzenellenbogen, *Ha-Ma'yan* (Tishrei, 1965), 9–14).

Labor Ideology in Europe. In modern times, from the Haskalah period in the 19th century, the alienation of the Jews in the *galut* from manual labor, particularly from agricultural production, was increasingly regarded as the root of evil in the "Jewish problem," while "Jewish parasitism" became a key word in modern anti-Semitism. The famous Yiddish term "luftmenshen," i.e., people who willy-nilly make a living from all kinds of petty, superfluous, mediating occupations, instead of useful work, emerged in the peculiar atmosphere of the Russian Pale of Settlement, which in the late 19th and early 20th century was a kind of huge "reservation" consisting of a network of towns and townlets in which masses of Jews were compelled to live "on air." The reaction in Jewish society to this condition took many social and political forms, including waves of mass emigration from Russia to the West and the yearning for a "return to the soil," particularly in Erez Israel. There were also attempts at "productivization" in Russia itself, as, e.g., in the Jewish agricultural settlements in southern Russia, the fostering of crafts and artisanship among Jewish youth, etc. Most of these trends were linked to elaborate ideologies, which, according to their originator's basic concepts, were either religious (as, e.g. Ḥayyim Landau, the founder of Ha-Po'el ha-Mizrachi and his followers), or socialist or Zionist and Zionist-Socialist (Naḥman Syrkin: Ber Borochov). In the early stages of the pioneering movement in Erez Israel, the ideology of labor was elevated to a basic philosophy of the reborn Jew rooted in the soil of his homeland (A. D. Gordon). This philosophy was largely instrumental in reversing in the Land of Israel the social structure of the "nonproductive" Jewish population in the European Diaspora. The ideology of productivization was also the motive force of endeavors of Jewish settlement on the land in Argentina, Brazil, and, in the 1930s, in Soviet Birobidzhan.

5 CHARITY

The obligation to render help to the poor and to the needy and to give them gifts is stated many times in the Bible and was considered by the rabbis of all ages to be one of the cardinal *mitzvot* of Judaism.

In the Bible. The Bible itself legislates several laws which are in effect a sort of tax for the benefit of the poor. Among these are *leket, shikhhah* and *pe'ah* as well as the special institutionalized tithe for the poor. The institution of the sabbatical (Heb: *Shemittah*) and Jubilee year was in order "that the poor of thy people may eat" (Ex. 23:11) as well as to cancel debts about which the warning was given "If there be among you a needy man, one of your brethren, within thy gates, in thy land which the Lord thy God giveth thee, thou shalt not harden thy heart nor shut thy hand from thy needy brother; but thou shalt surely open thy hand unto him and shalt surely lend him sufficient for his need in that which he wanteth. Beware that there be not a base thought in thy heart, saying 'The seventh year, the year of release, is at hand'; and thine eye be evil against thy needy brother and thou give him nought; and he say unto the Lord against thee and it be sin in thee. Thou shalt surely give him, and thy heart shall not be grieved when thou givest unto him; because that for this thing the Lord thy God will bless thee in all thy work...." (Deut. 15:7–10). The Pentateuch also insists that the needy be remembered when the festivals are celebrated, e.g., "And thou shalt rejoice before the Lord thy God, thou, and thy son, and thy daughter, and thy man-servant, and thy maid-servant, and the Levite that is within thy gates, and the stranger, and the fatherless and the widow that are in the midst of thee" (16:11, 14). The Bible expects Israel to be aware of the needs of the poor and the stranger (who is considered to be in an inferior economic position) because Israel itself had experienced this situation in Egypt: "Love ye therefore the stranger; for ye were strangers in the land of Egypt" (10:19) and promises "for this thing the Lord thy God will bless thee in all thy work and in all that thou puttest thy hand unto" (15:10).

Charity is an attribute of God Himself: "For the Lord your God, He is God of gods, and Lord of lords . . . He doth execute justice for the fatherless and widow and loveth the stranger, in giving him food and raiment" (10:17, 18), a theme which was developed at considerable length by the psalmist (cf. Ps. 145:15, 16; 132:15). Both the prophets Isaiah and Ezekiel considered charity as an indispensable requirement for a life of piety. Indeed, Isaiah proclaims that the "acceptable day to the Lord" is not the fast which only consists of afflicting the soul and wearing sackcloth and ashes but rather the day on which bread is dealt to the hungry, the poor that are cast out are brought into the house and the naked clothed (Is. 58:5-7); Ezekiel (16:49) attributes the destruction of Sodom to its lack of charity, "neither did she strengthen the hand of the poor and needy." "A woman of valor" is one who "stretcheth out her hand to the poor; Yea, she reacheth forth her hands to the needy" (Prov. 31:20). Charity to the poor is equated with "lending to the Lord, and his good deed will He repay unto him" (ibid., 19:17). The virtue of charity and the fact that it deserves reward from God is stressed over and over in the arguments in the book of Job (22:5-9; 29:12,13). Following the precedent in the Pentateuch, the book of Esther (9:12) makes sending gifts to the poor a part of the new festival it inaugurates (Purim), and when Ezra and Nehemiah taught the people anew the meaning of Rosh Ha-Shanah, they told them, "Go your way, eat the fat, and drink the sweet and send portions unto him for whom nothing is prepared" (Neh. 8:10).

In the Talmud and Rabbinic Literature. Although the idea of charity and almsgiving is spread throughout the whole of the Bible, there is no special term for it. The rabbis of the Talmud, however, adopted the word צְדָקָה *(zedakah)* for charity and it is used (but not exclusively so) throughout rabbinic literature in the sense of helping the needy by gifts. It has been suggested that the word *zedakah* in this sense already appears in Daniel (4:24) and in the Apocrypha (Ben Sira 3:30; 7:10 and Tobit 4:7; 12:8–9); in some of the verses the context would seem to bear out such a supposition. All this indicates, however, is that the term had come into use in the post-biblical period; in Talmud times it was entirely accepted to the extent that the rabbis interpreted biblical passages where the word certainly does not mean charity in the sense of their own usage. The word has since passed into popular usage and is almost exclusively used for charity. The term חֶסֶד *(hesed,* "loving-kindness"), which is used widely in the Bible, has taken on the meaning of physical aid, or lending without interest.

CHARITY AS ZEDAKAH. The word *zedakah* literally means "righteousness" or "justice"; by their very choice of word the rabbis reveal a great deal of their attitude to the subject, for they see charity not as a favor to the poor but something to which they have a right, and the donor, an obligation. In this way they teach "The poor man does more for the householder (in accepting alms) than the householder does for the poor man (by giving him the charity)" (Lev. R. 34:8) for he gives the householder the opportunity to perform a *mitzvah.* This attitude stemmed from the awareness that all men's possessions belong to God and that poverty and riches are in His hand. This view is aptly summed up in *Avot* (3:8): "Give unto Him of what is His, seeing that thou and what thou hast are His" and is further illustrated in a story told of Rava. A poor man came before Rava who asked him what he usually had for his meal. The man replied, "Fatted chicken and old wine." "But do you not" said Rava "feel worried that you are a burden on the community?" "Do I eat what is theirs?" said the man, "I eat what is God's" (exegesis to Ps. 145:15). At that point Rava's sister brought him a gift of a fatted chicken and some old wine which Rava understood to be an omen and apologized to the poor man (Ket. 67b).

The importance the rabbis attached to the *mitzvah* of *ẓedakah* can be understood from R. Assi who stated that *ẓedakah* is as important as all the other commandments put together (BB 9a) and from R. Eleazar who expounded the verse "To do righteousness *(ẓedakah)* and justice is more acceptable to the Lord than sacrifice" (Prov. 21:3) to mean that charity is greater than all the sacrifices (Suk. 49b). *Ẓedakah*, to the rabbis, hastens the redemption (BB 10a), ensures that the doer will have wise, wealthy, and learned sons (BB 19b), and atones for sins (BB 9a). Giving charity is the way in which man can "walk after the Lord your God" (Deut. 13:5) and saves from death (Prov. 1:2). Together with Torah and service (i.e., prayer), the practice of charity is one of the pillars on which the world rests (Avot 1:2). Giving charity does not impoverish and not giving is tantamount to idolatry (Ket. 68a). Charity is an act of devotion and a complement to prayer; as such the wise give charity just before praying as it is written, "and I, in righteousness *(ẓedek)* will see Thy face" (Ps. 17:15; BB 9a).

Since *ẓedakah* is considered a biblical commandment the rabbis found it necessary—as in the case of every other *mitzvah*—to define it in minute detail, e.g., who is obligated to give, who is eligible to receive, how much should be given and in what manner. These laws are scattered throughout the Talmud and were codified by Maimonides in his *Yad* in *Hilkhot Mattenot Aniyyim*, the first six chapters of which deal with the laws of *leket, shikhḥah*, and *pe'ah*, and the last four, with the general laws of charity. In the *Tur* and Shulḥan Arukh the laws are codified in *Yoreh De'ah* 247–59.

GIVERS AND RECEIVERS OF CHARITY. Everybody is obliged to give charity; even one who himself is dependent on charity should give to those less fortunate than himself (Git. 7a). The court can compel one who refuses to give charity—or donates less than his means allow—to give ac-

פאה

Engraving showing a poor man gleaning wheat, representing the tractate *Pe'ah*. From a title page of the Hebrew-Latin Mishnah illustrated by Mich. Richey, Amsterdam, 1700–04. Jerusalem, J.N.U.L.

cording to the court's assessment. The recalcitrant can even be flogged, and should he still refuse, the court may appropriate his property in the assessed sum for charity (Ket. 49b: Maim. Yad. Mattenot Aniyyim 7:10).

For the purposes of charity a poor man is one who has less than 200 zuz (200 dinar—each of which coins is the equivalent of 96 barley grains—of a mixture of 7/8 bronze and 1/8 silver). This sum is the criterion if it is static capital (i.e., not being used in business); if, however, it is being used, the limit is 50 zuz (*ibid.*, 9:13). A man with more than these sums is not entitled to take *leket, shikhhah*, and *pe'ah*, the poor man's tithe or charity—and he who does will be 169 reduced to real poverty (*ibid.*, 10:19). Charity should be dispensed to the non-Jewish poor in order to preserve good relations; however, charity should not be accepted from them unless it is entirely unavoidable. Women take precedence over men in receiving alms, and one's poor relatives come before strangers. The general rule is "the poor of your own town come before the poor of any other town," but this rule is lifted for the poor of Erez Israel who take precedence over all (Sh. Ar., YD 251:3). A traveller in a strange town who is out of funds is considered to be poor and may take charity even though he has money at home. When he returns to his home he is not obliged to repay the charity he has taken (Pe'ah 5:4). A man is not obliged to sell his household goods in order to maintain himself but is eligible for charity (Pe'ah 8:8); even if he owns land, houses, or other property, he is not required to sell them at a disadvantage if the prices are lower than usual (BK 7a–b). It is permitted to deceive a poor man who, out of pride, refuses to accept charity, and to allow him to think that it is a loan; but a miser who refuses to use his own means is to be ignored (Ket. 67b).

THE AMOUNT OF CHARITY TO BE GIVEN. To give a tenth of one's wealth to charity is considered to be a "middling" virtue, to give a 20th or less is to be "mean"; but in Usha the rabbis enacted that one should not give more than a fifth lest he become impoverished himself and dependent on charity (Ket. 50a; Maim. Yad loc. cit., 7:5). The psychological needs of the poor should be taken into consideration even though they may appear to be exaggerated. Thus a once wealthy man asked Hillel for a horse and a runner to go before him, which Hillel supplied; on another occasion, when Hillel could not afford to hire a runner for him, Hillel acted as one himself (Ket. 67a). This attitude is based on the interpretation of the verse "thou shalt surely open thy hand unto him . . . for his need which he wanteth" (Deut. 15:8), the accent being on "his" and "he"; however, on the basis of the same verse the rabbis

taught that "you are required to maintain him but not to

enrich him," stressing the word "need" (Ket. 67a). "We must be more careful about charity than all the other positive *mitzvot* because *zedakah* is the criterion of the righteous (*zaddik*), the seed of Abraham, as it is written 'For I have singled him [Abraham] out, that he may instruct his children and his posterity to keep the way of the Lord by doing what is just [*zedakah*; Gen. 18:19]' ... and Israel will only be redeemed by merit of charity, as it is written 'Zion shall be redeemed with justice, And they that return of her with righteousness [*zedakah*; Isa. 1:17]'" (Maim. Yad, loc. cit. 10:1).

MANNER OF DISPENSING CHARITY. This appreciation of the importance of charity led the rabbis to be especially concerned about the manner in which alms are to be dispensed. The prime consideration is that nothing be done that might shame the recipient. "R. Jonah said: It is not written 'Happy is he who gives to the poor,' but 'Happy is he who considers the poor' (Ps. 41:2): i.e., he who ponders how to fulfill the command to help the poor. How did R. Jonah act? If he met a man of good family who had become impoverished he would say, 'I have heard that a legacy has been left to you in such a place; take this money in advance and pay me back later.' When the man accepted it he then said to him, 'It is a gift'" (TJ, Pe'ah 8:9, 21b). When R. Yannai saw somebody giving a zuz to a poor man in public he said, "It were better not to have given rather than to have given him and shamed him" (Ḥag. 5a). Out of consideration for the sensibilities of the poor the rabbis considered the best form of almsgiving to be that in which neither the donor nor the recipient knew each other: "Which is the *zedakah* which saves from a strange death? That in which the giver does not know to whom he has given nor the recipient from whom he has received" (BB 10a), and R. Eliezer saw the "secret" giver as being greater than Moses (BB 9b). Stories are told throughout the Talmud illustrating this principle and relating how the pious used to devise ingenious methods of giving alms so as to remain anonymous (Ket. 67b.; Ta'an. 21b–22a, et al.).

Carved wood charity drum, London, early 19th century. It was designed for the Five Shillings Sabbath Charity, and from it were
172 drawn tickets entitling the poor to meals. London Museum.

For the same reason it is important to receive the poor in good humor, and even if one cannot afford to give, one must at least appease the poor with words (Lev. R. 34:15; Maim Yad loc. cit. 10:5).

Maimonides (Yad, loc. cit. 10:7–12) lists eight ways of giving *zedakah* which are progressively more virtuous: to give (1) but sadly; (2) less than is fitting, but in good humor; (3) only after having been asked to; (4) before being asked; (5) in such a manner that the donor does not know who the recipient is; (6) in such a manner that the recipient does not know who the donor is; and (7) in such a way that neither the donor nor the recipient knows the identity of the other. The highest form of charity is not to give alms but to help the poor to rehabilitate themselves by lending them money, taking them into partnership, employing them, or giving them work, for in this way the end is achieved without any loss of self-respect at all.

"CHARITY WARDENS." "In every town where there are Jews they must appoint 'charity wardens' *[gabba'ei zedakah]*, men who are well-known and honest that they should collect money from the people every Sabbath eve and distribute it to the poor . . . We have never seen or heard of a Jewish community which does not have a charity fund" (Yad, loc. cit. 9:1–3). Because the charity warden was involved in the collection and distribution of public funds, special care was taken to ensure that there should not be even the slightest suspicion of dishonesty. The actual collection had to be made by at least two wardens who were not permitted to leave each other during the course of it. The distribution of the money was to be made by at least three wardens in whose hands lay the decision as to whom to give and how much. Besides money, food and clothing were also distributed. It seems that the poor were registered with the fund and mendicants who went from door to door begging were not to be given any sizable sums (BB 9a); the fund did, however, supply the needs of strangers. Apart from maintaining the poor, the fund was also used for redeeming captives and dowering poor brides, both of

A Jewish soup kitchen at Spitalfields, in London's East End, 1879.
Cecil Roth Collection.

which were considered to be among the most virtuous of
acts. In addition to the fund *(kuppah)* there were also
communal soup kitchens *(tamḥui)* at which any person
with less than enough for two meals was entitled to eat
(Yad, loc. cit. 9:13).

Collecting and distributing charity is to some extent
distasteful work and at times even humiliating. In order to
encourage men to undertake it, the rabbis interpreted
several scriptural verses as extolling the wardens who are

considered to be "eternal stars" and greater even than the givers (BB 8a, 9a). R. Yose, however, prayed "May my lot be with those who collect charity rather than with those who distribute it" (Shab. 118b), apparently preferring the risk of humiliation to that of misjudgment.

Charity is a form of vow, and a promise to give must be fulfilled immediately (Yad, loc. cit. 8:1). Generally speaking the charity money must be used for the purpose for which it was given and it is forbidden to divert the funds to some other cause.

THE ACCEPTING OF CHARITY. When necessary, accepting charity is perfectly legitimate and no shame attaches itself to the poor who are otherwise unable to support themselves. However, one is advised to do everything in one's power to avoid having to take alms: "Make your Sabbath a weekday (by not eating special food or wearing good clothes) rather than be dependent on other people" (Pes. 112a); and, "even a wise and honored man should do menial work (skinning unclean animals) rather than take charity" (Pes. 113a). The greatest of the sages did physical labor in order to support themselves and remain independent. "A person who is really entitled to take charity but delays doing so and so suffers rather than be a burden to the community will surely be rewarded and not die before he reaches a position in which he will be able to support others. About such a person was it written: 'Blessed is the man that trusteth in the Lord' (Jer. 17:7)" (Yad, loc. cit. 10:18).

6 PROSELYTES

There is a considerable amount of evidence of a widespread conversion to Judaism during the period of the Second Temple, especially the latter part of the period, and the word *ger,* which in biblical times meant a stranger, or an alien, became synonymous with a proselyte.

Proselytism was obviously widespread among the ordinary people. The statement of the New Testament that the Pharisees "compass sea and land to make one proselyte" (Matt. 23:15), suggesting a vigorous and active proselytization may possibly be an exaggeration, but on the other hand, the near pride which the rabbis took in the claim that some of their greatest figures were descended from proselytes (see below) point to an openhanded policy toward their acceptance. Such incidents as the different approach of Shammai and Hillel to the request to be taught the principles of Judaism by a potential proselyte (Shabb. 31a) and the incidental mention of "Judah the Ammonite proselyte" (Ber. 28a) point to the fact that the movement was not confined to the upper classes. In fact Josephus states explicitly that in his day the inhabitants of both Greek and barbarian cities evinced a great zeal for Judaism (Contra Ap. 2. 39).

It was during this period that the detailed laws governing the acceptance of proselytes were discussed and codified, and they have remained standard in Orthodox Judaism.

Laws of Conversion. The procedure, established by the *tannaim,* according to which a non-Jew may be accepted into the Jewish faith, was elucidated as follows: "In our days, when a proselyte comes to be converted, we say to him: 'What is your objective? Is it not known to you that today the people of Israel are wretched, driven about, exiled, and in constant suffering?' If he says: 'I know of this and I do not have the merit,' we accept him immediately and we inform him of some of the lighter precepts and of some of the severer ones . . . we inform him of the chastisements for the transgression of these precepts . . . and we also inform him of the reward for observing these precepts . . . we should not overburden him nor be meticulous with him . . ." (Yev. 47a; cf. Ger. 1, in: M. Higger, *Sheva Massekhtot Ketannot* (1930), 68–69). This text refers to a person who converted through conviction. The *halakhah* also accepts a posteriori, proselytes who had converted in order to marry, to advance themselves, or out of fear (Yev. 24b, in the name of Rav, see TJ, Kid. 4:1, 65b–d; Maim. Yad, Issurei Bi'ah 13:17; Sh. Ar., YD 268:12). The acceptance of a proselyte "under the wings of the Divine Presence" is equivalent to Israel's entry into the covenant, i.e., with circumcision, immersion, and offering a sacrifice (Ger. 2:4, in: M. Higger; loc. cit. 72).

A proselyte had to sacrifice a burnt offering either of cattle or two young pigeons. R. Johanan b. Zakkai instituted that in those times when sacrifice was no longer possible, a proselyte was not obliged to set aside money for the sacrifice (Ker. 9a). Therefore, only circumcision and immersion remained. R. Eliezer and R. Joshua disagreed as to whether someone who immersed himself but was not circumcised or vice versa could be considered a proselyte. According to R. Eliezer, he is a proselyte, even if he performed only one of these commandments. R. Joshua, however, maintained that immersion was indispensable. The halakhic conclusion is that "he is not a proselyte unless he has both been circumcised and has immersed himself" (Yev. 46). The act of conversion must take place before a *bet din,* consisting of three members; a conversion carried out by the proselyte when alone is invalid (Yev. 46b–47a). There is a suggestion that the three members of the *bet din* must be witnesses only to his acceptance of the precepts but not to the immersion. Maimonides, however, decided (Yad,

Issurei Bi'ah 13:7), that a proselyte who immersed himself in the presence of two members only is not a proselyte. The schools of Shammai and Hillel differed on the issue of a proselyte who had already been circumcised at the time of his conversion: "Bet Shammai states: 'One must draw from him the blood of circumcision'; Bet Hillel states: 'One need not draw the blood of circumcision from him'" (Tosef., Shab. 15:9; TB, Shab. 135a). Most of the rabbinic authorities decide in favor of Bet Shammai (Tos. to Shab. 135a; Maim. Yad, Issurei Bi'ah 14:5; Sh. Ar., YD 268:1), and "who hast sanctified us with Thy commandments and hast commanded us to circumcise proselytes and to draw from them the blood of the covenant" (Shab. 137b) is said in the circumcision benediction of proselytes.

A proselyte must observe all the precepts that bind Jews. The statement: "There shall be one law for the citizen and for the stranger that dwelleth amongst you" (Ex. 12:49), which refers to the paschal lamb, the sages interpreted to mean that the stranger (proselyte) was the equal of the citizen concerning all the precepts of the Torah (Mekh. Pisha, 15). They tried to equalize the status of the proselyte and that of the Jew; certain differences stemming from the origin of the convert, however, remained. According to an anonymous Mishnah, a proselyte may not confess himself after taking out the tithes since the statement occurs in the confession "the land which Thou hast given to us"; nor does he read the section on the first fruits, where the statement is: "which the Lord hath sworn unto our fathers to give unto us." The proselyte, praying by himself must say: "the God of the Fathers of Israel"; in the synagogue he says: "the God of your Fathers" (Ma'as. Sh. 5:14; Bik. 1:4). According to one tradition, R. Judah permitted a proselyte to read the section on the first fruits, claiming that Abraham was the father of the whole world (TJ, Bik. 1:4, 64a; but in Tosef., Bik. 1:2 this permission is only extended to the Kenites). The Palestinian *amoraim,* R. Joshua b. Levi and R. Avihu, agreed with R. Judah. The authorities (particularly R. Samson in his commentary to

Bikkurim (ibid.), and Maimonides in his letter to Obadiah the Proselyte, below) in permitting a proselyte to say "the God of our Fathers" in the prayers based themselves on the same rationale.

A proselyte terminates all former family ties upon conversion and "is considered a newly born child." His Jewish name is not associated with that of his father and he is referred to as "the son of Abraham (our father)." Later, it became the custom to name the proselyte himself after the first Jew who knew his Creator "Abraham the son of Abraham." According to the letter of the law, a proselyte may marry his relatives. The sages, however, decreed against this "So that they should not say: 'We have come from a greater sanctity to a lesser sanctity'" (Yev. 22a, Yad, Issurei Bi'ah 14:12). The disqualifications pertaining to testimony of relatives in judicial cases of family members do not apply to the proselyte; his relatives also may not inherit from him. If no heirs were born to him after his conversion, his property and his possessions are considered not to belong to anyone, and whoever takes hold of them becomes their owner (BB 3:3, 4:9; Git. 39a; Yad, Zekhi'ah u-Mattanah 1:6).

A proselyte may marry a Jewish woman, even the daughter of a priest (Kid. 73a; Yad, Issurei Bi'ah 19:11; Sh. Ar., EH 7:22). A female proselyte, however, cannot marry a kohen, unless she was converted during childhood, not later than the age of three years and one day (Yev. 60b; Kid. 78a). R. Yose permits the marriage of the daughter of a male or female proselyte to a kohen; R. Eliezer b. Jacob, however, disputes the matter. The statement "From the day of the destruction of the Temple, the kohanim have preserved their dignity and followed the opinion of R. Eliezer b. Jacob" shows that tradition tended toward the latter's opinion. The *amoraim,* however, decided that he be followed only in those cases where the marriage has not yet taken place. If a female proselyte is already married to a kohen, she is not bound to leave him (Kid. 4:7; TB, Kid. 78b; Yad, Issurei Bi'ah 19:12). A proselyte may also marry a *mamzer* ("bastard"). According to some opinions, the permission may extend over ten generations, while others claim it should be only until his heathen origin is forgotten (Kid. 72b, 75a).

A proselyte cannot be appointed to any public office. The rabbis based their decision on the verse: "Thou shalt appoint over thee a king from among thy brothers—appointments shall be only from among thy brothers." This injunction does not apply to a proselyte whose mother or father are of Jewish origin (Yev. 45b; Kid. 76b; Tos. Sot. 41b, Yad, Melakhim 1:4). A proselyte may not hold the office of judge in a criminal court; he may act as such in a civil court (Sanh. 36b) and also judge a fellow proselyte, even in a criminal law case (Rashi to Yev. 102a). Unless one of his parents was born Jewish, most authorities bar a proselyte from acting as judge even in a civil court (Alfasi on Sanh. 4:2, Yad, Sanh. 2:9, 11:11). Others are of the opinion that even in a civil court he can only judge a fellow proselyte (Tos. Yev. 45b; RaShBA on Yev. 102a).

Appreciation of the Proselyte. In the Talmud and the Midrashim, as well as in other contemporary literature, the accepted attitude toward proselytes is usually positive. There is, however, strong evidence in rabbinic sources that some authorities were opposed to the concept of conversion and proselytes. Those scholars who ignore or obliterate such evidence cannot be justified. The differences in outlook found in rabbinic sources can partly be explained by disparities in character and temperament. However, the deciding factors were usually contemporary conditions and the personal experiences of the rabbis. R. Eliezer b. Hyrcanus, who was under ban, objected to the acceptance of proselytes (Eccles. R. 1:8). When Aquila the Proselyte wondered and asked: "Is this all the love which the Lord hath given unto the proselyte, as it is written 'and He loveth the stranger to give him bread and clothing?'" R. Eliezer was angry with him, but R. Joshua comforted him, saying: "Bread means Torah . . . clothing means the *tallit:* the man
180 who is worthy to have the Torah, will also acquire its

precepts; his daughters may marry into the priesthood and their grandsons will sacrifice burnt offerings on the altar." (Gen. R. 70:5). It is possible that R. Eliezer's negative attitude may have been influenced by his contacts with the first Christians. He may have seen that many of the new heretics were proselytes who had relapsed and it is only concerning these that he said, "They revert to their evil ways" (BM 59b). The same R. Eliezer also states: "When a person comes to you in sincerity to be converted, do not reject him, but on the contrary encourage him" (Mekh. Amalek 3). From his time, proselytes out of conviction were mentioned in the benediction for the righteous and the pious in the *Amidah* (Meg. 17b). The bitter experience of Jews with proselytes in times of war and revolt influenced the negative attitude to conversion. Proselytes and their offspring became renegades, often slandering their new religion and denouncing the Jewish community and its leaders to the foreign rulers. In Josephus there is a description of Hellenist proselytes who apostatized and returned to their evil ways (Jos., Apion 2:123). Reference to the situation which existed after the destruction of the Temple and the abortive revolt which followed it is made in the *baraita* statement: "Insincere proselytes who wear *tefillin* on the heads and on their arms, *zizit* in their clothes, and who fix *mezuzot* on their doors—when the war of Gog and Magog will come. . . each one of them will remove the precepts from himself and go on his way. . . " (Av. Zar. 3b). At the time of the revolt of Bar Kokhba the expression "they impede the arrival of the Messiah" (Nid. 13b), referred to such proselytes. At the same epoch, R. Nehemiah taught: a proselyte who converted in order to marry or converted to enjoy the royal table or to become a servant of Solomon, proselytes who converted from fear of the lions (see: II Kings 17:24–28), proselytes who converted because of a dream, or the proselytes of Mordecai and Esther, are not acceptable as proselytes, unless they convert themselves (as) at the present time (Yev. 24b), i.e., by conviction in times of political decline, oppressions, persecutions, and lack of any material benefit. R. Simeon b. Yoḥai, upon seeing Judah b. Gerim ("a son of proselytes"), who was responsible for the rabbi's criticism of the Romans reaching the ears of the rulers, said: "Is this one still in the world!" and set his eyes upon him, turning him into a heap of bones (Shab. 33b–34a). This experience throws light on the commentary of R. Simeon: "Those who feared the Lord were a hindrance to Israel . . . the best of the gentiles, you should put to death . . ." (Mekh. Va-Yeḥi 2). His real opinions, however, found expression in the commentary (Mekh. Nezikim (Mishpatim) 18): "It is said—'And those that are beloved by Him are compared to the sun when it rises in all its strength'; Now who is greater—he who loves the king or he whom the king loves? One must say—he whom the king loves, as the verse says: 'and He loves the stranger [proselyte]' "; the statement of R. Ḥiyya: "Do not have any faith in a proselyte until 24 generations have passed because the inherent evil is still within him" (Mid. Ruth Zuta on 1:12); and other statements of *amoraim* who despised proselytes: "Proselytes are as hard for Israel [to endure] as a sore" (Yev. 47b) were prompted by the bad experiences Jews had with proselytes who had turned national or religious recreants. To these the rabbis referred: "The proselytes who left Egypt with Moses, made it [the Golden Calf] and said to Israel: These are your gods" (Ex. R. 42:6). The rabbis distinguished between three categories of proselytes: "Proselytes are of three types: There are some like Abraham our Father, some like Hamor, and some that are like heathens in all respects" (SER 27). In the teachings of the *amoraim* the basic tone is that of the tannaitic statement: "Proselytes are beloved; in every place He considers them as part of Israel" (Mekh. *ibid.*). They too made efforts "not to close the door before the proselytes who may come" *(ibid).* In the third century, R. Johanan and R. Eleazar separately deduced from different verses that "the Holy One, Blessed be He, exiled Israel among the nations only in order to increase their numbers with the addition of proselytes" (Pes. 87b). R. Eleazar also said:

"Whoever befriends a proselyte is considered as if he created him" (Gen. R. 84:4). There are numerous other statements which praise proselytes (e.g., Tanḥ. Lekh Lekha 6; Num. R. 8:9; Mid. Ps. 146:8). A tendency to increase the honor of the proselytes and to glorify conversion can perhaps be found in the tradition which traces the origins of such great personalities as R. Meir, R. Akiva, Shemaiah, and Avtalyon to proselytes. They were descendants of such wicked men as Sisera, Sennacherib, Haman, and Nero (Git. 56a, 57b; Sanh. 96b). The name of R. Akiva's father does not appear explicitly in the Talmud, but *Dikdukei Soferim, ibid.,* 9 (1878), 283 and also Maimonides' introduction to *Mishneh Torah* relate that Joseph, the father of R. Akiva, was a proselyte by conviction. The last of the Babylonian *amoraim,* R. Ashi, said that the destiny of the proselytes had also been determined at Mount Sinai (Shab. 146a). Most of the rabbis of the Talmud observed the tradition: "When a proselyte comes to be converted, one receives him with an open hand so as to bring him under the wings of the Divine Presence" (SER 7; Lev. R. 2:9).

Post Talmudic. During the following era the proponents of the two ruling monotheistic religions—in contrast to polytheism—regarded abandonment of their faith and transfer to another religion as a capital offense. The canons of the Church forbade proselytism and Christian rulers fiercely opposed any tendency to adopt Jewish religious customs. The number of proselytes diminished in Christian countries, and those who endangered their lives by adherence to Israel were generally compelled to flee to lands beyond the bounds of the rule of the Church.

A talmudist who was a proselyte by conviction sent halakhic queries to Maimonides, who addressed him in respectful terms: "Master and teacher, the intelligent and enlightened Obadiah, the righteous proselyte," and wrote to him, "You are a great scholar and possess an understanding mind, for you have understood the issues and known the right way." In his letters to this proselyte, Maimonides expresses high appreciation of proselytism and the proselyte: he permits him to pray:

> ... as every native Israelite prays and recites blessings ... any-
> one who becomes a proselyte throughout the generations and
> anyone who unifies the Name of the Holy One as it is written
> in the Torah is a pupil of our father Abraham and all of them
> are members of his household ... hence you may say, Our
> God, and the God of our fathers; for Abraham, peace be upon
> him, is your father ... for since you have entered beneath the
> wings of the Divine Presence and attached yourself to Him,
> there is no difference between us and you. ... You certainly
> recite the blessings: Who has chosen us; Who has given us;
> Who has caused us to inherit; and Who has separated us.
> For the Creator has already chosen you and has separated
> you from the nations and has given you the Torah, as the
> Torah was given to us and to proselytes. ... Further, do not
> belittle your lineage: if we trace our descent to Abraham,
> Isaac, and Jacob, your connection is with Him by Whose
> word the universe came into being.

(Resp. Rambam (ed. Freimann), no. 42). Concerning the
vexations and humiliating words violently addressed to this
proselyte by certain Jews, Maimonides writes to him:

> Toward father and mother we are commanded honor and
> reverence, toward the prophets to obey them, but toward
> proselytes we are commanded to have great love in our inmost
> hearts. ... God, in His glory, loves proselytes. ... A man who
> left his father and birthplace and the realm of his people at a
> time when they are powerful, who understood with his insight,
> and who attached himself to this nation which today is a des-
> pised people, the slave of rulers, and recognized and knew that
> their religion is true and righteous ... and pursued God ...
> and entered beneath the wings of the Divine Presence ... the
> Lord does not call you fool [Heb. *kesil*], but intelligent [*maskil*]
> and understanding, wise and walking correctly, a pupil of
> Abraham our father ...

With the decline in the number of proselytes by
conviction, the fundamental attitude of the medieval Jewish
scholars toward proselytism as a phenomenon of profound
religious significance did not change, and some of them
continued to consider that the purpose of Israel's dispersion
among the nations was to gain proselytes. Moses b. Jacob

of Coucy (mid-13th century) explains to his contemporaries that they must act uprightly toward gentiles since "so long as they [i.e., Jews] act deceitfully toward them, who will attach themselves to them?" (*Semag,* Asayin 74). Isaiah b. Mali di Trani the Younger permits the teaching of the books of the Prophets and the Hagiographa to gentiles, because he regards them as consolation spoken to Israel, "and as a result he [the gentile] may mend his ways" (*Shiltei Gibborim,* Av. Zar., ch. 1).

In Modern Times. The Jewish attitude to proselytism at the beginning of the modern period was inclined to be negative; aspirations to win over people of other faiths to Judaism dwindled. However, the *bet din* has no authority to repudiate proselytes wishing to convert despite the admonitions concerning the gravity of such a step; the Shulḥan Arukh and the other *posekim* of the period left the laws concerning proselytism in force, but examination of the texts reveals, and at times it is even expressly stated, that it was only a formal duty to accept proselytes, and, indeed, attempts at active conversion were infrequent.

With the relative toleration that began to prevail in the ruling circles and among intellectuals in the 17th century, especially in Western Europe, the negative attitude to Christianity among Jews diminished. There was a growing tendency not to regard Christianity as an idolatrous religion but to look upon its adherents as being subject to the Noachide Laws who are absolved from the belief in absolute monotheism. Such a view left no room for conversion efforts to bring Christians under the wings of the *Shekhinah.*

The Enlightenment strengthened this inclination to religious contraction. The slogan of religious toleration discouraged propaganda activities among the different faiths. The *maskilim* pointed with pride to the resemblance between the principles of Enlightenment and the aims of Judaism—which, in their opinion, were tolerance. Emphasis on Jewish tolerance and abandonment of all active proselytizing became a fixed principle in modern Jewish apologetics. This apologetical attitude even influenced study of the past, and historical accounts tended to ignore that active Jewish proselytizing had occurred, as if Judaism had never desired to make converts. There was no change from the psychological point of view in the self-defensive attitude of Judaism even after it had been granted a status of juridical equality with the other religions of the state. Even though no legal obstacles now prevent proselytizing little attempt has been made to propagate conversion.

Recent Trends. Whereas in some countries of the Diaspora, particularly England and South Africa, there was a distinct tendency to adopt more stringent regulations for the acceptance of proselytes in the Orthodox community, it was generally appreciated that a greater leniency could be permitted in the State of Israel, since the prospective proselytes, most of whom were either partners in, or the children of, mixed marriages, would become much more integrated in the Jewish people than would be likely in the Diaspora. Despite this the rabbinical authorities were slow to alleviate the difficulties in the way of applicants for proselytization. They normally insisted on a year's postponement of consideration after making application, and on the ability and undertaking of the candidate to adhere to the requirements of Orthodox Judaism. From 1948 to 1968, 2,288 proselytes were accepted by the rabbinical courts of Israel, out of a total of 4,010 who applied. A tendency toward leniency became more pronounced at the beginning of the 1970s as a result of two factors. One was the expectation of an increased immigration from Soviet Russia where, owing to prevailing circumstances, intermarriage had taken place on an unprecedented scale; and the other was the situation created by the amendment to the Law of Return adopted by the Knesset in 1970. Two provisions made the need for an acceleration of proselytization urgent. The first was that the law was extended to include the partners, children, and grandchildren of mixed marriages who were not Jews according to *halakhah,* and the second that, whereas in Israel only those converted in accordance with *halakhah* were registered as Jews, in the case of immigrants, conversion by Reform and Conservative rabbis was accepted by the civil authorities for these immigrants to be registered as Jews. The resulting anomaly, that these non-Orthodox proselytes were regarded as Jews by the civil authorities while their conversion was not accepted by the Orthodox rabbinate, which was the only legal body determining personal status, had to be reduced as much as possible. In 1971 the Ministry for Religious Affairs, for the first time, established schools for prospective proselytes in Israel, at the Orthodox kibbutzim of Sa'ad and Lavi, where candidates may undergo an intensive course in Judaism.

There have also been a number of instances of the conversion of Muslims to Judaism (see A. Rotem, in: *Maḥanayim,* no. 92 (1964), 159).

7 CRUELTY TO ANIMALS

The rules concerning the treatment of animals are based on the principle that animals are part of God's creation toward which man bears responsibility. Laws and other indications in the Pentateuch and the rest of the Bible make it clear not only that cruelty to animals is forbidden but also that compassion and mercy to them are demanded of man by God. According to rabbinic tradition, interpreting the biblical record, mankind was not allowed to eat meat until after the Flood, although the sacrifice of animals to God had been previously allowed (Gen. 1:29; 9:3). Once permitted, the consumption of meat remained surrounded with many restrictions (the Dietary Laws). According to the rabbis, the Hebrew word for "desireth" in the verse, "When the Lord thy God shall enlarge thy border and thou shalt say: 'I will eat flesh,' because thy soul desireth to eat flesh . . ." (Deut. 12:20), has a negative connotation; hence, although it is permitted to slaughter animals for food, this should be done in moderation. It has been suggested that the Jewish method of slaughter, particularly the laws that the knife be exceedingly sharp and without the slightest notch, were motivated by consideration for the animal because this method is the most painless. The biblical Sabbath laws also suggest consideration for animals ("Thou shall not do any manner of work . . . nor thine ox, nor thine ass, nor any of thy cattle" Ex. 20:10; Deut. 5:14; "but on the seventh day thou shalt rest; that thine ox and thine ass may have rest" (Ex. 23:12)), as do the prohibitions against muzzling an ox as it threshes (Deut. 25:4), and slaughtering an animal and its young on the same day (Lev. 22:28). One reason for the commandment to let the fields lie fallow in the Sabbatical year is that "the poor of thy people . . . and the beast of the field" may eat from them (Lev. 25:6–7). This same idea is inherent in the commandment "If thou see the ass of him that hateth thee lying under its burden . . . . thou shalt surely release it with him" (Ex. 23:5), and in the requirement to release the parent bird before taking the young (Deut. 22:6–7). (However, there is a difference of opinion in the Talmud as to the reason for these last *mitzvot* (see below).) Indications of the same consideration appear in the narrative sections of the Bible. The angel rebuked Balaam for smiting his ass (Num. 22:32), and God Himself admonished Jonah "and should not I have pity on Nineveh, that great city, wherein are more than sixscore thousand persons . . . and also much cattle?" (Jonah 4:11). God is also praised as the One who satisfied all living creatures (Ps. 145:9–16), and for giving the beasts and the birds their food (Ps. 147:9).

In view of all this, the rabbis based a great deal of their legislation and interpretation on the principle of *za'ar ba'alei ḥayyim*. As one the seven Noachide Laws, the prohibition to eat the flesh of a living animal, applies also to non-Jews (Sanh. 56a–57a, 59a–b; Tosef., Av. Zar. 8:4–6). The dietary laws limiting the killing of animals are discussed at great length, and the rabbis recommend moderation in eating even permitted meat. The rabbis were not completely opposed to killing animals—giving priority to human needs—but they were entirely against wanton killing as they were against causing pain to animals. It is forbidden to inflict a blemish on an animal (Ḥul. 7b). Many acts otherwise forbidden on the Sabbath are permitted when their purpose is to relieve animals' pain on the grounds that cruelty to animals is biblically prohibited (Shab. 128b). The accepted (although not unanimous) view is that the commandment to help unload (Ex. 23:5, see above) is motivated by consideration for animals, which is thus regarded as a principle of biblical force (Maim. Yad, Roẓe'aḥ u-Shemirat Nefesh, 13; Tur., ḤM, 272) and thus it is permitted to unload a burden from a laboring animal even on the Sabbath (Maim. Yad, Shabbat 21:9–10). It is permitted to ask a non-Jew to milk cows on the Sabbath—an act that would be otherwise forbidden. The rabbis ordained that one should not recite the festive benediction *She-Heheyanu* before the act of ritual slaughter or before putting on new leather shoes because the enjoyment is at the cost of the animal. On the basis of the verse "I will give grass in thy fields for thy cattle, and thou shalt eat and be satisfied" (Deut. 11:15), the rabbis decided that "it is forbidden for a man to eat before he has fed his animal **because the animal is mentioned first**" (Ber. 40a). This decision accordingly passed into the *halakhah* and was subsequently codified (Maim. Yad, Avadim, 9:8). Out of the same consideration they also legislated that "a man is not permitted to buy animals unless he can properly provide for them" (TJ, Yev. 15:3, 14d; TJ, Ket. 4:8, 29a). The principle of kindness to animals played no less a part in the *aggadah* than it did in the *halakhah*. It is as though God's treatment of man will be according to the latter's treatment of animals. This is suggested by the juxtaposition of the promise of long life with the *mitzvah* of sending the parent bird away before taking the young (Deut. 22:6–7). R. Judah ha-Nasi was divinely punished because he did not show mercy to animals, and the punishment was removed only when his attitude improved, and Moses and David were considered fit to be leaders of Israel only after they had been shepherds (TJ, Kil. 9:3, 32a; BM 85a). In later rabbinic literature, both halakhic and ethical, great prominence is also given to demonstrating God's mercy to animals, and to the importance of not causing them pain (see R. Margaliot (ed.), *Sefer Hasidim* (1957), 589, 667, 668, 670; **M.** Cordovero, *Palmtree of Deborah* (1966), ch. 2–3). Even the necessary inflicting of pain is frowned upon as "cruel."

The rabbinical attitude toward hunting is entirely negative. Harsh things are said about those who hunt even for a living. R. Ezekiel Landau said that "the only hunters we know of (in the Bible) are Nimrod and Esau; it is not the way of the children of Abraham, Isaac, and Jacob."

Medieval Jewish philosophers used the principle of *za'ar ba'alei ḥayyim* to explain various *mitzvot*. It was suggested that the reason for not plowing with an ox and an ass together (Deut. 22:10) is that the ox, being the stronger, would cause pain to the ass (Ibn Ezra, *ibid.*). Philosophers from R. Joseph Albo to R. Abraham Isaac Kook discussed the question of why it is permitted to eat meat at all and, indeed, from the talmudic statement that "the *am ha-areẓ* (i.e., "the poor") is forbidden to eat meat" (Pes. 49b), it would seem that its authors were also sensitive to the problem (see D. Cohen, in: *La-Ḥai Ro'i* (Memorial A. Y. Raanan Kook; 1961), 201–54).

Part Four:

LAW

1 JUSTICE

It has been widely stated that justice is the moral value which singularly characterizes Judaism both conceptually and historically. Historically, the Jewish search for justice begins with biblical statements like "Justice (Heb. *zedek*), justice shall ye pursue" (Deut. 16:20). On the conceptual side, justice holds a central place in the Jewish world view, and many other basic Jewish concepts revolve around the notion of justice.

God's primary attribute of action (see Attributes of God) is justice (Heb. *mishpat;* Gen. 18:25; Ps. 9:5). His commandments to men, and especially to Israel, are essentially for the purpose of the establishment of justice in the world (see Ps. 119:137–44). Men fulfill this purpose by acting in accordance with God's laws and in other ways imitating the divine quality of justice (Deut. 13:5; Sot. 14a; Maimonides, *Guide,* 1:54, 3:54). This process of establishing justice in the world is to be completed in the messianic reign of universal justice (see Isa. 11:5ff.; Deut. R. 5:7). All history, therefore, like the Torah itself, which is its paradigm, begins and ends with justice (Ex. R. 30:19).

The two main biblical terms for justice are *zedek* and *zedakah.* They refer to both divine and human justice, as well as to "the works of justice" (Ex. 9:27; Prov. 10:25; Ps. 18:21–25). This justice is essentially synonymous with holiness (Isa. 5:16). In the Bible, furthermore, "justice" is so consistently paired with "mercy" or "grace" (*hesed;* Isa. 45:19; Ps. 103:17ff.), that by talmudic and later times the term *zedakah* has come to mean almost exclusively "charity" or "works of love" (BB 10b), and the notion of "justice" is rendered by the terms "truth" (*emet*), "trust" *(emunah)*, and "integrity" *(yosher)*. Throughout the literature, finally, other values, particularly peace and redemption, are consistently associated with justice, as its components or products (Hos. 12:7; Ps. 15:1; Ta'an. 6:2). Ultimately, therefore, virtually the entire spectrum of ethical values is comprised in the notion of justice.

Jewish justice is different from the classic philosophic (Greek-Western) view of this concept. In the latter, justice is generally considered under the headings of "distributive" and "retributive." These are, of course, also comprised in *zedakah*, but while "distributive" and "retributive" justice are essentially procedural principles (i.e., how to do things), Jewish justice is essentially substantive (i.e., what human life should be like). Substantive justice depends on an ultimate (i.e., messianic) value commitment. This is also made clear by modern thinkers, such as Hermann Cohen, who regards the just society as the ideal society of univeral human dignity and freedom (*Ethik des reinen Willens* (1904), ch. 15; *Religion der Vernunft aus des Quellen des Judentums* (1929), ch. 19), and Ch. Perelman, who in his analysis of justice writes: ". . . in the end one will always come up against a certain irreducible vision of the world expressing nonrational [though justifiable] values and aspirations" (Perelman, *Justice* (1967), 54). Although Perelman does not claim to be discussing a particularly Jewish concept of justice, he is aware of the Jewishness of this ethos (cf. W. Kaufmann, in: *Review of Metaphysics, 23* (1969), 211, 224ff., 236). The substantive view of justice is concerned with the full enhancement of human and, above all, social life. Thus it suffuses all human relations and social institutions—the state (the commonplace dichotomy between individual and collective responsibility, often illustrated by the contrast between Ex. 20:5 and Ezek. 18, is transcended in the recognition of the dialectical interrelationship between the two, illustrated in Deut. 24:16 alongside Lev. 19:16 (see also Sanh. 73a), and in the contemporary involvement of the individual citizen in the collective actions of his nation), lawcourts (e.g., II Chron.

A sitting of the Sanhedrin illustrating the mishnaic tractate *Sanhedrin* on courts of justice and criminal procedure. Detail from a title page on a Hebrew-Latin edition of the Mishnah with engravings by Mich. Richey, Amsterdam, 1700–1704. Jerusalem, J.N.U.L.

19:6; Maim. Yad, Sanhedrin, 23:8–10), economics (Lev. 19:36), and private affairs—and, indeed, the single positive ordinance encumbent also on all non-Jews is the establishment of judiciaries (Sanh. 56a).

Justice is not contrasted with love, but rather correlated with it. In rabbinic literature, Jewish philosophy, and

מתנות

Woman receiving a *ketubbah*. Detail from a title page of a Latin-Hebrew Mishnah, Amsterdam, 1700–04. Jerusalem, J.N.U.L. with engravings by Mich. Richey.

Kabbalah, God is described as acting out of the two "attributes of lawfulness and compassion" (PR 5:11, 40:2: Maimonides, *Guide* 3:53).

The critical problem pertaining to justice is that of theodicy: if God is just and rules the world, how can the successes of evil be explained? The problem of theodicy, a recurrent theme in literature, is raised by the Psalmist and is the theme of Job. It is the subject of E. Wiesel's story, written in the wake of the Holocaust, in which three rabbis subpoena God to a trial and find Him guilty. In the history of Jewish thought many solutions to the problem have been suggested, among them the essentially neoplatonic notion that evil is privation, i.e., that it is not something positive in 197 itself but merely the absence of good (*Guide* 3:18–25); the view that evil and suffering constitute trials of the just, or, in rabbinic literature, "afflictions of love," i.e., that God tests the righteous by causing them to suffer in this world; and the doctrine of reward and punishment in *Olam ha-Ba* (Sanh. 90b–92a; Albo, *Sefer ha-Ikkarim,* 1:15).

The rabbis regard Moses as the ideal of strict unbending justice, in contrast to Aaron, who is the prototype of the ideal of peace, and they interpret the incident of the Golden Calf as exemplifying the problem arising from the clash of these two ideals (cf. Sanh. 6a–7b and parallels). In the same context they suggest that compromise in legal cases may constitute a denial of justice *(ibid.).*

A reply to, though not a resolution of, the problem of theodicy in our time may be attempted in two directions: (a) to protest against injustice in the tradition of Job, Ḥoni ha-Me'aggel, and the ḥasidic leader Levi Isaac of Berdichev, which is possible only before a responsible authority, i.e., a just God; (b) to regard justice as a normative, rather than a descriptive, concept, as does Cohen, who writes that "justice maintains the tension between reality and the eternal ideal" (*Religion der Vernunft,* p. 569). According to this view, justice can be striven for and looked for only in the future—whether the future of mankind as a whole (the days of the Messiah) or of the individual—i.e., in God, whose justice in judgment is affirmed in the blessing recited in the hour of death, "blessed be the just judge."

Man is obliged to imitate God by acting on the principle of compassionate equity (Micah 6:8; Mak. 24b; BM 30b, 83a), and—at the final consummation of history—justice and mercy become identical.

2 LAW AND MORALITY

In the Bible. In the Pentateuch, legal and moral norms are not distinguished by any definitional criteria. The manner of presentation of both is via revelation—moral norms are not presented as wisdom but rather as prophetic revelation. Thus the two remain indistinguishable as to authority. The basis of adherence to the system as a whole is the fact that it constitutes divine command. Even in the form of presentation, no distinction is made between the two types. The apodictic form, for example, is used both for the prohibition on murder (Ex. 20:13) and the command to love one's neighbor (Lev. 19:18). On the critical issue of enforcement, no textual distinction exists on which to base enforced and nonenforced forms or between humanly enforced and divinely enforced ones. The premise of the pentateuchal code is that no propounded norm of human behavior is either optional or lacking in enforcement. Indeed the sanction system is one in which human punishment and divine retribution function as equal components of a single scheme.

This single corpus of legal-moral behavioral norms was distinct from Ancient Near-Eastern legal-moral systems in a number of significant respects. First, the very unity of morality and law in the Pentateuch created a new basis of authority for the behavioral precepts of Hebrew civilization. Secondly, in the Torah individualistic morality gave way to national morality which was addressed to the people of Israel as a corporate moral entity. Thus the national entity was made party to the maintenance of the mandated standards of behavior and could be held responsible for the breach of such norms by individual citizens. Thirdly, despite the exclusivity of the covenantal relationship between God and the Jewish people, God's role in the enforcement of legal-moral behavioral norms is clearly pictured as universal. Thus Cain, the generation of the flood, Sodom, the seven Canaanite nations, and others, are all pictured as subjects of divine retribution for illegal-immoral behavior though they were not parties to the covenant.

In the prophetic literature, no new realm of purely moral concern was created. The breaches of social morality which play such a prominent part in the prophetic critique of the Jewish people were all premised on the identical legal-moral behavioral norms. The "immorality" of the people was in reality their "illegal" behavior. The major shift which distinguishes the literary prophets from their predecessors was that the notion of corporate legal-moral responsibility was given a vital new component. In the Pentateuch, national doom was threatened for cultic sins in particular and for neglect of the divine commandments in general. The prophets introduced the notion that the most decisive factor in the corporate fate of the nation was that aspect of mandated legal-moral behavioral norms which encompassed social relations. Thus when Amos threatens national doom and exile, he speaks of the sins of the normal life context, of social, economic, and political behavior, but maintains complete silence with regard to the sin of idolatry. In Isaiah and Micah too, the threat of national destruction is created by social corruption—the violation of the legal-ethical behavioral norms of everyday life. Failure to observe the divine command results in the corporate punishment of the nation whether the sin is cultic or legal-moral in nature.

The Talmudic Period. There was not yet any development of a specific moral order as distinct from the legal system in the talmudic period. However, it is already clearly recognized in tannaitic literature that legal sanctions could not enforce every form of behavior which was morally desirable. Indeed Mishnah and Tosefta make occasional references to situations where, despite justification, one party lacks any legal recourse against the other and ". . . he has nothing but resentment *[taromet]* against him" (e.g., BM 4:6, 6:1; Tosef., Git., 3:1; BM 4:22). This recognition of a gap between sanctionable behavior and behavior which though desirable is not enforceable produced three types of relationships between the two realms: morality as a direct source of law; morality as a source of private, higher standards of legal liability; and morality in legal form.

MORALITY AS A DIRECT SOURCE OF LAW. The tannaitic period was particularly rich in social legislation motivated by the desire to expand the scope of enforcement to encompass as broad as possible a range of morally desirable behavior. Two terms in particular were often used to indicate the presence of a moral interest as the basis for tannaitic legislation:

(1) "In the interest of peace" *(mi-penei darkhei shalom)*. This term is a composite, indicating that the legislative purpose of the statute is the prevention of communal conflict which would result from some immoral practice not otherwise limited by law. The specific forms of immoral behavior viewed by the *tannaim* as likely to produce communal conflict included: unequal distribution of religious honors, threat to the good reputation of a group or an individual, taking by force where property rights are uncertain, unearned benefit from the labor or initiative of another, and the exclusion of groups from societal privileges and responsibilities. In all of these instances, the methods used to avoid the conflict were either to legalize a status quo which was both orderly and fair, or to extend legal rights to situations or persons otherwise excluded (e.g. Git. 5:8–9; Tosef. Pe'ah 3:1; Ḥul. 10:13; Git. 5 (3):4–5).

(2) "For the benefit of society" *(mi-penei tikkun ha-olam)*. This tannaitic term is also a composite, reflecting the presence of a moral interest being translated into an enforceable legal norm. The Mishnah (Git. 4:3–5:3) contains an entire codex of such statutes. The unique character of the situations governed "for the benefit of

society" is that the moral interest involved, while produced by an existing or incipient legal relationship, affects primarily persons outside the relationship itself. The legislation affecting that relationship is thus primarily designed to have general communal benefit. Some of the moral interests dealt with in this type of legislation are the prevention of bastardy (the *Mamzer*) and of abandoned wives (the *Agunot*), the deterrence of theft and of non-punishable injurious behavior, the encouragement of lending and of returning lost property, the encouragement of care for orphans and destitute children, and the encouragement of public service in the area of law and medicine (e.g., Git. 4:2–5:3; 9:4; Tosef. Ter. 1:12–13; Git. 4 (3): 5–7; 8 (6):9).

The *amoraim* did not themselves use *darkhei shalom* or *tikkun ha-olam* as bases for further translation of morality into law. However, their awareness that in tannaitic legislation morality was being used as a source of law is clearly indicated through their use of the notion of the prevention of hostility *(mi-shum eivah)* as a legislative end. While no legislation in tannaitic literature is described as having been designed to prevent hostility, the *amoraim* often ascribe that very purpose to tannaitic legislation. Thus tannaitic legislation giving a husband the right to his wife's earnings is viewed by the *amoraim* as motivated by the desire to prevent ill-feeling or hostility *(eivah)* between them (Ket. 58b). The source of the ill-feeling would be the inequality resulting from the husband's being obliged to support his wife without being entitled to ownership of whatever she earns. This recognition, that legislation based on the tendency of ill-feeling to undermine an existing relationship was an attempt to cure legislatively the underlying inequality, led the *amoraim* to limit the application of the statute to those situations where its motivating moral interest was relevant. Thus where the marital relationship is in any case about to be terminated, ill-feeling may be a matter of indifference (BM 12b), and further, where the relationship must be terminated by law, ill-feelings between the parties may actually be functional (Yev. 90b) and therefore the law designed to prevent such hostility is inapplicable.

The role of morality as a source of law continued into the legal work of the *amoraim* themselves, although it shifted from the realm of legislation to that of juridical interpretation. Two standards of moral behavior, one positive and one negative, predominate in this amoraic process:

(1) "And thou shalt do that which is right and good" (Deut. 6:18; *ve-asita ha-yashar ve-ha-tov*). Two amoraic laws are based on this verse: (a) Property taken by a creditor in payment of a debt may be redeemed at any time (i.e., absence of injury to the creditor; BM 35a); and (b) Right of an abutting property owner to first purchase is preserved despite sale of the property (i.e., absence of injury to the original owner; BM 108a). In both cases doing the "right and good" involves the restoration of a legal right which a person had lost through no fault of his own.

(2) "Her ways are ways of pleasantness" (Prov. 3:17; *darkhei no'am*). The fact that "pleasantness" was viewed as a basic characteristic of biblical law dictated to the *amoraim* the rejection of any juridical interpretation which could lead to the establishment of a law that could cause either the loss of personal dignity or injury to a marital relationship (e.g., Suk. 32b; Yev. 15a). The principle, however, operated in a negative fashion only, to preclude any particular juridical alternative which contravened the moral qualities of "pleasantness."

MORALITY AS A SOURCE OF PRIVATE, HIGHER STANDARDS OF LEGAL LIABILITY. There are occasions which arise in any legal system where, despite the existence of a law prohibiting certain action, the hands of the court are tied because of evidentiary or procedural principles. The absence of enforcement in such instances, while producing an inequity in that particular case, could only be remedied by the abandonment of a principle which on balance is of value to the legal system. In the attempt to minimize such injustice, the *tannaim*, and subsequently the *amoraim* also, attempted to use the threat of divine retribution as a means of inducing the wrongdoer to remedy the injury of his own free choice, and to reject the exemption which the system was obliged to allow him. It was in this specific particular context that the rabbis often asserted that while the defendant was "exempt by human law, he is liable by divine law" (*hayyav be-dinei shamayim*; e.g., BK 6:4. An entire codex of such situations where "his case is passed on for divine judgment" is found in Tosef. BK 6:16–17). A similar case of moral pressure being brought to bear to emphasize the need for voluntary rectification where the judiciary is unable to act is reflected in the phrase "the sages are greatly pleased with him" (*ru'ah hakhamin nohah heimenno*; e.g., Shev. 10:9. For the reverse formulation, see BB 8:5). The moral pressure for this type of behavior led the *amoraim* to use similar formulations to urge self-judgment even in cases where the initial liability itself was in doubt (BM 37a). In such cases the *amoraim* suggest that a man assume liability upon himself if "he wishes to fulfill his duty in the sight of heaven."

Two uniquely amoraic devices supplement the above as moral means of urging an individual to accept higher standards of civil liability where he has indeed been the cause of injury to another. Both are literary legal fictions in that they attempt to explain tannaitic statements or actions which in reality might have been based on completely different reasons. (a) Pious behavior *(middat hasidut)*. Each time that the *amora* Rav Hisda suggests that a particular tannaitic statement constituted a suggestion of especially righteous behavior it is part of an attempt to resolve an inner contradiction in a Mishnah (e.g., BM 52b; Shab. 120a; Hul. 130b). While the Talmud on one occasion rejects R. Hisda's suggestion for some alternative resolution (Shab. 120a), the device itself, and its frequent acceptance by the *amoraim*, gives recognition to their use of moral persuasion to encourage private adoption of the highest possible standards of civil liability. Indeed R. Hisda may well have been pointing out a more general phenomenon, that of recording dissenting opinions in the Mishnah in order that such higher standards remain as a personal option. (b) Beyond the limit of the law *(li-fenim mi-shurat ha-din)*. This device too, emerging from the school of Rav, is used consistently to resolve the disparity between existing law and the behavior of some earlier scholar (e.g., BK 99b; BM 30b; Ket. 97a; Ber. 45b). While it may be the case that in each instance the scholar behaved in full accord with the law of his own time, the exemption from liability not yet having become applicable, the significance of the amoraic suggestion lies in its openness to the acceptance and desirability of such private assumption of higher standards of legal liability. Indeed, by eradicating the time difference between the existing law and earlier behavior, the *amoraim* in effect maintain the viability of the entire history of legal development as a source of rules devised to produce the result most morally desirable in any particular case. While in their talmudic usage none of these devices leads to enforceable law, many *rishonim* and *aharonim* insist on the partial or total enforceability of a good number of the laws denominated as *dinei shamayim, middat ḥasidut* and *li-fenim mi-shurat ha-din* (e.g., *Rema* ḤM 12:2; PDRS: 132–153, 151) Thus, while formal legislation was basically absent and no admission would be made that juridical interpretation really involved the creation of new law, such reinterpretations to create higher standards of enforceability were in fact part of the continuity of the process of the use of morality as a source of new law. In this way the use of morality to create private, higher standards of liability has often led to the eventual adoption of those new standards as law for everyone.

MORALITY IN LEGAL FORM. The impact of morality on Jewish law has been felt in a third way, as a result of rabbinic formulation of moral principles in legal form. The unwillingness of the rabbinic mind to accept seriously any substantial gap between the two realms is evidenced by the gradual assimilation into the realm of law, of forms of behavior which were not initially enforceable but were formulated in the terminology of illegal behavior. The two prime categories in this pattern are where immoral behavior is compared to illegal action and where the seriousness of the behavior is indicated by a disproportionate penalty.

(1) "As if . . ." *(ke-illu)*. The term *ke-illu*, in its legal usage (like *na'asah ke*), usually introduces a legal fiction (BM 34a; Yev. 13:3). In its usage in the process of grading the moral significance of behavior it creates fictional analogies to legal or illegal behavior. Thus a person who conducts himself with humility is as one who offers all the sacrifices (Sot. 5b), while one who honors an evil person is as one who worships idols (Tosef. Av. Zar. 6(7):16). In tannaitic usage, this device is used almost exclusively to encourage behavior which is not legally mandatory (except where it is used in exegesis in the form, "Scripture considers him as if . . ."; e.g., Sanh. 4:5). In such instances, the weight of the divine legal prohibition is used to bolster moral pronouncements which otherwise lack any authority. The fact that *amoraim* began to extend this comparative device to add the weight of divine law to the authority of rabbinic law (e.g., Ber. 35a) introduced the possibility that the first half of the formula was not merely unenforceable moral teaching, but was itself legally binding in its own right. It was then only a short step to the frequent conclusions of *rishonim* that behavior which is compared to illegal action must itself be illicit (e.g., Sot. 3:4; cf. Yad, Talmud Torah 1:13).

(2) Disproportionate penalty, such as "liable to the death penalty" *(ḥayyav mitah)*. While the Bible lays down the penalty of death at the hands of the court for a variety of crimes, the *tannaim* had already begun using the ascription of the death penalty to crimes for which clearly no court would prescribe such punishment. This exaggerated penalty was an effective way of communicating rabbinic feelings about the enormity of misbehavior. The *amoraim* made extensive use of this device to indicate their indignation at immoral behavior. Thus, in a passage which makes manifestly clear that it is aimed at emphasis rather than true legal liability, the Talmud says, "A mourner who does not

let his hair grow long and does not rend his clothes is liable to death" (MK 24a). Similarly the rabbis asserted that, "Any scholar upon whose garment a [grease] stain is found is liable to death" (Shab. 114a). Again, however, the very use of legal terminology in formulating the moral position led to the conclusion that the behavior so described was indeed legally prohibited, and it was therefore often considered as this by the *rishonim* (cf. instances in Sanh. 58b, 59a, and codes). Thus in the constant growth of the scope of the law the morality of one generation frequently became the law of the next.

3 THE 613 COMMANDMENTS

The total number of the biblical commandments (precepts and prohibitions) is given in rabbinic tradition as 613. R. Simlai, a third century sage, states: "613 commandments were revealed to Moses at Sinai, 365 being prohibitions equal in number to the solar days, and 248 being mandates corresponding in number to the limbs of the human body" (Mak. 23b). The number 613 (usually known by the Hebrew mnemonic, תַּרְיַ״ג (TaRYaG— ת = 400, ר = 200, י = 10, ג = 3), is found as early as tannaitic times.

Works enumerating the commandments are numerous (see Jellinek, *Kunteres Taryag,* 1878), but the majority of the lists conform to one of four methods of enumeration: (1) The earliest lists, those of the anonymous *azharot,* are divided simply into two lists of positive and prohibitive precepts, with little attention being paid to the internal classification. (2) The threefold division into positive commandments, prohibitions, and biblical portions. (3) Classification of the precepts under the tenfold headings of the Decalogue. (4) Independent logical classification of the two lists of positive and prohibitive precepts. This is the method of Maimonides and his school.

Mandatory Commandments.

God.

The Jew is required to [1]believe that God exists and to [2]acknowledge His unity; to [3]love, [4]fear, and [5]serve Him. He is also commanded to [6]cleave to Him (by associating with and imitating the wise) and to [7]swear only by His name. One must [8]imitate God and [9]sanctify His name.

Torah.

The Jew must [10]recite the *Shema* each morning and evening and [11]study the Torah and teach it to others. He should bind *tefillin* on his [12]head and [13]his arm. He should make [14] *zizit* for his garments and [15]fix a *mezuzah* on the door. The people are to be [16]assembled every seventh year to hear the Torah read and [17]the king must write a special copy of the Torah for himself. [18]Every Jew should have a Torah scroll. One should [19]praise God after eating.

Temple, and the Priests.

The Jews should [20]build a Temple and [21]respect it. It must be [22]guarded at all times and the [23] Levites should perform their special duties in it. Before entering the Temple or participating in

1. Ex. 20:2
2. Deut. 6:4
3. Deut. 6:5
4. Deut. 6:13
5. Ex. 23:25:
6. Deut. 10:20
7. Deut. 10:20
8. Deut. 11:13 (Deut. 6:13 and also 13:5)
9. Lev. 22:32
8. Deut. 28:9

10. Deut. 6:7
11. Deut. 6:7
12. Deut. 6:8
13. Deut. 6:8
14. Num. 15:38
15. Deut. 6:9

16. Deut. 31:12
17. Deut. 17:18
18. Deut. 31:19
19. Deut. 8:10

20. Ex. 25:8
22. Num. 18:4
21. Lev. 19:30
23. Num. 18:23

its service the priests [24]must wash their hands and feet; they must also [25]light the candelabrum daily. The priests are required to [26]bless Israel and to [27]set the shewbread and frankincense before the Ark. Twice daily they must [28]burn the incense on the golden altar. Fire shall be kept burning on the altar [29]continually and the ashes should be [30]removed daily. Ritually unclean persons must be [31]kept out of the Temple. Israel [32]should honor its priests, who must be [33]dressed in special priestly raiment. The priests should [34]carry the Ark on their shoulders, and the holy anointing oil [35]must be prepared according to its special formula. The priestly families should officiate in [36]rotation. In honor of certain dead close relatives the priests should [37]make themselves ritually unclean. The high priest may marry [38]only a virgin.

Sacrifices.

The [39]tamid sacrifice must be offered twice daily and the [40]high priest must also offer a meal-offering twice daily. An additional sacrifice (musaf) should be offered [41]every Sabbath, [42]on the first of every month, and [43]on each of the seven days of Passover. On the second day of Passover [44]a meal offering of the first barley must also be brought. On Shavuot a [45]musaf must be offered and [46]two loaves of bread as a wave offering. The additional sacrifice

24. Ex. 30:19
25. Ex. 27:21
26. Num. 6:23

27. Ex. 25:30
28. Ex. 30:7
29. Lev. 6:6

30. Lev. 6:3
31. Num. 5:2

32. Lev. 21:8

33. Ex. 28:2
34. Num. 7:9
35. Ex. 30:31

36. Deut. 18:6-8
37. Lev. 21:2-3
38. Lev. 21:13

39. Num. 28:3

40. Lev. 6:13

41. Num. 28:9
42. Num. 28:11

43. Lev. 23:36
44. Lev. 23:10

45. Num. 28:26-27

46. Lev. 23:17

must also be made on [47]Rosh Ha-Shanah and [48]on the Day of Atonement when the [49]Avodah must also be performed. On every day of the festival of [50]Sukkot a *musaf* must be brought as well as on the [51]eighth day thereof.

Every male Jew should make [52]pilgrimage to the Temple three times a year and [53]appear there during the three pilgrim Festivals. One should [54]rejoice on the Festivals.

On the 14th of Nisan one should [55]slaughter the paschal lamb and [56]eat of its roasted flesh on the night of the 15th. Those who were ritually impure in Nisan should slaughter the paschal lamb on [57]the 14th of Iyyar and eat it with [58]*maẓẓah* and bitter herbs.

Trumpets should be [59]sounded when the festive sacrifices are brought and also in times of tribulation.

Cattle to be sacrificed must be [60]at least eight days old and [61]without blemish. All offerings must be [62]salted. It is a *mitzvah* to perform the ritual of [63]the burnt offering, [64]the sin offering, [65]the guilt offering, [66]the peace offering and [67]the meal offering.

Should the Sanhedrin err in a decision its members [68]must bring a sin offering which offering must also be brought [69]by a person who has unwittingly transgressed a *karet* prohibition (i.e., one which, if done deliberately, would incur *karet*). When in doubt as to whether one has transgressed such a prohibition a [70]"suspensive" guilt offering must be brought.

47. Num. 29:1–2
48. Num. 29:7–8
49. Lev. 16
50. Num. 29:13
51. Num. 29:36
52. Ex. 23:14
53. Ex. 34:23; Deut. 16:16
54. Deut. 16:14
55. Ex. 12:6
56. Ex. 12:8
57. Num. 9:11
58. Num. 9:11; Ex. 12:8
59. Num. 10:10; Num. 10:9
60. Lev. 22:27
61. Lev. 22:21
62. Lev. 2:13
63. Lev. 1:2
64. Lev. 6:18
65. Lev. 7:1
66. Lev. 3:1
67. Lev. 2:1; 6:7
68. Lev. 4:13
69. Lev. 4:27
70. Lev. 5:17–18

For [71] stealing or swearing falsely and for other sins of a like nature, a guilt offering must be brought. In special circumstances the sin offering [72] can be according to one's means.

One must [73] confess one's sins before God and repent for them.

A [74] man or [75] a woman who has a seminal issue must bring a sacrifice; a woman must also bring a sacrifice [76] after childbirth.

A leper must [77] bring a sacrifice after he has been cleansed.

One must [78] tithe one's cattle. The [79] first born of clean (i.e., permitted) cattle are holy and must be sacrificed. The firstborn of man must be [80] redeemed. The firstling of the ass must be [81] redeemed; if not [82] its neck has to be broken.

Animals set aside as offerings [83] must be brought to Jerusalem without delay and [84] may be sacrificed only in the Temple. Offerings from outside the land of Israel [85] may also be brought to the Temple.

Sanctified animals [86] which have become blemished must be redeemed. A beast exchanged for an offering [87] is also holy.

The priests should eat [88] the remainder of the meal offering and [89] the flesh of sin and guilt offerings; but consecrated flesh which has become [90] ritually unclean or [91] which was not eaten within its appointed time must be burned.

71. Lev. 5:15, 21–25; 19:20–21
72. Lev. 5:1–11
73. Num. 5:6–7
74. Lev. 15:13–15
75. Lev. 15:28–29
76. Lev. 12:6
77. Lev. 14:10
78. Lev. 27:32
79. Ex. 13:2
80. Ex. 22:28; Num. 18:15
81. Ex. 34:20
82. Ex. 13:13
83. Deut. 12:5–5
84. Deut. 12:14
85. Deut. 12:26
86. Deut. 12:15
87. Lev. 27:33
88. Lev. 6:9
89. Ex. 29:33
90. Lev. 7:19
91. Lev. 7:17

Vows.

A Nazirite must [92]let his hair grow during the period of his separation. When that period is over he must [93]shave his head and bring his sacrifice.

A man must [94]honor his vows and his oaths which a judge can [95]annul only in accordance with the law.

Ritual Purity.

Anyone who touches [96]a carcass or [97]one of the eight species of reptiles becomes ritually unclean; food becomes unclean by [98]coming into contact with a ritually unclean object. Menstruous women [99]and those [100]lying-in after childbirth are ritually impure. A [101]leper, [102]a leprous garment, and [103]a leprous house are all ritually unclean. A man having [104]a running issue is unclean, as is [105]semen. A woman suffering from [106]running issue is also impure. A [107]human corpse is ritually unclean. The purification water (mei niddah) purifies [108]the unclean, but it makes the clean ritually impure. It is a mitzvah to become ritually clean [109]by ritual immersion. To become cleansed of leprosy one [110]must follow the specified procedure and also [111]shave off all of one's hair. Until cleansed the leper [112]must be bareheaded with clothing in disarray so as to be easily distinguishable.

92. Num. 6:5
93. Num. 6:18
94. Deut. 23:24
95. Num. 30:3
96. Lev. 11:8, and 24
97. Lev. 11:29–31
98. Lev. 11:34
99. Lev. 15:19
100. Lev. 12:2
101. Lev. 13:3
102. Lev. 13:51
103. Lev. 14:44
104. Lev. 15:2
105. Lev. 15:16
106. Lev. 15:19
107. Num. 19:14
108. Num. 19:13, 21
109. Lev. 15:16
110. Lev. 14:2
111. Lev. 14:9
112. Lev. 13:45

The ashes of [113]the red heifer are to be used in the process of ritual purification.

Donations to the Temple.

If a person [114]undertakes to give his own value to the Temple he must do so. Should a man declare [115]an unclean beast, [116a] house, or [117]a field as a donation to the Temple, he must give their value in money as fixed by the priest. If one unwittingly derives benefit from Temple property [118]full restitution plus a fifth must be made.

The fruit of [119]the fourth year's growth of trees is holy and may be eaten only in Jerusalem. When you reap your fields you must leave [120]the corners, [121]the gleanings, [122]the forgotten sheaves, [123]the misformed bunches of grapes and [124]the gleanings of the grapes for the poor.

The first fruits must be [125]separated and brought to the Temple and you must also [126]separate the great heave offering (terumah) and give it to the priests. You must give [127]one tithe of your produce to the Levites and separate [128]a second tithe which is to be eaten only in Jerusalem. The Levites [129]must give a tenth of their tithe to the priests.

In the third and sixth years of the seven year cycle you should [130]separate a tithe for the poor instead of the second tithe. A declaration

113. Num. 19:2–9

114. Lev. 27:2–8
117. Lev. 27:16, 22–23

119. Lev. 19:24
120. Lev. 19:9
121. Lev. 19:9
123. Lev. 19:10

125. Ex. 23:19
126. Deut. 18:4

128. Deut. 14:22
129. Num. 18:26

115. Lev. 27:11–12
116. Lev. 27:14

118. Lev. 5:16

122. Deut. 24:19
124. Lev. 19:10

127. Lev. 27:30; Num. 18:24

130. Deut. 14:28

131. Deut. 26:13
132. Deut. 26:5
133. Num. 15:20
134. Ex. 23:11
135. Ex. 34:21
136. Lev. 25:10
137. Lev. 25:9
138. Lev. 25:24
139. Lev. 25:29–30
140. Lev. 25:8
141. Deut. 15:3
142. Deut. 15:3
143. Deut. 18:3
144. Deut. 18:4
145. Lev. 27:21, 28

[131]must be recited when separating the various tithes and [132]when bringing the first fruits to the Temple.

The first portion of the [133]dough must be given to the priest.

The Sabbatical Year.

In the seventh year (*shemittah*) everything that grows is [134]ownerless and available to all; the fields [135]must lie fallow and you may not till the ground. You must [136]sanctify the Jubilee year (50th) and on the Day of Atonement in that year [137]you must sound the *shofar* and set all Hebrew slaves free. In the Jubilee year all land is to be [138]returned to its ancestral owners and, generally, in a walled city[139]the seller has the right to buy back a house within a year of the sale.

Starting from entry into the land of Israel, the years of the Jubilee must be [140]counted and announced yearly and septennially.

In the seventh year [141]all debts are annulled but [142]one may exact a debt owed by a foreigner.

Concerning Animals for Consumption.

When you slaughter an animal you must [143]give the priest his share as you must also give him [144]the first of the fleece. When a man makes a *ḥerem* (a special vow) you must [145]distinguish between that which belongs to the Temple (i.e., when God's name was mentioned in the vow) and between that which goes to the priests. To be fit for consumption, beast and fowl must be [146]slaughtered according to the law and if they are not of a domesticated species [147]their blood must be covered with earth after slaughter. Set the parent bird [148]free when taking the nest. Examine [149]beast, [150]fowl, [151]locusts and [152]fish to determine whether they are permitted for consumption.

The Sanhedrin should [153]sanctify the first day of every month and reckon the years and the seasons.

Festivals.

You must [154]rest on the Sabbath day and [155]declare it holy at its onset and termination. On the 14th of Nisan [156]remove all leaven from your ownership and on the night of the 15th [157]relate the story of the exodus from Egypt; on that night [158]you must also eat *mazzah*. On the [159]first and [160]seventh days of Passover you must rest. Starting from the day of the first sheaf (16th of Nisan) you shall [161]count 49 days. You must rest on [162] Shavuot, and on [163] Rosh Ha-Shanah; on the Day of Atonement you must [164]fast and [165]rest. You must also rest on [166]the first and [167]the eighth day of Sukkot during which festival you shall [168]dwell in booths

146. Deut. 12:21
147. Lev. 17:13
148. Deut. 22:7
149. Lev. 11:2
150. Deut. 14:11
151. Lev. 11:21
152. Lev. 11:9
153. Ex. 12:2; Deut. 16:1
154. Ex. 23:12
155. Ex. 20:8
156. Ex. 12:15
157. Ex. 13:8
158. Ex. 12:18
159. Ex. 12:16
160. Ex. 12:16
161. Lev. 23:35
162. Lev. 23
163. Lev. 23:24
164. Lev. 16:29
165. Lev. 16:29, 31
166. Lev. 23:35
167. Lev. 23:36

168. Lev. 23:42
170. Num. 29:1

173. Deut. 17:15
175. Ex. 23:2
176. Deut. 16:18
177. Lev. 19:15

and 169take the four species. On Rosh Ha-Shanah 170you are to hear the sound of the *shofar.*

Community.

Every male should 171give half a shekel to the Temple annually. You must 172obey a prophet and 173appoint a king. You must also 174obey the Sanhedrin; in the case of division, 175yield to the majority. Judges and officials shall be 176appointed in every town and they shall judge the people 177impartially.

Whoever is aware of evidence 178must come to court to testify. Witnesses shall be 179examined thoroughly and, if found to be false, 180shall have done to them what they intended to do to the accused.

When a person is found murdered and the murderer is unknown the ritual of 181decapitating the heifer must be performed.

Six cities of refuge should be 182established. The Levites, who have no ancestral share in the land, shall 183be given cities to live in.

You must 184build a fence around your roof and remove potential hazards from your home.

Idolatry.

Idolatry and its appurtenances 185must be destroyed, and a city which has become perverted must be 186treated according to the law. You are commanded to 187destroy the seven Canaanite nations,

182. Deut. 19:3
183. Num. 35:2

185. Deut. 12:2; 7:5
186. Deut. 13:17

169. Lev. 23:40
171. Ex. 30:12-13
172. Deut. 18:15
174. Deut. 17:11

178. Lev. 5:1
179. Deut. 13:15
180. Deut. 19:19

181. Deut. 21:4

184. Deut. 22:8

187. Deut. 20:17

and [188]to blot out the memory of Amalek, and [189]to remember what they did to Israel.

War.

The regulations for wars other than those commanded in the Torah [190]are to be observed and a priest should be [191]appointed for special duties in times of war. The military camp must be [192]kept in a sanitary condition. To this end, every soldier must be [193]equipped with the necessary implements.

Social.

Stolen property must be [194]restored to its owner. Give [195]charity to the poor. When a Hebrew slave goes free the owner must [196]give him gifts. Lend to [197]the poor without interest; to the foreigner you may [198]lend at interest. Restore [199]a pledge to its owner if he needs it. Pay the worker his wages [200]on time; [201]permit him to eat of the produce with which he is working. You must [202]help unload an animal when necessary, and also [203]help load man or beast. Lost property [204]must be restored to its owner. You are required [205]to reprove the sinner but you must [206]love your fellow as yourself. You are commanded [207]to love the proselyte. Your

188. Deut. 25:19
189. Deut. 25:17

190. Deut. 20:11–12

191. Deut. 20:2
192. Deut. 23:14–15
193. Deut. 23:14

194. Lev. 5:23

195. Deut. 15:8;
     Lev. 25:35–36
196. Deut. 15:14

197. Ex. 22:24
198. Deut. 23:21

199. Deut. 24:13;
     Ex. 22:25
200. Deut. 24:15
201. Deut. 23:25–26
202. Ex. 23:5
203. Deut. 22:4

204. Deut. 22:1;
     Ex. 23:4
205. Lev. 19:17
206. Lev. 19:18
207. Deut. 10:19

weights and measures [208]must be accurate.

Family.

Respect the [209]wise; [210]honor and [211]fear your parents. You should [212]perpetuate the human race by marrying [213]according to the law. A bridegroom is to [214]rejoice with his bride for one year. Male children must [215]be circumcised. Should a man die childless his brother must either [216]marry his widow or [217]release her (ḥalizah). He who violates a virgin must [218]marry her and may never divorce her. If a man unjustly accuses his wife of premarital promiscuity [219]he shall be flogged, and may never divorce her. The seducer [220]must be punished according to the law. The female captive must be [221]treated in accordance with her special regulations. Divorce can be executed [222]only by means of a written document. A woman suspected of adultery [223]has to submit to the required test.

Judicial.

When required by the law [224]you must administer the punishment of flogging and you must [225]exile the unwitting homicide. Capital punishment shall be by [226]the sword, [227]strangulation, [228]fire, or [229]stoning, as specified. In some cases the body of the executed [230]shall be hanged, but it [231]must be brought to burial the same day.

Slaves.

Hebrew slaves [232]must be treated according to the special laws for them. The master should [233]marry his Hebrew maidservant or [234]redeem her. The alien slave [235]must be treated according to the regulations applying to him.

Torts.

The applicable law must be administered in the case of injury caused by [236]a person, [237]an animal or [238]a pit. Thieves [239]must be punished. You must render judgment in cases of [240]trespass by cattle, [241]arson, [242]embezzlement by an unpaid guardian and in claims against [243]a paid guardian, a hirer, or [244]a borrower. Judgment must also be rendered in disputes arising out of [245]sales, [248]inheritance and [246]other matters generally. You are required to [247]rescue the persecuted even if it means killing his oppressor.

Prohibitions.

Idolatry and Related Practices.

It is [1]forbidden to believe in the existence of any but the One God. You may not make images [2]for yourself or [3]for others to worship or for [4]any other purpose.

You must not worship anything but God either in [5]the manner

232. Ex. 21:2
233. Ex. 21:8
234. Ex. 21:8
235. Lev. 25:46

236. Ex. 21:18
237. Ex. 21:28
238. Ex. 21:33-34
239. Ex. 21:37-22:3
240. Ex. 22:4

241. Ex. 22:5
242. Ex. 22:6-8
243. Ex. 22:9-12
244. Ex. 22:13
245. Lev. 25:14

246. Ex. 22:8
247. Deut. 25:12
248. Num. 27:8

1. Ex. 20:3
2. Ex. 20:4
3. Lev. 19:4
4. Ex. 20:20
5. Ex. 20:5

prescribed for His worship or [6]in its own manner of worship.

Do not [7]sacrifice children to Molech.

You may not [8]practice necromancy or [9]resort to "familiar spirits" neither should you take idolatry or its mythology [10]seriously.

It is forbidden to construct a [11]pillar or [12]dais even for the worship of God or to [13]plant trees in the Temple.

You may not [14]swear by idols or instigate an idolator to do so, nor may you encourage or persuade any [15]non-Jew or [16]Jew to worship idols.

You must not [17]listen to or love anyone who disseminates idolatry nor [18]should you withhold yourself from hating him. Do not [19]pity such a person. If somebody tries to convert you to idolatry [20]do not defend him or [21]conceal the fact.

It is forbidden to [22]derive any benefit from the ornaments of idols.

You may not [23]rebuild that which has been destroyed as a punishment for idolatry nor may you [24]have any benefit from its wealth. Do not [25]use anything connected with idols or idolatry.

It is forbidden [26]to prophecy in the name of idols or prophecy [27]falsely in the name of God. Do not [28]listen to the one who prophesies for idols and do not [29]fear the false prophet or hinder his execution.

You must not [30]imitate the ways of idolators or practice their

7. Lev. 18:21
8. Lev. 19:31

11. Deut. 16:22
13. Deut. 16:21
14. Ex. 23:13

17. Deut. 13:9
18. Deut. 13:9

21. Deut. 13:9
22. Deut. 7:25
23. Deut. 13:17

25. Deut. 7:26
26. Deut. 18:20
27. Deut. 18:20

30. Lev. 20:23

6. Ex. 20:5

9. Lev. 19:31
10. Lev. 19:4
12. Lev. 20:1

15. Ex. 23:13
16. Deut. 13:12

19. Deut. 13:9
20. Deut. 13:9

24. Deut. 13:18

28. Deut. 13:3, 4

29. Deut. 18:22
32. Deut. 18:10
33. Deut. 18:10–11;

customs; ³¹divination, ³²soothsaying, ³⁴sorcery, ³⁵charming, ³⁶consulting ghosts or ³⁷familiar spirits and ³⁸necromancy are forbidden. Women must not ³⁹wear male clothing nor men ⁴⁰that of women. Do not ⁴¹tattoo yourself in the manner of the idolators.

You may not ⁴²garments made of both wool and linen nor may you shave (with a razor) the sides of ⁴³your head or ⁴⁴your beard. Do not ⁴⁵lacerate yourself over your dead.

Prohibitions Resulting from Historical Events.

It is forbidden to return to Egypt to ⁴⁶dwell there permanently or to ⁴⁷indulge in impure thoughts or sights. You may not ⁴⁸make a pact with the seven Canaanite nations or ⁴⁹save the life of any member of them. Do not ⁵⁰show mercy to idolators, ⁵¹permit them to dwell in the land of Israel or ⁵²intermarry with them. A Jewess may not ⁵³marry an Ammonite or Moabite even if he converts to Judaism but should not refuse (for reasons of genealogy alone) ⁵⁴a descendant of Esau or ⁵⁵an Egyptian who are proselytes. It is prohibited to ⁵⁶make peace with the Ammonite or Moabite nations.

The ⁵⁷destruction of fruit trees even in times of war is forbidden as is wanton waste at any time. Do not ⁵⁸fear the enemy and do not ⁵⁹forget the evil done by Amalek.

customs; [31]divination, [32]soothsaying, [34]sorcery, [35]charming, [36]consulting ghosts or [37]familiar spirits and [38]necromancy are forbidden. Women must not [39]wear male clothing nor men [40]that of women. Do not [41]tattoo yourself in the manner of the idolators.

You may not [42]garments made of both wool and linen nor may you shave (with a razor) the sides of [43]your head or [44]your beard. Do not [45]lacerate yourself over your dead.

Prohibitions Resulting from Historical Events.

It is forbidden to return to Egypt to [46]dwell there permanently or to [47]indulge in impure thoughts or sights. You may not [48]make a pact with the seven Canaanite nations or [49]save the life of any member of them. Do not [50]show mercy to idolators, [51]permit them to dwell in the land of Israel or [52]intermarry with them. A Jewess may not [53]marry an Ammonite or Moabite even if he converts to Judaism but should not refuse (for reasons of genealogy alone) [54]a descendant of Esau or [55]an Egyptian who are proselytes. It is prohibited to [56]make peace with the Ammonite or Moabite nations.

The [57]destruction of fruit trees even in times of war is forbidden as is wanton waste at any time. Do not [58]fear the enemy and do not [59]forget the evil done by Amalek.

31. Lev. 19:26; Deut. 18:10
34. Deut. 18:10–11
35. Deut. 18:10–11
36. Deut. 18:10–11
37. Deut. 18:10–11
38. Deut. 18:10–11
39. Deut. 22:5
40. Deut. 22:5
41. Lev. 19:28
42. Deut. 22:11
43. Lev. 19:27
44. Lev. 19:27
45. Deut. 16:1; Deut. 14:1: also Lev. 19:28
46. Deut. 17:16
47. Num. 15:39
48. Ex. 23:32:
49. Deut. 7:2
50. Deut. 7:2
51. Ex. 23:33
52. Deut. 7:3
53. Deut. 23:4
54. Deut. 23:8
55. Deut. 23:8
56. Deut. 23:7
57. Deut. 20:19
58. Deut. 7:21
59. Deut. 25:19

Blasphemy.

You must not [60]blaspheme the Holy Name, [61]break an oath made by It, [62]take It in vain or [63]profane It. Do not [64]try the Lord God. You may not [65]erase God's name from the holy texts or destroy institutions devoted to His worship. Do not [66]allow the body of one hanged to remain so overnight.

Temple.

Be not [67]lax in guarding the Temple. The high priest must not enter the Temple [68]indiscriminately; a priest with a physical blemish may not [69]enter there at all or [70]serve in the sanctuary and even if the blemish is of a temporary nature he may not [71]participate in the service there until it has passed. The Levites and the priests must not [72]interchange in their functions. Intoxicated persons may not [73]enter the sanctuary or teach the Law. It is forbidden for [74]non-priests, [75]unclean priests or [76]priests who have performed the necessary ablution but are still within the time limit of their uncleanness to serve in the Temple. No unclean person may enter [77]the Temple or [78]the Temple Mount. The altar must not be made of [79]hewn stones nor may the ascent to it be by [80]steps. The fire on it may not be [81]extinguished nor may any other but the specified incense be [82]burned on the golden altar.

60. Lev. 24:16; rather Ex. 22:27
61. Lev. 19:12
62. Ex. 20:7
63. Lev. 22:32
64. Deut. 6:16
65. Deut. 12:4
66. Deut. 21:23

67. Num. 18:5

68. Lev. 16:2
69. Lev. 21:23
70. Lev. 21:17
71. Lev. 21:18
72. Num. 18:3
73. Lev. 10:9-11
74. Num. 18:4
75. Lev. 22:2
76. Lev. 21:6
77. Num. 5:3
78. Deut. 23:11
79. Ex. 20:25
80. Ex. 20:26
81. Lev. 6:6
82. Ex. 30:9

You may not 83manufacture oil with the same ingredients and in the same proportions as the anointing oil which itself 84may not be misused. Neither may you 85compound incense with the same ingredients and in the same proportions as that burnt on the altar. You must not 86remove the staves from the Ark, 87remove the breastplate from the ephod or 88make any incision in the upper garment of the high priest.

Sacrifices.

It is forbidden to 89offer sacrifices or 90slaughter consecrated animals outside the Temple. You may not 91sanctify, 92slaughter, 93sprinkle the blood of or 94burn the inner parts of a blemished animal even if the blemish is 95of a temporary nature and even if it is 96offered by Gentiles. It is forbidden to 97inflict a blemish on an animal consecrated for sacrifice.

Leaven or honey may not 98be offered on the altar, neither may 99anything unsalted. An animal received as the hire of a harlot or as the price of a dog 100may not be offered.

Do not 101kill an animal and its young on the same day.

It is forbidden to use 102olive oil or 103frankincense in the sin offering or 104, 105, in the jealousy offering (sotah). You may not 106substitute sacrifices even 107from one category to the

83. Ex. 30:32	84. Ex. 30:32	
	85. Ex. 30:37	
86. Ex. 25:15	87. Ex. 28:28	
	88. Ex. 28:32	
89. Deut. 12:13	91. Lev. 22:20	
90. Lev. 17:3–4	92. Lev. 22:22	
94. Lev. 22:22	93. Lev. 22:24	
95. Deut. 17:1	96. Lev. 22:25	
	97. Lev. 22:21	
	98. Lev. 2:11	
99. Lev. 2:13		
100. Deut. 23:19		
101. Lev. 22:28		
104. Num. 5:15	102. Lev. 5:11	
105. Num. 5:15	103. Lev. 5:11	
	107. Lev. 27:26	

other. You may not [108]redeem the firstborn of permitted animals. It is forbidden to [109]sell the tithe of the herd or [110]sell or [111]redeem a field consecrated by the *ḥerem* vow.

When you slaughter a bird for a sin offering you may not [112]split its head.

It is forbidden to [113]work with or [114]to shear a consecrated animal. You must not slaughter the paschal lamb [115]while there is still leaven about; nor may you leave overnight [116]those parts that are to be offered up or [117]to be eaten.

You may not leave any part of the festive offering [118]until the third day or any part of [119]the second paschal lamb or [120]the thanksgiving offering until the morning.

It is forbidden to break a bone of [121]the first or [122]the second paschal lamb or [123]to carry their flesh out of the house where it is being eaten. You must not [124]allow the remains of the meal offering to become leaven. It is also forbidden to eat the paschal lamb [125]raw or sodden or to allow [126]an alien resident, [127]an uncircumcised person or an [128]apostate to eat of it.

A ritually unclean person [129]must not eat of holy things nor may [130]holy things which have become unclean be eaten. Sacrificial meat [131]which is left after the time-limit or [132]which was slaughtered with wrong intentions must not be eaten. The heave offering must

106. Lev. 27:10
108. Num. 18:17
109. Lev. 27:33
110. Lev. 27:28
111. Lev. 27:28
112. Lev. 5:8
113. Deut. 15:19
114. Deut. 15:19
115. Ex. 34:25
116. Ex. 23:10
117. Ex. 12:10
118. Deut. 16:4
119. Num. 9:13
120. Lev. 22:30
121. Ex. 12:46
122. Num. 9:12
123. Ex. 12:46
124. Lev. 6:10
125. Ex. 12:9
126. Ex. 12:45
127. Ex. 12:48
128. Ex. 12:43
129. Lev. 12:4
130. Lev. 7:19
131. Lev. 19:6—8
132. Lev. 7:18

not be eaten by [133]a non-priest, [134]a priest's sojourner or hired worker, [135]an uncircumcised person, or [136]an unclean priest. The daughter of a priest who is married to a non-priest may not [137]eat of holy things.

The meal offering of the priest [138]must not be eaten, neither may [139]the flesh of the sin offerings sacrificed within the sanctuary or [140]consecrated animals which have become blemished.

You may not eat the second tithe of [141]corn, [142]wine, or [143]oil or [144]unblemished firstlings outside Jerusalem. The priests may not eat the [145]sin-offerings or the trespass-offerings outside the Temple courts or [146]the flesh of the burnt-offering at all. The lighter sacrifices [147]may not be eaten before the blood has been sprinkled. A non-priest may not [148]eat of the holiest sacrifices and a priest [149]may not eat the first-fruits outside the Temple courts.

One may not eat [150]the second tithe while in a state of impurity or [151]in mourning; its redemption money [152]may not be used for anything other than food and drink.

You must not [153]eat untithed produce or [154]change the order of separating the various tithes.

Do not [155]delay payment of offerings—either freewill or obligatory—and do not [156]come to the Temple on the pilgrim festivals without an offering.

133.	Lev. 22:10	134.	Lev. 22:10
135.	Lev. 22:10	136.	Lev. 22:4
137.	Lev. 22:12		
139.	Lev. 6:23	138.	Lev. 6:16
140.	Deut. 14:3		
144.	Deut. 12:17	141.	Deut. 12:17
145.	Deut. 12:17	142.	Deut. 12:17
146.	Deut. 12:17	143.	Deut. 12:17
147.	Deut. 12:17	148.	Deut. 12:17
149.	Ex. 29:33		
150.	Deut. 26:14	152.	Deut. 26:14
151.	Deut. 26:14		
153.	Lev. 22:15	154.	Ex. 22:28
155.	Deut. 23:22		
156.	Ex. 23:15		

Do not [157]break your word.

Priests.

A priest may not marry [158]a harlot, [159]a woman who has been profaned from the priesthood, or [160]a divorcee; the high priest must not [161]marry a widow or [162]take one as a concubine. Priests may not enter the sanctuary with [163]overgrown hair of the head or [164]with torn clothing; they must not [165]leave the courtyard during the Temple service. An ordinary priest may not render himself [166]ritually impure except for those relatives specified, and the high priest should not become impure [167]for anybody in [168]any way.

The tribe of Levi shall have no part in [169]the division of the land of Israel or [170]in the spoils of war.

It is forbidden [171]to make oneself bald as a sign of mourning for one's dead.

Dietary Laws.

A Jew may not eat [172]unclean cattle, [173]unclean fish, [174]unclean fowl, [175]creeping things that fly, [176]creatures that creep on the ground, [177]reptiles, [178]worms found in fruit or produce or [179]any detestable creature.

157. Num. 30:3

158. Lev. 21:7
159. Lev. 21:7
160. Lev. 21:7
161. Lev. 21:14
162. Lev. 21:15
163. Lev. 10:6
164. Lev. 10:6
165. Lev. 10:7
166. Lev. 21:1
167. Lev. 21:11
168. Lev. 21:11
169. Deut. 18:1
170. Deut. 18:1
171. Deut. 14:1

172. Deut. 14:7
173. Lev. 11:11
174. Lev. 11:13
175. Deut. 14:19
176. Lev. 11:41
177. Lev. 11:44
178. Lev. 11:42
179. Lev. 11:43

An animal that has died naturally [180]is forbidden for consumption as is [181]a torn or mauled animal. One must not eat [182]any limb taken from a living animal. Also prohibited is [183]the sinew of the thigh (gid ha-nasheh) as is [184]blood and [185]certain types of fat (helev). It is forbidden [186]to cook meat together with milk or [187]eat of such a mixture. It is also forbidden to eat [188]of an ox condemned to stoning (even should it have been properly slaughtered).

One may not eat [189]bread made of new corn or the new corn itself, either [190]roasted or [191]green, before the omer offering has been brought on the 16th of Nisan. You may not eat [192]orlah or [193]the growth of mixed planting in the vineyard.

Any use of [194]wine libations to idols is prohibited, as is [195]gluttony and drunkenness. One may not eat anything on [196]the Day of Atonement. During Passover it is forbidden to eat [197]leaven (ḥamez) or [198]anything containing an admixture of such. This is also forbidden [199]after the middle of the 14th of Nisan (the day before Passover). During Passover no leaven may be [200]seen or [201]found in your possession.

Nazirites.

A Nazirite may not drink [202]wine or any beverage made from grapes; he may not eat [203]fresh grapes, [204]dried grapes, [205]grape seeds

181. Ex. 22:30
184. Lev. 7:26
186. Ex. 23:19

189. Lev. 23:14
190. Lev. 23:14
191. Lev. 23:14

194. Deut. 32:38

198. Ex. 13:20
199. Deut. 16:3

201. Ex. 12:19

202. Num. 6:3
203. Num. 6:3

180. Deut. 14:21
182. Deut. 12:23
183. Gen. 32:33
185. Lev. 7:23
187. Ex. 34:26
188. Ex. 21:28

192. Lev. 19:23
193. Deut. 22:9

195. Lev. 19:26; Deut. 21:20
196. Lev. 23:29
197. Ex. 13:3

200. Ex. 13:7

204. Num. 6:3

or [206]grape peel. He may not render himself [207]ritually impure for his dead nor may he [208]enter a tent in which there is a corpse. He must not [209]shave his hair.

Agriculture.

It is forbidden [210]to reap the whole of a field without leaving the corners for the poor; it is also forbidden to [211]gather up the ears of corn that fall during reaping or to harvest [212]the misformed clusters of grapes, or [213]the grapes that fall or to [214]return to take a forgotten sheaf.

You must not [215]sow different species of seed together or [216]corn in a vineyard; it is also forbidden to [217]crossbreed different species of animals or [218]work with two different species yoked together.

You must not [219]muzzle an animal working in a field to prevent it from eating.

It is forbidden to [220]till the earth, [221]to prune trees, [222]to reap (in the usual manner) produce or [223]fruit which has grown without cultivation in the seventh year (shemittah). One may also not [224]till the earth or prune trees in the Jubilee year, when it is also forbidden to harvest (in the usual manner) [225]produce or [226]fruit that has grown without cultivation.

One may not [227]sell one's landed inheritance in the land of Israel permanently or [228]change the lands of the Levites or [229]leave the Levites without support.

205. Num. 6:4
206. Num. 6:4
207. Num. 6:7
208. Lev. 21:11
209. Num. 6:5
210. Lev. 23:22
211. Lev. 19:9
212. Lev. 19:10
213. Lev. 19:10
214. Deut. 24:19
215. Lev. 19:19
216. Deut. 22:9
217. Lev. 19:19
218. Deut. 22:10
219. Deut. 25:4
220. Lev. 25:4
221. Lev. 25:4
222. Lev. 25:5
223. Lev. 25:5
224. Lev. 25:11
225. Lev. 25:11
226. Lev. 25:11
227. Lev. 25:23
228. Lev. 25:33
229. Deut. 12:19

Loans, Business and the Treatment of Slaves.

It is forbidden to [230]demand repayment of a loan after the seventh year; you may not, however, [231]refuse to lend to the poor because that year is approaching. Do not [232]deny charity to the poor or [233]send a Hebrew slave away empty-handed when he finishes his period of service. Do not [234]dun your debtor when you know that he cannot pay. It is forbidden to [235]lend to or[236]borrow from another Jew at interest or [237]participate in an agreement involving interest either as a guarantor, witness, or writer of the contract.

Do not [238]delay payment of wages.

You may not [239]take a pledge from a debtor by violence, [240]keep a poor man's pledge when he needs it, [241]take any pledge from a widow or [242]from any debtor if he earns his living with it.

Kidnaping [243]a Jew is forbidden.

Do not [244]steal or [245]rob by violence. Do not [246]remove a landmark or [247]defraud.

It is forbidden [248]to deny receipt of a loan or a deposit or [249]to swear falsely regarding another man's property.

You must not [250]deceive anybody in business. You may not [251]mislead a man even verbally. It is forbidden to harm the stranger among you [252]verbally or [253]do him injury in trade.

230. Deut. 15:2
231. Deut. 15:9
232. Deut. 15:7
233. Deut. 15:13
234. Ex. 22:24
235. Lev. 25:37
236. Deut. 23:20
237. Ex. 22:24
238. Lev. 19:13
239. Deut. 24:10
240. Deut. 24:12
241. Deut. 24:17
242. Deut. 24:6
243. Ex. 20:13
244. Lev. 19:11
245. Lev. 19:13
246. Deut. 19:14
247. Lev. 19:13
248. Lev. 19:11
249. Lev. 19:11
250. Lev. 25:14
251. Lev. 25:17
252. Ex. 22:20

You may not [254]return or [255]otherwise take advantage of, a slave who has fled to the land of Israel from his master, even if his master is a Jew.

Do not [256]afflict the widow or the orphan. You may not [257]misuse or [258]sell a Hebrew slave; do not [259]treat him cruelly or [260]allow a heathen to mistreat him. You must not [261]sell your Hebrew maidservant or, if you marry her, [262]withhold food, clothing, and conjugal rights from her. You must not [263]sell a female captive or [264]treat her as a slave.

Do not [265]covet another man's possesions even if you are willing to pay for them. Even [266]the desire alone is forbidden.

A worker must not [267]cut down standing corn during his work or [268]take more fruit than he can eat.

One must not [269]turn away from a lost article which is to be returned to its owner nor may you [270]refuse to help a man or an animal which is collapsing under its burden.

It is forbidden to [271]defraud with weights and measures or even [272]to possess inaccurate weights.

Justice.

A judge must not [273]perpetrate injustice, [274]accept bribes or be

253. Ex. 22:20
254. Deut. 23:16
255. Deut. 23:17
256. Ex. 22:21
258. Lev. 25:42
257. Lev. 25:39
259. Lev. 25:43
260. Lev. 25:53
261. Ex. 21:8
262. Ex. 21:10
263. Deut. 21:14
264. Deut. 21:14
265. Ex. 20:17
266. Deut. 5:18
267. Deut. 23:26
268. Deut. 23:25
269. Deut. 22:3
270. Ex. 23:5
271. Lev. 19:35
272. Deut. 25:13
273. Lev. 19:15
274. Ex. 23:8

[275]partial or [276]afraid. He may [277]not favor the poor or [278]discriminate against the wicked; he should not [279]pity the condemned or [280]pervert the judgment of strangers or orphans.

It is forbidden to [281]hear one litigant without the other being present.

A capital case cannot be decided by [282]a majority of one.

A judge should not [283]accept a colleague's opinion unless he is convinced of its correctness; it is forbidden to [284]appoint as a judge someone who is ignorant of the law.

Do not [285]give false testimony or accept [286]testimony from a wicked person or from [287]relatives of a person involved in the case.

It is forbidden to pronounce judgment [288]on the basis of the testimony of one witness.

Do not [289]murder.

You must not convict on [290]circumstantial evidence alone.

A witness [291]must not sit as a judge in capital cases.

You must not [292]execute anybody without due proper trial and conviction.

Do not [293]pity or spare the pursuer.

Punishment is not to be inflicted for [294]an act committed under duress.

Do not accept ransom [295]for a murderer or [296]a manslayer.

Do not [297]hesitate to save another person from danger and do not

275. Lev. 19:15
276. Deut. 1:17
277. Lev. 19:15, rather Ex. 23:3
278. Ex. 23:6
279. Deut. 19:13
280. Deut. 24:17
281. Ex. 23:1
282. Ex. 23:2
283. Ex. 23:2
284. Deut. 1:17
285. Ex. 20:16
286. Ex. 23:1
287. Deut. 24:16
288. Deut. 19:15
289. Ex. 20:13
290. Ex. 23:7
291. Num. 35:30
292. Num. 35:12
293. Deut. 25:12
294. Deut. 22:26
295. Num. 35:31
296. Num. 35:32
297. Lev. 19:16

²⁹⁸leave a stumbling block in the way or ²⁹⁹mislead person by giving wrong advice.

It is forbidden ³⁰⁰to administer more than the assigned number of lashes to the guilty.

Do not ³⁰¹tell tales or ³⁰²bear hatred in your heart. It is forbidden to ³⁰³shame a Jew, ³⁰⁴to bear a grudge or ³⁰⁵to take revenge.

Do not ³⁰⁶take the dam when you take the young birds.

It is forbidden to ³⁰⁷shave a leprous scall or ³⁰⁸remove other signs of that affliction. It is forbidden ³⁰⁹to cultivate a valley in which a slain body was found and in which subsequently the ritual of breaking the heifer's neck (eglah arufah) was performed.

Do not ³¹⁰suffer a witch to live.

Do not ³¹¹force a bridegroom to perform military service during the first year of his marriage. It is forbidden to ³¹²rebel against the transmitters of the tradition or to ³¹³add or ³¹⁴detract from the precepts of the law.

Do not curse ³¹⁵a judge, ³¹⁶a ruler or ³¹⁷any Jew.

Do not ³¹⁸curse or ³¹⁹strike a parent.

It is forbidden to ³²⁰work on the Sabbath or ³²¹walk further than the permitted limits (eruv). You may not ³²²inflict punishment on the Sabbath.

It is forbidden to work on ³²³the first or ³²⁴the seventh day of

298.	Deut. 22:8	299.	Lev. 19:14
300.	Deut. 25:2–3		
301.	Lev. 19:16	302.	Lev. 19:17
303.	Lev. 19:17	305.	Lev. 19:18
304.	Lev. 19:18		
306.	Deut. 22:6	308.	Deut. 24:8
307.	Lev. 13:33	309.	Deut. 21:4
310.	Ex. 22:17	312.	Deut. 17:11
311.	Deut. 24:5	313.	Deut. 13:1
		314.	Deut. 13:1
315.	Ex. 22:27	316.	Ex. 22:27
318.	Ex. 21:17	317.	Lev. 19:14
320.	Ex. 20:10	319.	Ex. 21:15
321.	Ex. 16:29	322.	Ex. 35:3
		323.	Ex. 12:16

Passover, on [325] Shavuot, on [326] Rosh Ha-Shanah, on the [327]first and [328]eighth (*Shemini Azeret*) days of Sukkot and [329]on the Day of Atonement.

Incest and Other Forbidden Relationships.

It is forbidden to enter into an incestuous relationship with one's [330]mother, [331]step-mother, [332]sister, [333]step-sister, [334]son's daughter, [335]daughter's daughter, [336]daughter, [337]any woman and her daughter, [338]any woman and her son's daughter, [339]any woman and her daughter's daughter, [340]father's sister, [341]mother's sister, [342]paternal uncle's wife, [343]daughter-in-law, [344]brother's wife and [345]wife's sister.

It is also forbidden to [346]have sexual relations with a menstruous woman.

Do not [347]commit adultery.

It is forbidden for [348]a man or [349]a woman to have sexual intercourse with an animal.

Homosexuality [350]is forbidden, particularly with [351]one's father or [352]uncle.

It is forbidden to have [353]intimate physical contact (even without actual intercourse) with any of the women with whom intercourse is forbidden.

A *mamzer* may not [354]marry a Jewess.

Harlotry [355]is forbidden.

A divorcee may not be [356]remarried to her first husband if, in the meanwhile, she had married another.

A childless widow may not [357]marry anybody other than her late husband's brother.

A man may not [358]divorce a wife whom he married after having raped her or [359]after having slandered her.

An eunuch may not [360]marry a Jewess.

Castration [361]is forbidden.

The Monarchy.

You may not [362]elect as king anybody who is not of the seed of Israel.

The king must not accumulate an excessive number of [363]horses, [364]wives, or [365]wealth.

353. Lev. 18:6
354. Deut. 23:3

355. Deut. 23:18
356. Deut. 24:4

357. Deut. 25:5

358. Deut. 22:29
359. Deut. 22:19

360. Deut. 23:2

361. Lev. 22:24

362. Deut. 17:15

363. Deut. 17:16

364. Deut. 17:17
365. Deut. 17:17

4 REASONS FOR THE COMMANDMENTS

The search for "reasons" for the commandmets *(ta'amei ha-mitzvot)* of the Torah springs from a tendency to transcend mere obedience to them by investing them with some intrinsic meaning. The Pentateuch itself offers reasons for some commandments (e.g., Ex. 22:26; 23:9; Deut. 11:19; 17:16–17; 23:4–5) and emphasizes the "wisdom" of the Law (Deut. 4:6–8). It also differentiates between *mishpatim* ("ordinances") and *hukkim* ("statutes") without, however, offering any clear principle of division. Classical rabbinic literature contains a more formal discussion of the problem. The *mishpatim* are said to represent laws that would have been valid even without having been "written" in the Torah, such as the prohibitions against robbery, idolatry, incest, and murder, while the *hukkim,* such as the prohibition of swine's flesh and the wearing of garments made of both wool and flax are "decrees" of God. It is to the latter class that "the evil inclination" and the gentiles object (Sifra, Lev. 18:4, par. 140). From the second century onward Christian attacks on "the Law" provoked many Jewish replies stressing the importance of the *mitzvot:* the commandments were given for the sole purpose of purifying man (Gen. R. 41:1—for parallels see Theodor Albeck ed. (1965), 424–5); they strengthen man's holiness (Mekh. 89a); they enable Israel to acquire merit (Mak. 3:16). R. Simeon b. Yoḥai is known to have favored the exposition of the reasons of Scripture *(doresh ta'amei dikera),* but he did not go beyond offering exegetical observations (Kid. 68b, et al.). The *ta'amei ha-Torah* ("reasons of the commandments") are not revealed and should not be revealed (Pes. 119a; cf. Sanh. 21b); the "yoke of the commandments" is to be cherished without probing its reasons. No detailed rationalization of the commandments is to be found in the rabbinic sources.

Hellenistic Literature. The need for a rational explanation of the Mosaic law was expressed for the first time in the Hellenistic period; it was motivated by a desire to present the Jewish religion to the pagan world as a legislation designed to produce a people of the highest virtue. The *Letter of Aristeas* describes the dietary laws and other commandments, e.g., those concerning sacrifices, wearing of *ẓiẓit*, the *mezuzah*, and *tefillin*, as divinely ordained means for awakening holy thoughts and forming character (cf. 142–4, 147, 150ff., 169). In IV Maccabees (5:23–24) divine law is identified with reason and held to be the chief aid to a virtuous life (cf. 1:15–17, 30ff.; 5:7, 25–26).

PHILO. Philo offered the first systematic exposition of the reasons for the commandments in several of his works. He presented the law of Moses as the ideal law envisaged by the philosophers, that is, the law that leads men to live according to virtue (H. A. Wolfson, *Philo*, 2 (1947), 200ff.). The laws of Moses are divided into positive and negative laws and into those relating to man and those relating to God, and they are all subsumed under the Ten Commandments. Aside from these classifications, the laws of Moses also fall into the following four categories: (1) beliefs; (2) virtuous emotions; (3) actions symbolizing beliefs; and (4) actions symbolizing virtues. However, under the influence of Judaism this fourfold classification of philosophic virtues is expanded to include such religious virtues as faith, piety, prayer, and repentance. Unlike the natural law, the Mosaic law is revealed by God; nevertheless, it is in accord with human nature. Every law in it has a rational purpose (*ibid.*, 305–6). In the explanation of some laws, particularly those involving the sacrifices and festivals, Philo used the allegorical method. Elsewhere he tried to present the Mosaic legislation as a form of government that combines the best features of the three types of rule described as good by Plato and Aristotle, namely, monarchy, aristocracy, and democracy (382ff.).

Medieval Philosophy. SAADIAH GAON. Saadiah Gaon was the first Jewish thinker to divide the commandments into those obligatory because they are required by reason (Ar. *'aqliyyāt,* Heb. *sikhliyyot*) and those given through revelation (Ar. *sam'iyyāt,* Heb. *shimiyyot*). In making this distinction he followed the parallel teachings of the Mu'tazilite Kalām but also added a Platonic account. According to the Mu'tazilite exposition, the rational laws are divided into three kinds: gratitude, reverence, and social conduct; and from these three categories he derived many special laws. In his Platonic exposition he showed the rational character of certain laws by pointing out the damaging effects of the acts prohibited: Theft and robbery, for example, undermine the economic basis of society, and untruthfulness destroys the harmony of the soul. Discussing the revelational laws, Saadiah holds that while they are primarily an expression of God's will, they have some rational aspects or "usefulness," although he repeatedly reminds himself that God's wisdom is superior to man's. For example, the holy seasons enable man to pursue spiritual matters and human fellowship; the priesthood guides and helps people in time of stress; and dietary laws combat animal worship (*Book of Beliefs and Opinions,* 3:5, 1–3).

KARAITES. While the Rabbanites eventually went on to formulate other "reasons of the commandments," the Mu'tazilite approach, exemplified by Saadiah, remained in force among the Karaites throughout the medieval period. Joseph al-Baṣīr and Jeshua b. Judah emphasized the validity of the moral law prior to revelation. Aaron b. Elijah differentiated between *mitzvot sikhliyyot* ("rational laws") and *mitzvot toriyyot* ("Toraitic laws"; *Eẓ Ḥayyīm,* ed. F. Delitzsch (1841) chap. 102). Elijah Bashyazi (b.c. 1420) spoke of the rational ordinances as those precepts "established and planted in man's heart" and known prior to revelation (see L. Nemoy, *Karaite Anthology* (1952), 241ff.).

BAḤYA IBN PAQUDA. Baḥya combined Saadiah's division of the commandments with another classification also derived from Mu'tazalite sources, that of "duties of the members [of the body]" (Ar. *farā'iḍ al-jawāriḥ*, Heb. *ḥovot ha-evarim*) and "duties of the hearts" (Ar. *farā'iḍ al-qulūb*, Heb. *ḥovot ha-levavot*). The "duties of the members" are of two kinds: duties obligatory by virtue of reason and duties neither enjoined nor rejected by reason, e.g., the prohibition of eating milk and meat together. The "duties of the hearts," on the other hand, are of an intellectual and attitudinal kind, such as belief in God, trust in Him, and fear and love of Him (*Ḥovot ha-Levavot*, Introduction). Baḥya emphasized "duties of the hearts" (3:3) and asserted that it is only on account of the weakness of the intellect that the revelational commandments are necessary. Unlike Saadiah, however, he does not try to explain the revelational laws in terms of usefulness for specific ends; they are simply expressions of piety and, thereby, effective aids to the attainment of the perfect life of attachment to God.

JOSEPH IBN ẒADDIK. Joseph ibn Ẓaddik stressed gratitude as the most fundamental duty to God, who out of love created the world and gave it His commandments. Accepting the distinction between rational and revelational commandments, Ibn Ẓaddik held that even the latter have a "subtle meaning" *(sod dak, inyan dak)*. The observance of the Sabbath, for example, teaches the createdness of the world and points to the bliss of the world-to-come (*Sefer ha-Olam ha-Katan*, S. Horovitz, ed. (1903), 59–64).

JUDAH HALEVI. Judah Halevi's classifications of the commandments were under three headings: (1) rational laws *(sikhliyyot)*, also termed psychic laws *(nafshiyyot)*, such as those having to do with belief in God, justice, and gratitude (*Kuzari*, 2:48; 3:11); (2) governmental laws *(minhagiyyot)*, which are concerned with the functioning and well-being of society *(ibid.);* and (3) revelational laws *(shimiyyot)*, or divine laws *(elohiyyot)* 239 whose main function is to elevate the Jew to communion with God and whose highest manifestation is prophecy. God alone is capable of determining the revelational laws, which in themselves are neither demanded nor rejected by reason (1:98; 2:23; 3:53). For Halevi the revelational laws are supreme and the rational and governmental laws are only a "preamble" (2:48).

ABRAHAM IBN EZRA. Abraham ibn Ezra dealt with the subject of the commandments in his commentaries on the Torah and in his small treatise *Yesod Mora*. He distinguished between laws which are implanted in the human heart prior to revelation *(pikkudim)* and laws which prescribe symbolic acts reminding us of such matters as creation, e.g., observance of the Sabbath, and the exodus from Egypt, e.g., the observance of Passover (*Yesod Mora*, ch. 5; Commentary to Gen. 26:5; Short Commentary to Ex. 15:26). In addition he speaks of "obscure commandments" *(mitzvot ne'elamot)*, which have no clear-cut reason. Certain of these commandments he tried to explain as prohibitions of acts contrary to nature, e.g., seething a kid in its mother's milk, and others, as serving utilitarian purposes, e.g., the separation of the leper as a sanitary measure (Lev. 13:45-46) and the dietary laws in order to prevent injurious influences to body and soul (Comm. to Lev. 19:23; 11:43). Astrological motifs are employed in the interpretation of the sanctuary and its parts, the garments of the high priest, and the sacrifices.

ABRAHAM IBN DAUD. Abraham ibn Daud who initiated the Aristotelian trend in medieval Jewish philosophy, abandoned the Kalām terms "rational" and "revelational" and replaced them with "generally known" (Ar. *mashhūrāt*, a translation of the Greek *endoxa;* Heb. *mefursamot*) and "traditional" (Ar. *maqbūlāt*, Heb. *mekubbalot*). This change of terminology reflects the Aristotelian view that good and evil are not a matter of demonstrative knowledge but of opinion (*Topics*, 1:1; cf. Maimonides, *Millot ha-Higgayon*, ch. 8; Guide 1:2). Ibn Daud assumed that the "generally known" laws, i.e., the laws of social conduct, are identical in all religions and, therefore, that the formation of states composed of different religious communities is possible, no matter how opposed their religions may be (*Sefer ha-Emunah ha-Ramah*, ed. S. Weil (1852), 5:2, 75).

MAIMONIDES. Maimonides, like Ibn Daud, discarded as illegitimate the distinction between "rational" and "revelational" laws. In his view, all laws set forth in the Torah have a "cause" (Ar. *'illa*, Heb. *illah*), that is, a "useful purpose" (Ar. *ghāya mufīda*, Heb. *takhlit mo'ilah*), and follow from God's wisdom, not from an arbitrary act of His will. In some cases, such as the prohibitions against killing and stealing, their utility is clear, while in others, such as the prohibitions against sowing with diverse seeds, it is not. Maimonides identified the former commandments with the laws known as *mishpatim* ("ordinances") and the latter, with those known as *ḥukkim* ("statutes"). Although general laws, e.g., the institution of sacrifices, have a reason, particular laws, e.g., the number of animals for a particular sacrifice, do not (Guide, 3:26, 31). There are two overall purposes of the Torah: the welfare of the soul, in which man finds his ultimate perfection in this world and the next, and the welfare of the body, which is a means to the welfare of the soul. For the welfare of the soul the law promotes correct opinions, and for the welfare of the body it sets down norms for the guidance of society and the individual. To promote opinions, the law fosters two kinds of beliefs: absolutely true beliefs, such as the existence and unity of God, and beliefs necessary for the well-being of the state, such as God's anger in punishing evildoers (Guide, 3:27–28, 31–32).

Introducing a new method of interpretation of Jewish law, Maimonides regarded many *ḥukkim* of the Torah as directed toward the abolition of the idolatrous practices of the ancient pagans, as described in a tenth-century book by Ibn Waḥshiyya, known as the *Nabatean Agriculture*. He even maintained that it is the first intention of the law to put an end to idolatry (Guide, 3:29). Another method that Maimonides used to explain certain laws is described by the

term "gracious ruse" (Ar. *talaṭṭuf;* Heb. *ormah*), which is
borrowed from the Greek philosopher Alexander of
Aphrodisias (c. 200; see S. Pines' introduction to his
translation of the Guide, lxxii ff.). Thus, for example, God
graciously tolerated the customary mode of worship
through animal sacrifice, but transferred it from idols to His
own name and through this "ruse" effaced idolatry (3:32).
However, in marked contrast to the utilitarian treatments
of the commandments in Maimonides' *Guide of the
Perplexed* is the deeply religious approach of his *Mishneh
Torah.* The *ḥukkim,* including the sacrifices, appear in the
latter work as important vehicles of the spiritual life (cf.
Yad, Me'ilah, end; Temurah, end; Mikva'ot, end).

Ḥasdai Crescas and Joseph Albo. The approach of
Ḥasdai Crescas is of an entirely different nature. Crescas
rejected the notion, implicit in the views of his predecessors,
e.g., Maimonides, that the Torah had to adapt itself to the
low level of religion prevalent at the time of its revelation,
an assumption which tended to render part of the
commandments obsolete. He was also the first to introduce
theological instead of moral or metaphysical concepts for
the interpretation of the commandments. In this context it
is important to recall that Crescas was concerned with
refuting Christian theological notions and the charge of the
apostate Abner of Burgos that Judaism had succumbed to
philosophy. In his polemic with Christianity Crescas
accepted the notion of original sin (*Or Adonai,* 2:2,6), but
argued that all *mitzvot* are means of redemption from the
"poison" injected into Eve by the serpent. Unlike the
Aristotelians who saw intellectual perfection as the final
goal of the Torah, Crescas maintained that its ultimate
purpose is to instill the love of God in man (*ibid.,* 2:6, 2).

Crescas' pupil Joseph Albo continued his master's
polemics against Christian attacks on the Mosaic law,
arguing that it is more perfect than any other law and that
the Gospels are really no law at all. Distinguishing three
kinds of laws, Albo held that natural law *(ha-dat ha-tivit)*
contains those rules that are indispensable for the merest

association of men; that conventional law *(ha-dat ha-nimusit)* promotes virtues according to human opinion, or the "generally known" *(ha-mefursam)*; and that divine law *(ha-dat ha-Elohit)* guides man to true happiness, which is the bliss of the soul and eternal life *(Sefer ha-Ikkarim* 1:7, and passim; see I. Husik, in *Hebrew Union College Annual* 2 (1925), 381ff.; R. Lerner, in *Ancients and Moderns,* ed. J. Cropsey, 1964).

Modern Jewish Thought. Modern Jewish thought, marked by a deep crisis of traditional beliefs and halakhic authority, dealt with the subject of reasons for divine commandments on various levels.

MOSES MENDELSSOHN. Moses Mendelssohn distinguished three layers within the body of Jewish teachings: (1) religion par excellence, consisting of eternal truths that all enlightened men hold in common; (2) historical truths concerning the origin of the Jewish nation, which faith accepts on authority; and (3) laws, precepts, commandments, and rules of life revealed by God through words and Scripture as well as oral tradition *(Jerusalem* (1783), 113–5). Revealed legislation prescribes only actions, not faith nor the acceptance of eternal truths. The actions prescribed by the revealed law are the "ceremonies," and the specific element of Judaism, therefore, is the ceremonial laws.

In opposition to Spinoza, who considered the Mosaic legislation a state law designed only to promote the temporal happiness of the Jewish nation, Mendelssohn contended that Mosaic laws transcend state law, because of its twofold goal: actions leading to temporal happiness and meditation on eternal and historical truths leading to eternal happiness *(ibid.,* 116). Every ceremony has a specific meaning and a precise relation to the speculative aspect of religion and morality *(ibid.,* 95). Since the Mosaic law is more than a state law, those of its parts which apply to the individual remain valid even after the destruction of the Jewish state and should be steadfastly observed *(ibid.,* 127–9). Moreover, it retains its important function as a bond between Jews everywhere, which is essential as long as 243 polytheism, anthropomorphism, and religious usurpation continue to rule the earth (letter to Herz Homberg, in *Gesammelte Schriften*, 5 (1844), 669). Mendelssohn's polemics against Spinoza were taken up again in the late 19th-early 20th century by Hermann Cohen (cf. his *Juedische Schriften*, ed. B. Strauss, 3 (1924), 290–372).

NINETEENTH-CENTURY PHILOSOPHERS. Isaac Noah Mannheimer and Michael Sachs wrote against the alarming neglect of observance of the ceremonial law in the period of Emancipation. They reemphasized the significance of ceremonial law in terms borrowed partly from Mendelssohn and partly from Kant's vindication of the *cultus* as a means of furthering morality. Of great moment was Leopold Zunz's forthright stand on behalf of the rite of circumcision, which occasioned his study of the ceremonial law as a whole (*Gutachten ueber die Beschneidung*, in Zunz, Schr, 2 (1876), 190–203). Abraham Geiger recognized only the validity of those ceremonies which proved capable of promoting religious and moral feelings (*Nachgelassene Schriften*, ed. L. Geiger, 1 (1875), 254ff., 324–5, 486–8). Under the influence of the German philologist Friedrich Cruezer and Hegel, theologians began to view the rituals prescribed in the Torah, especially the sacrificial cult, as merely symbolic expressions of ideas (see for example, D. Einhorn, *Das Prinzip des Mosaismus*, 1854). Defending an orthodox position, Samson Raphael Hirsch evolved a system of symbolism based chiefly on ethical values in order to give fresh meaning to the totality of *halakhah* (*Nineteen Letters*, sections *Edoth* and *Horeb;* see *Horeb*, trans. by I. Grunfeld, 1 (1962), 108).

TWENTIETH-CENTURY PHILOSOPHERS. In the 20th century Leo Baeck spoke of two fundamental religious experiences, that of mystery *(Geheimnis)* and that of commandment *(Gebot)*, which in Judaism are intertwined in a perfect unity (*Essays*, trans. by W. Kaufmann (1958), 171, 173). For Franz Rosenzweig there is a difference between commandment and law. God is not a lawgiver—He commands, and each act of *mitzvah* accomplishes the task of "unifying" Him, an assertion that Rosenzweig formulated in terms of kabbalistic doctrine (*Der Stern der Erloesung*, 3rd ed. (1954), 2:114ff.; 3:187–94).

Part Five

RITUAL AND STUDY

1 PRAYER

In the Bible. The concept of prayer is based on the conviction that God exists, hears, and answers (Ps. 65:3; cf. 115:3–7)—that He is a personal deity. In a sense it is a corollary of the biblical concept that man was created "in the image of God" (Gen. 1:26–27), which implies, inter alia, that there is a fellowship with God. Although prayer has an intellectual base, it is essentially emotional in character. It is an expression of man's quest for the Divine and his longing to unburden his soul before God (Ps. 42:2–3 [1–2]; 62:9[8]). Hence prayer takes many forms: petition, expostulation, confession, meditation, recollection (anamnesis), thanksgiving, praise, adoration, and intercession. For the purpose of classification, "praise" is distinguished from "prayer" in the narrower, supplicatory sense, and "ejaculatory" from formal, "liturgical" prayer. But the source is the same; in its irresistable outpouring, the human heart merges all categories in an indivisible "I–Thou" relationship. Thus prayer and praise may intermingle (I Sam. 2:1–10) and supplication and thanksgiving follow in close succession (Ps. 13:1–5, 6). Indeed many scriptural passages might be called "para-prayers"—they seem to hover between discourse and entreaty (Ex. 3:1–12), meditation and petition (Jer. 20:7ff.), or expostulation and entreaty (Job, passim). It has been estimated (Koehler-Baumgartner) that there are 85 prayers in the Bible, apart from 60 complete psalms and 14 parts of psalms that can be so termed; five psalms are specifically called prayers (Ps. 17, 86, 90, 102, 142). But such liturgical statistics depend on the definition given to prayer.

THE CHARACTER OF PRAYER. Despite its multifaceted

character, biblical prayer is essentially a simple human reaction. The rabbis called it "the service in the heart" (Ta'an. 2a); the expression has its roots in biblical thought (Hos. 7:14; Ps. 108:2; 111:1). But the needs of man are so numerous and complex that prayer inevitably came to reflect the vast range of human moods, fears, hopes, feelings, desires, and aspirations. In early times—in the patriarchal age—a simple invocation, a calling upon the name of the Lord (Gen. 12:8; 21:33), would suffice. The approach to God at this stage was marked by spontaneity, directness, and familiarity—God was near. Yet the future was veiled by mystery; man was often undecided how to act. Hence the request for a sign or oracle addressed directly to God (Gen. 24:12–14), or indirectly through a priest (I Sam. 14:36–37) or prophet (II Kings 19:2ff.). From this stratum grew the magnificent prayers for understanding and guidance (Num. 6:24–26; I Kings 3:6ff.; Ps. 119:33ff.).

But in emergency man does not merely want to know the future; he seeks to determine it by entreating God's help. Thus Jacob (in a votive supplication) prayed for essential material needs (Gen. 28:20ff.); Eliezer for the success of his mission (Gen. 24:12–14); Abraham for the salvation of Sodom (Gen. 18:23–33); Moses for erring Israel (Ex. 32:31–32); Joshua for divine help in the hour of defeat (Josh. 7:6–9); Hezekiah for deliverance from Sennacherib (II Kings 19:15–19); the prophets on behalf of their people (Jer. 14:1ff.; 15:1ff.; Amos 7:2ff.); Daniel for Israel's restoration (Dan. 9:3–19); Ezra for the sins of his people (Ezra 9:6–15); and Nehemiah for the distress of his people (Neh. 1:4–11). Solomon's noble dedication prayer at the consecration of the Temple (I Kings 8:12–53) includes almost every type of prayer—adoration, thanksgiving, petition, and confession. It also strikes a universal note (8:41ff.) so often echoed by the prophets. The spectrum of biblical prayer thus ranges from the simplest material needs to the highest spiritual yearnings (Ps. 51:1ff.; 119:1ff.), transcending, like prophecy, the horizon of history and reaching to the realm of eschatology (Isa. 66:22–23).

There was an early relationship between sacrifice and prayer (Gen. 13:4; 26:25), which persisted until the destruction of the Second Temple. The sacrifice suggested man's submission to the will of God; the prayer often provided a commentary on the offering. But the two are not necessarily linked. It is noteworthy that the sacrificial regulations make no liturgical provisions (except for the Day of Atonement, Lev. 16:21); but actually the offerings were themselves a dramatic form of prayer. Contrariwise, prayer could replace sacrifice (Ps. 141:2). In the synagogue, prayer, accompanied by Scripture reading and exposition, entirely took the place of altar offerings.

Examples of prayers of intercession have already been cited. The intercessor, whether prophet, priest, king, or national leader, does not point to the need for an intermediary in worship: "The Lord is near to all who call upon Him in truth" (Ps. 145:18). The intercessor is one who, by his innate spiritual attributes, lends weight to the entreaty. The ultimate criterion still remains not the worthiness of the pleader but of those for whom he is pleading (Ezek. 14:14, 20).

THE ACCESSORIES OF PRAYER. Prayer, unlike sacrifice, could be offered up anywhere (Gen. 24:26; Dan. 6:11 in the upper chamber; Ezra 9:5ff.), but there was a natural tendency to prefer a sacred site (e.g., Shiloh or Gibeon). Eventually the Temple at Jerusalem became the major place of prayer (Isa. 56:7); those who could not be there physically at least turned toward it when worshiping (Dan. 6:11; cf. Ps. 5:8 [7]). In time to come the Temple would be a house of prayer for all nations (Isa. 56:7). The synagogue had its origin during the Babylonian exile; originally a place of assembly, it became in due course a house of prayer and study. The emphasis on congregational prayer began to grow but private prayer was never abolished. The heart and not the hour dictated the occasion for prayer. Day and night the Heavenly Father could be entreated (e.g., I Sam. 15:11; Ps. 86:3; 88:2[1]). But the need for regularity brought about a synchronization of the times of prayer and of sacrifice: morning worship corresponded to the morning oblation (Ps. 5:4[3]), afternoon orisons to the late afternoon sacrifice (I Kings 18:36; Ezra 9:5). Nightfall provided yet another occasion for worship, so that prayers came to be offered thrice daily (Ps. 55:18; Dan. 6:11; though twice in I Chron. 23:30). The seven times a day mentioned in Psalms 119:164 mean "often" or "constantly."

In the Bible no particular gestures are prescribed in connection with prayer. But certain postures developed naturally to lend emphasis to the content of the prayer: standing, which is normal (I Sam. 1:26; I Kings 8:22); kneeling (Dan. 6:11; Ezra 9:5); prostration (Josh. 7:6); head bowed (Gen. 24:26; Neh. 8:6); hands stretched out or uplifted (I Kings 8:22; Ps. 28:2); face between knees (I Kings 18:42); and even sitting (II Sam. 7:18). More important accompaniments of prayer were fasting, mourning, and weeping (Isa. 58:2-5; Joel 2:12); but the ultimate criterion remained earnestness of heart (Joel 2:13).

Originally prayer was undoubtedly spontaneous and personal; but the need to organize religion gave rise to liturgical patterns and musical renderings (Ezra 2:65; I Chron. 16). Prayer formulas are found already in the Pentateuch (Deut. 21:7ff.; 26:5-15). The Psalms provide examples of fuller liturgical development, including formalized choral and instrumental features. Thus, the response "Amen" occurs in Numbers 5:22, Psalms 41:14, etc.: a prayer before the reading of the Torah in Nehemiah 8:6; a doxology in Nehemiah 9:5, 32; a typical review of God's dealings with Israel leading to a confession and a pledge in Nehemiah 9:6-10:1 (9:38).

ANSWER TO PRAYER. That prayer is answered is an accepted biblical verity (e.g., Gen. 19:17-23; Num. 12:9ff.); but Scripture is no less emphatic that not all prayers are answered (Gen. 18:17ff.; Isa. 29:13ff.). Ritual is not enough, while hypocritical worship is an abomination (Isa. 1:15; Amos 4:4ff.); and there are occasions when intercession is forbidden (Jer. 7:16; 11:14). It is at this point that the biblical concept of prayer is seen in its true inwardness. Paganism regarded worship as a form of magic, whereby the deity could be compelled to fulfill the worshiper's wishes; the moral element was wholly absent. In biblical faith the divine response is essentially linked to ethical and spiritual values. Man, as it were, answers his own prayer (Gen. 4:7), and fundamentally the answer is a significant change of spirit and outlook. Abraham learned the lesson of faith (Gen. 15:1-6); Moses became his people's deliverer (Ex. 3:2-4:18); Isaiah was transformed into a prophet (Isa. 6:5-8). Prayer and prophecy were probably closely correlated, the former providing spiritual soil in which the revelatory seed took root (Jer. 1:6ff.; Hab. 1:13-2:3). In many instances prayer assumes a tempestuous character (Jer. 12; Ps. 22; Job, passim [cf. 16:17]), but the storm always ends in newfound faith and peace. At times, moreover, God answers before He is appealed to (Isa. 65:24; cf. Dan. 9:20ff.), for man not only beseeches God, but God also seeks man (Isa. 50:2; 65:12). The "I-Thou" relationship is reciprocal.

In sum, the Bible conceives prayer as a spiritual bridge between man and God. It is a great instrument of human regeneration and salvation, worthy even of martyrdom (Dan. 6:11). Rooted in faith (Ps. 121) and moral integrity (Ps. 15), it banishes fear (Ps. 23) and asks, in its noblest formulations, only the blessing of divine favor (Num. 6:24-26). Clothed in language of simple but matchless beauty, it is imbued with religious love and a sense of sweet fellowship with God. Both the Christian and Muslim liturgies have been profoundly influenced by the spirit, thought, and forms of biblical prayer.

In the Apocryphal Literature. There are a number of references to prayer in the apocryphal books, including the idea of the living offering up prayers on behalf of the dead (II Mac. 12:44-45). The apocryphal work, The Prayer of Manasseh, is a penitential prayer. The biblical concept that God is near to those who suffer is also developed (Ecclus. 35:13-17). Prayer is associated with the giving of alms

(Ecclus. 7:10), and there is a national prayer for deliverance from an enemy (Ecclus. 36:1–17).

In Rabbinic Thought. On the biblical verse "And serve Him with all your heart" (Deut. 11:13), the rabbis commented "What is service of the heart? This is prayer" (Ta'an. 2a). "Service" *(avodah)* in this context is connected with the Temple and its worship, for which prayer is seen as a substitute. On the other hand, the saying of R. Eleazar that prayer is dearer to God than good works and sacrifices (Ber. 32b), though hyperbolic, may nonetheless be intended to express the real superiority of prayer. Possibly, the tension in this matter is to be perceived in the two reasons given for the statutory prayers of the day. According to one opinion, these were ordained by the patriarchs, while another view has it that they correspond to the perpetual offerings in Temple times (Ber. 26b).

The obligation of offering up prayer, though supported by a scriptural verse, is considered to be rabbinic, not biblical (Ber. 21a). Prayers are to be recited three times a day: morning, afternoon, and night (Ber. 4:1). In addition to the statutory prayers and private prayers of various kinds, public prayers were offered in times of distress; prayers for rain, for instance, in times of drought (Ta'an. 2:1–5).

THE VALUE OF PRAYER AND CONCENTRATION IN PRAYER. Prayer stands high in the world of values (Ber. 6b). God Himself prays, His prayer being that His mercy might overcome His judgment (Ber. 7a). Nevertheless, the study of the Torah occupies a higher rung than prayer, and some scholars, whose main occupation was study, only prayed periodically (Shab. 11a; RH 35a). A rabbi who spent too much time on his prayers was rebuked by his colleague for neglecting eternal life to engage in temporal existence (Shab. 10a). Communal prayer is of greater significance than private prayer (Ber. 8a; Deut. R. 2:12). Too much reflection on one's prayers in the expectation that these will be answered was discouraged (Ber. 32b). Prayer should be offered with proper concentration *(kavvanah)* on the words uttered in God's presence (Ber. 31a). R. Eliezer said: "He that makes his prayer a fixed task, his prayer is not supplication" (Ber. 4:4). R. Simeon b. Nethanel said: ". . . and when thou prayest make not thy prayer a fixed form, but [a plea for] mercies and supplications before God" (Avot 2:13). One way of avoiding the deadening familiarity of a "fixed form" was to recite a new prayer each day (TJ, Ber. 4:3, 8a). When R. Eliezer was asked by his disciples to teach them the ways of life that they might learn them and by following attain the life of the world to come, part of his reply was: "When you pray, know before Whom you stand" (Ber. 28b). A person who has just returned from a journey and is consequently unable to concentrate properly, should not pray until three days have elapsed (Er. 65a).

PROPER FORMS OF PRAYER. Not every prayer is valid. A prayer for God to change the past, for instance, is a "vain prayer" (Ber. 9:3). The impossibility of God answering every prayer addressed to Him is acknowledged in the account of the prayer of the high priest on the Day of Atonement who used to pray before the rainy season that the prayers of the travelers who required fair weather should not be allowed to enter God's presence (Yoma 53b). A man should not only pray for himself but should also think of others, using the plural form "grant us" rather than the singular "grant me" (Ber. 29b–30a). If a man needs something for himself but prays to God to grant that very thing to his neighbor who needs it, such an unselfish prayer causes God to grant him his wish first (BK 92a). Man should never despair of offering supplication to God "even if a sharp sword rests upon his neck" (Ber. 10a). In praising God, man should be circumspect, using only the standard forms of praise found in Scripture and established for use in prayer (Ber. 33b). Prayers of thanksgiving, particularly in the form of the benediction (berakhah), are repeatedly enjoined by the rabbis (Ber. 6:1–3), as well as praise of God for His wondrous works and the marvelous beings He has created (Ber. 9:1–2; Ber. 58b).

THE ADDRESSING OF PRAYERS DIRECTLY TO GOD. R.

Judah said that if a human being is in trouble and wishes to invoke the aid of his patron he must first stand at the door and call out to a servant or a member of the patron's family and he may or may not be allowed to enter. But it is otherwise with God. God says, "When a man is in trouble, do not cry out to the angel Michael or to the angel Gabriel but to Me and I will answer immediately" (TJ, Ber. 9:1, 13a). On the other hand, R. Johanan said: "When one petitions for his needs in Aramaic, the ministering angels do not heed him, for they do not understand Aramaic" (Shab. 12b). Possibly a distinction is to be made between the angels bringing man's prayers to God and direct intercession, with the angels as intermediaries between man and God (cf. Tob., 12:12, 15). Some men were renowned for their capacity to pray and to have their prayers answered, so that great scholars, less gifted in this direction, would ask these saints to pray on their behalf (Ber. 34b). A number of miracle tales are told to illustrate the immediacy of God's response to the prayers of such men (Ta'an. 3:8; Ta'an. 23a–b).

In Medieval Thought. Although medieval Jewish thinkers profoundly considered major theological problems, there is surprisingly little discussion in their writings of the intellectual difficulties involved in prayer. One of the few discussions as to why prayer should be necessary, since God knows man's needs, is that of Joseph Albo (Ikkarim 4:18). Albo replies that the act of turning to God in prayer is itself one of the conditions upon which God's help depends, just as it depends on other forms of human effort.

MAIMONIDES. True to his doctrine of theological negation, Maimonides in the standard liturgy only permits the use of those divine attributes in prayer which have been ordained by the "prophets," and he is opposed to the indiscriminate writing of hymns (Guide, 1:59; cf. Ibn Ezra to Eccles. 5:1). In spite of the talmudic statement that the obligation to pray is of rabbinic origin *(mi-de-rabbanan)*, Maimonides observes that this only applies to the number, form, and times of prayer, and that it is a biblical duty for the Jew to pray daily (Yad, Tefillah, 1:1). The need for adequate concentration in prayer *(kavvanah)* is particularly stressed in the Middle Ages and formed part of the general tendency prevalent among medieval Jewish thinkers who stressed greater inwardness in religious life. Baḥya ibn Paquda *(Ḥovot ha-Levavot,* 8:3, 9) remarks that prayer without concentration is like a body without a soul or a husk without a kernel. Maimonides' definition of *kavvanah* reads: "*Kavvanah* means that a man should empty his mind of all other thoughts and regard himself as if he were standing before the Divine Presence" (Yad, Tefillah, 4:16; cf. H. G. Enelow, in: *Studies in Jewish Literature Issued in Honor of Prof. Kaufmann Kohler* (1913), 82–107).

THE KABBALISTS. The kabbalists stress the difficulty of petitionary prayer to a God who is unchanging. They advance the view that prayer cannot, in fact, be offered to God as He is in Himself *(Ein Sof),* but only to God as He is manifested in the ten divine potencies (the *Sefirot*). God Himself is, therefore, not entreated directly to show mercy, for example, but prayer is directed to God as He is manifested in the *Sefirah* of loving-kindness. As a result of the power of man's prayer, this potency might function on earth. The magical nature of kabbalistic prayer and the dangers of setting up the *Sefirot* as divine intermediaries were the topic of much subsequent debate (Ribash, Resp. no. 157). The kabbalists, in fact, substituted for the older doctrine of *kavvanah* the concept of special intentions *(kavvanot)* i.e., meditations on the realm of *Sefirot.* Instead of concentrating on the plain meaning of the prayers, the kabbalist dwells on the realm of divine potencies and directs his mind, when reciting the words, to the supernal mysteries which govern and are controlled by them (see I. Tishby, *Mishnat ha-Zohar,* 2 (1961), 247–306).

The Ḥasidim. In Ḥasidism, the kabbalistic type of *kavvanot* yields to a far more emotional involvement and attachment *(devekut)* to God. "The metamorphosis which took place in the meaning of *kavvanot* at the advent of Ḥasidism, and more explicitly after the Great Maggid [Dov Baer of Mezhirech], consists in this—that an origi-

"Ḥasidim in a *bet midrash*" by Isidor Kaufmann. New York, Oscar Gruss Collection. Photo Frank Darmstaedter, New York.

nally intellectual effort of meditation and contemplation had become an intensely emotional and highly enthusiastic act" (Weiss, in: JJS, 9 (1958), 163–92). In Ḥasidism, prayer is a mystical encounter with the Divine, the heart leaping in ecstasy to its Source. Violent movements in prayer were not unusual; some of the ḥasidic groups even encouraged their followers to turn somersaults during their prayers (Dubnow, *Hasidut*, 112–5).

Prayer is frequently seen in Ḥasidism as man's most important religious activity. R. Shneur Zalman of Lyady, the founder of the intellectual Ḥabad sect in Ḥasidism, writes: "For although the forms of the prayers and the duty of praying three times a day are rabbinic, the idea of prayer is the foundation of the whole Torah. This means that man knows God, recognizing His greatness and His splendor with a serene and whole mind, and an understanding heart. Man should reflect on these ideas until his rational soul is awakened to love God, to cleave to Him and to His Torah, and to desire His commandments" (M. Teitelbaum, *Ha-Rav mi-Ladi u-Mifleget Ḥabad*, 2 (1914), 219).

In Ḥabad Ḥasidism, the true meaning of prayer is contemplation on the kabbalistic scheme whereby God's infinite light proceeds through the whole chain of being, from the highest to the lowest. Man should reflect on this until his heart is moved in rapture, but he should not engage in prayer for the sake of the pleasure such rapture will bring him; he must take care not to confuse authentic ecstasy with artificial spiritual titivation (Dov Baer of Lubavich, *Kunteres ha-Hitpa'alut*). Many ḥasidic groups, otherwise strictly conformist, disregarded the laws governing prayer at fixed times on the grounds that these interfere with the need for adequate preparation and with the spontaneity which is part of the prayer's essence.

In Modern Thought. The early reformers were much concerned about such questions as prayers for the restoration of sacrifices or the return to Zion, and whether prayer might be recited in the vernacular. Very few challenges, however, were presented to the idea of prayer as such in its traditional understanding. In the 20th century, Jewish thinkers began to consider the basic philosophical problems surrounding prayer. Petitionary prayer was felt to be especially difficult in the light of scientific views regarding cause and effect. A definite move away from the idea of prayer as a means of influencing God and toward its function as a way to affect man's attitudes can be observed. "Self-expression before God in prayer has thus a double effect; it strengthens faith in God's love and kindness, as well as in His all-wise and all-bountiful prescience. But it also chastens the desires and feelings of man, teaching him to banish from his heart all thoughts of self-seeking and sin, and to raise himself toward the purity and the freedom of the divine will and demand" (K. Kohler, *Jewish Theology* (1918), 275).

The tendency in some circles to reinterpret the God-idea itself in impersonal terms has cast prayer into a different

light. It is seen as an attempt by man to attune himself to

those powers in the universe which make for human self-fulfillment and as a reaching out to the highest within his own soul. Defenders of the traditional view of God and of prayer to Him have, however, not been lacking. (See *Proceedings of the Rabbinical Assembly of America*, 17 (1953), 151–238, for these two opinions).

2 STUDY

The study of the Torah (Hebrew: *talmud Torah*) as a supreme religious duty is one of the most typical and far-reaching ideas of rabbinic Judaism. Talmudic literature is full of references to the *mitzvah* of Torah study, especially of the difficult halakhic portions which require the fullest application. C. G. Montefiore (*A Rabbinic Anthology* (1938), introd., 17), though more than a little unsympathetic to this side of rabbinism, observes: "For all these legal discussions, all this 'study of the Law,' all these elaborations and minutiae, were to the Rabbis the breath of their nostrils, their greatest joy and the finest portion of their lives."

An early Mishnah (Peah 1:1), after describing such duties as honoring parents and performing acts of benevolence among the *mitzvot* for which there is reward both in this world and the next, concluded that the study of the Torah is "equal to them all." A tannaitic treatise, *Baraita Kinyan Torah* (Avot 6), devoted to the ideal of Torah study, contains the advice (6:4): "This is the way of the Torah: a morsel of bread with salt to eat, water by measure to drink; thou shalt sleep on the ground, and live a life of hardship, whilst thou toilest in the Torah. If thou doest thus, happy shalt thou be, and it shall be well with thee; happy shalt thou be—in this world, and it shall be well with thee—in the world to come." Quoting the verse, "This is the Law (Torah): when a man dieth in a tent" (Num. 19:14), the third-century teacher Resh Lakish taught: "The words of the Torah become firmly established only for one who kills himself (in study) for it" (Ber. 63b). Dedicated students, "toiling in the Torah," were found to number in the thousands in the great Palestinian and Babylonian academies during the first five centuries of the present era. Only against such a background of unqualified devotion does the saying of the second-century R. Jacob become intelligible: "If a man was walking by the way and studying and he ceased his study to declare, 'How fine is this tree!' or 'How fine is this plowed field!' Scripture reckons it to him as though he were guilty against his own soul" (Avot 3:7). Of Rava it was said (Shab. 88a) that he was once so engrossed in his studies that he was unaware that his fingers were spurting blood. It was taken for granted that a scholar would be incapable of diverting his mind from Torah study; hence it was ruled that a scholar is forbidden to remain in unclean alleyways where Torah should not be studied (Ber. 24b).

The ideal of Torah study had a twofold aim. First it was believed to lead to the practical observances, since without knowledge of what it is that the Torah enjoins full observance is impossible. "An empty-headed man cannot be a sin-fearing man, nor can an ignorant person be pious" (Avot 2:5). Secondly, Torah study was itself a religious duty of the highest order. This dual function of study is presumably given expression in the discussion said to have taken place in the early part of the second century: "R. Tarfon and the Elders were once reclining in the upper story of Nithza's house in Lydda, when this question was put to them: 'Which is greater, study or practice?' R. Tarfon replied: 'Practice is greater.' R. Akiva replied: 'Study is greater for it leads to practice.' Then they all answered and said: Study is greater, for it leads to practice" (Kid. 40b). Yet study without any intention of carrying out the precepts was seen as having no value. "Whoever says that he has only [an interest] in the study of the Torah, he does not even have [the study of] the Torah" (Yev. 109b). There is evidence of tension between the scholarly ideal and that of extraordinary piety without learning. The famous scholars were committed to Torah study as the highest pursuit, yet they were compelled to recognize the achievements of men of outstanding piety who were in no way renowned for their learning. The scholars yielded only grudgingly, as in the tale (Ber. 34b) of the miracle-working saint, R. Ḥanina b. Dosa, who prayed successfully for the recovery of R. Johanan b. Zakkai's son, whereas the prayers of R. Johanan would have accomplished nothing. When R. Johanan's wife asked him, "Is Ḥanina greater than you are?" he replied, "No; but he is like a servant of the king who can enter his presence at any time whereas I am like a nobleman who is allowed only to appear at fixed times."

The qualifications for study were carefully mapped out, 48 "excellences" by which the Torah is acquired being listed (perhaps for rehearsal by the prospective student):

By study, by the hearing of the ear, by the ordering of the lips, by the understanding of the heart, by the discernment of the heart, by awe, by reverence, by humility, by cheerfulness; by attendance on the Sages, by consorting with fellow-students, by close argument with disciples; by assiduity, by knowledge of Scripture and Mishnah; by moderation in business, in worldly occupation, pleasure, sleep, conversation, and jesting; by long-suffering, by a good heart, by faith in the Sages, by submission to sorrows; by being one that recognizes his place and that rejoices in his lot and that makes a fence around his words and claims no merit for himself; by being one that is beloved, that loves God, that loves mankind, that loves well-doing, that loves rectitude, that loves reproof, that shuns honor and boasts not of his learning, and delights not in rendering decisions; that helps his fellow to bear his yoke, and that judges him favorably, and that establishes him in the truth and establishes him in peace; and that occupies himself assiduously in his study; by being one that asks and makes answer, that hearkens and adds thereto; that learns in order to teach and that learns in order to practice; that makes his teacher wiser; that retells exactly what he has heard, and reports a thing in the name of him that said it (Avot. 6:6).

The demands made on the student were thus both of intellect and of character. The successful student acquired in addition to factual knowledge the capacity for skill in debate. Of particularly brilliant scholars it was said that they were able to provide 24 answers to every problem

(Shab. 33b; BM 84a). It was not unusual for teachers to encourage their disciples to cultivate alertness of mind by appearing on occasion to act contrary to the Law, to see whether the error would be spotted (Ber. 33b; Ḥul. 43b; Nid. 4b). The debators were compared to mighty warriors taking part in the "battles of the Torah" (Sanh. 111b). Another comparison was that to competent craftsmen. The "craftsmen and the smiths" (II Kings 24:14) were identified with the scholars and said to possess acute reasoning powers (Sif. Deut. 321). Of a text presenting severe problems of interpretation it was said that neither a carpenter nor his apprentice could provide the correct solution (Av. Zar. 50b). In similar vein keen scholars were compared to builders (Ber. 64a), to pearl divers capable of reaching great depths in pursuit of treasure (BK 91a), and to weavers (Ber. 24a). The purveyor of the difficult halakhic teachings was compared to a dealer in precious stones for the connoisseur, whereas the more popular but less profound aggadic teacher was compared to the retailer of cheap tinsel goods which all can afford to buy (Sot. 40a).

While the saying of R. Judah in the name of Rav, that a man should study the Torah even if his motives were not of the purest (she-lo li-Shemah), was generally accepted because the right motive would eventually emerge (Pes. 50b), the rabbinic ideal was that of Torah "for its own sake" (li-Shemah). R. Meir said: "Whoever labors in the Torah for its own sake merits many things; and not only that, but the whole world is indebted to him: he is called a friend, beloved, a lover of the All-present, a lover of mankind; it clothes him in meekness and reverence; it fits him to become just, pious, upright and faithful; it keeps him far from sin, and brings him near to virtue; through him the world enjoys counsel and sound knowledge, understanding and strength" (Avot 6:1). The Sifrei (Deut. 41 and 48) remarks: "Suppose you say, I am learning Torah that I may get rich, or that I may be called Rabbi, or that I may gain reward (from God)—the teaching of Scripture is: 'To love the Lord your God' (Deut. 11:13)." "Suppose you say, I   263 will learn Torah in order to be called learned, to have a seat in the academy, to have endless life in the world to come—the teaching is: 'To love the Lord your God.'"

From the rabbinic period and onward great centers of Jewish learning were established. In Palestine there was the academy at the sea-coast village of Jabneh, which came into especial prominence after the destruction of the Temple; at Lydda under the guidance of R. Eliezer b. Hyrcanus and R. Tarfon; at Bene-Berak under R. Akiva; at Usha in Galilee; and there were also centers in Sepphoris, Tiberias, and Caesarea. R. Yose b. Kisma said: "I was once walking by the way, when a man met me and greeted me and I returned his greeting. He said to me, 'Rabbi, from where are you?' I said to him, 'I come from a great city of sages and scribes.' He said to me, 'If you are willing to dwell with us in our place, I will give you a thousand golden dinars and precious stones and pearls.' I said, 'If you were to give me all the silver and gold and precious stones in the world, I would not dwell anywhere but in a home of the Torah'" (Avot 6:9). "Homes of the Torah" rose to a position of importance in third-century C.E. Babylonia. At the beginning of this century two Palestinian-trained scholars, Rav and Samuel, returned to their native Babylonia, the former to found the academy at Sura, the latter to revive the long-established academy at Nehardea. When Nehardea was destroyed during the Roman-Persian wars in the year 259 C.E., Samuel's disciple, R. Judah b. Ezekiel, founded an academy at Pumbedita which existed as a sister and rival institution of Sura for over eight centuries. After the decline of Sura and Pumbedita in the 11th century, new schools sprang up in North Africa and Europe to take their place. The schools of Paris, Troyes, Narbonne, Metz, Worms, Speyer, Altona, Cordoba, Barcelona, and Toledo were renowned in the Middle Ages. From the 16th century, Poland, with its own academies, emerged as the Jewish intellectual center.

Yet it should not be imagined that the rabbinic ideal of Torah study was for the scholar alone. It was binding on every Jew as a *mitzvah*. R. Johanan said in the name of R.

Simeon b. Yohai, "Even though a man reads no more than the *Shema* morning and evening he has thereby fulfilled the precept of 'This book of the law shall not depart'" (Josh. 1:8). It is, however, forbidden to say this in the presence of the ignorant (who would draw the consequence that detailed Torah study is not important). But Rava said it is meritorious to say it in the presence of the ignorant (so that they should not despair of having no part in Torah study; Men. 99b). There is no doubt that the rabbinic ideal was devotion to Torah study on the part of every Jew. Maimonides follows his rabbinic mentors in ruling (Yad, Talmud Torah 1:8): "Every man in Israel is obliged to study the Torah, whether he is firm of body or a sufferer from ill-health, whether a young man or of advanced age with his strength abated. Even a poor man who is supported by charity and obliged to beg at doors, and even one with wife and children to support, is obliged to set aside a period for Torah study by day and by night, as it is said: Thou shalt meditate therein day and night."

The Laws of Study. Three benedictions are to be recited before studying the Torah (Singer, Prayer 5). Since the whole of the Jew's waking life is a time for study these benedictions are recited at the beginning of each day and suffice for the whole day's study. It is considered meritorious to set aside a fixed time each day for Torah study, preferably in the company of others. Each community is expected to have a special "house of study" *(bet ha-midrash),* the sanctity of which is greater than that of a synagogue. As evidence of this it is ruled that while it is not permitted to run from a *bet ha-midrash* to a synagogue it is proper to run from a synagogue to a *bet ha-midrash.* A person unable to study himself should assist in supporting students of the Torah, in whose learning he will then have a share (Sh. Ar., YD 246:1). The Psalmist (Ps. 19:19) speaks of the precepts as "rejoicing the heart." Consequently, it is forbidden to study the Torah during the week of mourning for a close relative or on the Ninth of Av. The rabbis believed in the psychological value of verbal expression and therefore advised that

"Teacher and Young Pupil" by Isidor Kaufman, oil on canvas,
N.Y., Oscar Gruss Collection. Photo Frank Darmstaedter.

Torah study should not be a purely mental exercise but the
words of the text should be uttered aloud, customarily with
a chant. Since the study of the Torah is equal to all the other
precepts, a man should not interrupt his studies to do a good
deed unless there is no one else to carry it out. At the completion of the study of a whole tractate of the Talmud it is
customary to celebrate the occasion with a festive meal.

Scope of Study. "At five years the age is reached for the
study of Scripture, at ten for the study of Mishnah, at thirteen for the fulfillment of the commandments, at fifteen for
the study of Talmud" (Avot 5:21). This may reflect the actual
ages when the young students were gradually introduced to
the more complex subjects of study. Elsewhere (Kid. 30a) it
is said that a man should divide his study time so that a
third is devoted to Scripture, a third to Mishnah, and a third
to Talmud. In the Middle Ages, especially in France and
Germany, most of the students' efforts were directed to the

study of the Babylonian Talmud, in particular to its halakhic portion, with a certain neglect of other topics. Typical is the admission of Rabbenu Tam (Tos. Kid. 30a s.v. *lo*) that the rabbinic schools relied on the fact that the Babylonian Talmud is full of all matters, containing Scripture and Mishnah. This tendency toward a certain narrowing of studies to the virtual exclusion of all except *halakhah* became more and more the norm in Russia and Poland. The medieval thinkers, however, not only urged the study of their discipline but tended to identify philosophical investigation with the highest type of Torah study. Maimonides (Yad, Yesodei ha-Torah 4:13) identified the esoteric disciplines known as the "Work of Creation" and "Work of the Chariot" with Aristotelian physics and metaphysics, respectively, and ranked them higher in the Jewish scale of studies than talmudic debates. Similarly, the kabbalists zealously regarded their subject—the "soul of the Torah" (Zohar III 152a)—as the highest pursuit. The kabbalist Ḥayyim Vital (*Sha'ar ha-Hakdamot*, introd.) recommended that a man should spend an hour or two each day on halakhic casuistry in order to remove the coarse "shell" which surrounds the "fruit," but should devote the rest of his study time to the true science of the kabbalistic mysteries. In the 16th century R. Moses Isserles (YD 246:4) summed up the rabbinic attitude as follows: "A man should only study Scripture, Mishnah, and Gemara, and the Codes based on them. In this way he will acquire this world and the next. But he should not study other sciences. However, it is permitted to study other sciences occasionally, provided that this does not involve in the reading of heretical works. This is called by the Sages 'strolling in Paradise.' A man must not 'stroll in Paradise' until he has filled his stomach with meat and wine, namely, the knowledge of that which is forbidden and that which is permitted and the laws of the precepts."

The rise of the ḥasidic movement in the 18th century presented a serious challenge to the ideal of Torah study as the supreme religious duty. The early ḥasidic masters accused the conventional scholars of engaging in Torah study for motives of fame, wealth, and prestige. Prayer, in the traditional scheme inferior to study, was frequently elevated by the Ḥasidim above study. In addition, the rabbinic ideal of *Torah li-Shemah* ("for its own sake") was interpreted in early Ḥasidism to mean attachment to God *(devekut)*, while studying, especially in the sense of intense concentration on the letters of the text, was believed to reveal on earth the divine forces by means of which God governs the world (see J. G. Weiss in: *Essays Presented to . . . I. Brodie* (1966), Heb. sec. 151–69). The comparatively large number of classical talmudic scholars among the second and third generations of ḥasidic masters prevented, however, any radical departure from the older ideal. In a statement which combines the older ideal with the new ḥasidic emphasis on attachment to God while studying, R. Shneour Zalman of Lyady describes (*Tanya,* ch. 5, *Likkutei Amarim* (1912), 17–19) the religious significance of even the legalistic debates:

> Behold, with regard to every kind of intellectual perception, when one understands and grasps an idea in one's mind, the mind seizes the idea and encompasses it in thought so that the idea is held, surrounded, and enclosed in the mind in which it is comprehended. Conversely, the mind is clothed by an idea it has grasped. For instance, when one understands fully a rule in the Mishnah or the Gemara, his mind seizes the rule and encompasses it and, at the same time, his mind is encompassed by the rule. Now, behold, this rule is the wisdom and will of the Holy One, blessed be He, for it rose in His will that, for instance, when A pleads thus and B thus the rule will be thus. And even if, in fact, a case of this kind will never come before the courts, nonetheless, seeing that it rose in the will and wisdom of the Holy One, blessed be He, that this is the rule, it follows that when a man knows and grasps this rule in his mind in accordance with the decision laid down in the Mishnah or the Gemara or the Codes he grasps, seizes hold of, and encompasses in his mind the will and wisdom of the Holy One, blessed be He, of whom no thought can conceive.

A less mystical approach is advocated in the famous broadside fired against the Ḥasidim by the disciple of the

Gaon of Vilna, R. Ḥayyim of Volozhin (*Nefesh ha-Ḥayyim*). R. Ḥayyim reiterates the conventional view that Torah study even out of ulterior motives is not to be despised and that, moreover, Torah for its own sake does not mean that the student should have God in mind when he studies the texts (such an attempt, R. Ḥayyim argues, would interfere with the intense concentration required for the mastery of the difficult halakhic studies he favored above all else). The student should have a few moments of prayer and devout thoughts before his actual studies and then he should immerse himself in the texts. For R. Ḥayyim (*Nefesh ha-Ḥayyim* (1874), 4:9, 40a) the Torah student has little need for the moralistic and devotional literature (*Musar*) in order to become God-fearing. The Torah itself possesses the property of inducing the fear of God in the hearts of its diligent students. A work in similar vein, from the same school, singing the praises of traditional Torah study, is *Ma'alot ha-Torah* by Abraham, brother of the Gaon of Vilna. The book expresses the ideal taught in the yeshivah of Volozhin and in the Lithuanian yeshivot influenced by it in the 19th and 20th centuries, in which, however, *Musar* did eventually come to occupy a considerable place.

In Western Europe, from the beginning of the 19th century, more and more time had to be found for secular studies, frequently to the detriment of Torah study. Samson Raphael Hirsch adapted the rabbinic ideal of "Torah and *Derekh Ereẓ*" ("worldly occupation") so that the latter came to embrace Western learning and culture. Moreover, the critical investigation of the classical sources known as *Juedische Wissenschaft* posed problems of its own for the traditional ideal of Torah study. In a sense the objective, "scientific" scholarship that is the ideal of this school is opposed to that of study as a devotional exercise, if only because it is far more difficult to treat as sacred texts those that are critically examined, and, conversely, acknowledging the sanctity of a text tends to prejudge critical questions regarding its background and authorship. The achievements of *Juedische Wissenschaft* have shed new light on many obscure corners of Jewish thought and history, but critics such as G. Scholem (*Perakim be-Yahadut*, ed. by E. Spicehandler and J. Petuchowsky (n.d.), 312–327) have questioned whether the movement has ever had any real religious significance. There have undoubtedly emerged two vastly different worlds of Jewish studies: the world of the yeshivot indifferent or even hostile to critical scholarship, and the world of modern learning with no formal interest in study as an act of religious worship. To date there has been little meeting between these two worlds.

3 SABBATH

In the Bible. The etiology of the Sabbath is given in Genesis 1:1–2:3, although the name of the day does not appear there: God worked six days at creating the world; on the seventh he ceased working *(shavat mi-kol mela'khto)*, blessed the day, and declared it holy (see 2:1–3). The special status of the seventh day and its name were disclosed to Israel in the episode of the manna. God supplied each day's need of manna for five days; on the sixth, a double portion was provided to last through the seventh day, on which no manna appeared. Correspondingly, the Israelites were commanded to go out, collect, and prepare each day's portion for the first five days; on the sixth, they were to prepare for two days; on the seventh they were not to go out at all but were to remain at home. Thus they learned that the seventh day was "a Sabbath of the Lord," which they must honor by desisting from their daily food-gathering labor (Ex. 16:22). The fourth of the Ten Commandments generalizes the lesson of the manna. All work *(mela'khah)* is banned on the Sabbath, which here for the first time is given a rationale, drawn directly from the formulation of Genesis 2:1–3 and expressly identifying the Sabbath with the seventh day of creation (Ex. 20:8–11). The meaning of the "blessedness" and "sanctity" of the day is inferable from the manna experience.

According to Exodus 23:12 and 34:21, work is to cease on the seventh day in order to give slaves and draft animals rest; this must be observed even during the critical seasons of plowing and harvest. Deuteronomy's version of the Ten Commandments embodies this humanitarian motive in its divergent rational of the Sabbath rest; Israel is to keep the

Sabbath so that its slaves might rest, and because God, who liberated it from Egyptian bondage, so commanded (Deut. 5:14–15). God's instructions concerning the building of the Tabernacle end, and Moses' conveyance of them to the people begins, with an admonition to keep the Sabbath, indicating its precedence even over the duty of building the sanctuary. The Sabbath is called a sign both of God's consecration of Israel, and of His six-day creation. The rulings are applied in the exemplary tale of Numbers 15:32ff. A man was found collecting wood (to make a fire) on the Sabbath. Apprehended by witnesses and brought before Moses, he was sentenced to death by stoning at the hands of the whole community. Besides the daily sacrificial offering, an additional one, amounting to the total offering of a weekday, was prescribed for the Sabbath (Num. 28:9–10; cf. Num. 28:3–8). Admonitions to observe the Sabbath are coupled once with reverence toward parents (Lev. 19:3; cf. the juxtaposition in the Decalogue), and twice with reverence toward the sanctuary (Lev. 19:30; 26:2). As a time marker, the Sabbath terminated the week. Thus in the Tabernacle cult, the weekly replacement of shew-bread occurred on the Sabbath (Lev. 24:8; I Chron. 9:32).

Only scraps of evidence are available concerning the nature of the Sabbath during the Monarchy. In the Northern Kingdom during the ninth and eighth centuries, Sabbath and New Moon are mentioned together as days when business activity was halted (Amos 8:5), and people paid visits to men of God (II Kings 4:23). From Hosea 2:13 it appears that the Sabbath, like the New Moon and the festival mentioned before it, was among "all the joys" of the North that were under God's doom; this is a precious attestation of the joyous character of the day. In eighth-century Judah, too, Sabbath and New Moon were popularly celebrated in sacred convocations held in the Jerusalem Temple (Isa. 1:13; cf. Lam. 2:6 for later times). Again, as a time marker, the Sabbath was the day on which the palace guard was changed weekly (II Kings 11:5–9). Esteem of the Sabbath rose just before, during, and after the Exile.

Jeremiah 17:19–27 berates the rulers and populace of Judah for condoning the hauling of burdens (market wares) into and within Jerusalem on the Sabbath. In an unprecedented prophecy, the fate of the dynasty and the city is made to depend upon the observance of the Sabbath. Ezekiel contains similar prophecies. Chapter 20:12ff. lays stress on the Sabbath as a sign of Israel's consecration to God; its significance is shown by juxtaposition with all the rest of the divine laws, the Sabbath alone being singled out by name. In catalogs of sins for which Jerusalem was doomed, desecration of the Sabbath occurs repeatedly. As part of his program for a reconstituted Israel, the prophet innovates the priestly duty of seeing that the Sabbath is kept holy (44:24). Noteworthy too is the increase in the number of animals prescribed for the Sabbath sacrifice from double that of the weekday to the befitting number seven (Ezek. 46:4). The Exilic "Isaiah" also singles out the observance of the Sabbath, juxtaposing it to all the rest of the covenant obligations as the precondition of individual and national restoration (56:2, 4, 6; 58:13: "If you call the Sabbath a delight/ That which the Lord has sanctified—a day to be honored"). This prophet looks to an eventual universalization of the Sabbath among all nations (66:23).

The prophets' estimate of the fateful importance of Sabbath observance was taken to heart in the fifth-century community of restored Jerusalem. The public confession of Nehemiah 9:14 once again singles out the Sabbath from all the "commandments, laws, and teachings" given to Israel through Moses. A special clause in the covenant subscribed to by the community's representatives forbids commerce with outsiders on Sabbaths and holy days (Neh. 10:32). Nehemiah enforced this clause rigorously as governor of Judah, reminding the indifferent aristocrats that for desecrating the Sabbath their ancestors had been visited with catastrophe (13:15–22).

HISTORICAL AND LITERARY-HISTORICAL CONSIDERATIONS. Evidence that in the period of the Monarchy the Sabbath was a popular, joyous holy day, marked by cessation of business and celebrated publicly and by the individual, in the Sanctuary and outside it, accords with the pentateuchal traditions that it was among the chief stipulations of the Mosaic covenant. The antiquity and interrelation of the various rationales given in the Pentateuch for the Sabbath are, however, problematic. Such rationales appear in both versions of the Decalogue. That of Exodus, associating the Sabbath with the Creation, is theocentric and sacramental. The sanctity of the day is grounded in an event in the life of God—His cessation from work, His rest, His blessing and consecration. Israel's observance of the day is imitative and out of respect for God's authority. The revelation of the day's sanctity exclusively to Israel—with the attendant obligation to keep it—is a sign of Israel's consecration to God. This rationale is worked out in the creation story, the Exodus Decalogue, and the two admonitions connected with the building of the Tabernacle. Critical analysis assigns all these passages to the Priestly Source (P); their interrelation is, in any event, beyond dispute. The Deuteronomic version of the Decalogue grounds the Sabbath, ambiguously, on the liberation of Israel from slavery. On the one hand, the humane concern of Exodus 23 over the welfare of slaves is involved, on the other, the authority of God to give such laws by virtue of His having redeemed Israel. Since none of these rationales is reflected in the meager extra-pentateuchal passages on the Sabbath, speculation on their age and interrelationship can be based only on internal evidence. Even if conceptual or literary development can be shown, absolute dating is impossible—all the more so when it is borne in mind that presently interrelated ideas may have arisen independently and contemporaneously, and in either case, before their literary embodiment. The compassionate ground of Exodus 23:12 is conceptually simpler than the historical-humanistic one of Deuteronomy. On the other hand, Deuteronomy's is tangential to the essence of the Sabbath day—its holiness. That is accounted for only by the cosmic-sacramental rationale

Three articles used in the *Havdalah* ceremony at the end of
the Sabbath. The gold goblet (German, early 17th century)
is flanked (left) by an 18th-century German silver candle
holder and by a silver and gilt spice box (Austria, 1817).
Jerusalem, Israel Museum. Photo David Harris, Jerusalem.

associated with the Exodus Decalogue. But if the rationale in
Exodus is the best developed, it is not necessarily the latest.

Deuteronomy's seems to have been substituted for it, as more in accord with the spirit of that work, in its version of the Sabbath commandment. Critics consider the sacramental (probably priestly) rationale an Exilic conception, since its esteem of the Sabbath as a sign of Israel's consecration agrees with the Exilic views of the importance of the day. But is a historical explanation really needed for the priestly esteem of a holy day whose centrality in Israel's life is vouched for by its inclusion in the Decalogue—the only holy day so honored? Distinctively Exilic is the appreciation of the Sabbath as a decisive factor in national destiny, and that is lacking in the priestly material as elsewhere in the Pentateuch. Warnings of doom for violation of the covenant laws single out idolatry (Ex. 23:24; Deut. 4:25ff.) as the fatal national sin; Leviticus 26:34–35, 43—of priestly provenance—adds neglect of the Sabbatical (fallow) Year to the causes of national doom. But violation of the Sabbath day is nowhere held to be a factor in Israel's downfall, nor is its observance a warrant of national well-being—as in Jeremiah, Ezekiel, the Exilic Isaiah, and Nehemiah. This suggests that the age of Jeremiah is the *terminus ad quem* of the pentateuchal material on the Sabbath. The increased regard for the Sabbath from Jeremiah's time on is to be connected with the danger of assimilation to the gentiles that loomed since the reign of Manasseh (cf. Zeph. 1), and greatly troubled the religious leaders of the Exile (Ezek. 20:32ff). With the Temple destroyed and the Jews dispersed, the distinctively Israelite day of rest, which allowed of public and private expression and which was not essentially bound up with a sacrificial cult, became a chief vehicle of identification with the covenant community. To mark oneself off from the gentiles by observing the peculiar, weekly "sign" of God's consecration of Israel was an act of loyalty which might well be counted the equivalent of the rest of the covenant commandments, while disregard of the Sabbath might well be considered as serious a breach of faith with the God of Israel as the worship of alien gods. Such in fact was the view of Exilic and post-Exilic thinkers who put forward the idea that the breaking of the Sabbath was a cause of the nation's collapse.

Speculation on the origin of the Sabbath has centered on the apparent Babylonian cognate, *šapattu*, the mid-month day of the full moon, called "the day of calming [the god's] heart"—apparently an auspicious day. The biblical combination of "New Moon and Sabbath" has been thought, accordingly, to reflect what were originally two holy days, one at the start, the other in the middle of the month. Another partial analogy to the Sabbath has been found in the "evil days" of the Babylonian month (mostly at seven-day intervals) on which the king's activity was severely restricted. How the *šapattu* might have been combined with the entirely distinct "evil days," become dissociated from the lunar cycle, and finally emerge as the joyous, weekly "Sabbath of the Lord" has not been persuasively explained. Nonetheless an ultimate connection between the biblical and the Babylonian phenomena seems likely. If so, the history of the Sabbath began with a radical severance from the past. The particularity of the biblical day was its positive sanctity—so that abstention from work on it expressed piety, and that sanctity was a divine ordinance—not a matter of lucky and unlucky times. It was perhaps first grounded on God's compassion toward workers, later brought into relation with the Creation, and later still with the Exodus.

In the Apocrypha. According to the Book of Maccabees, the Sabbath was at one time observed so strictly that on one occasion during the Maccabean revolt, the Jews allowed themselves to be killed rather than resist on the Sabbath (I Macc. 2:31–38). Later, it was decided that the Sabbath may be transgressed in order to save life (I Macc. 2:40–41). The Book of Jubilees (2:17–32 and 50:6–13) is extremely severe on Sabbath desecration, death being the penalty even for such offenses as walking any distance, fasts, or traveling on a ship on the Sabbath. The Book of Jubilees (50:8) also forbids marital relations on the Sabbath, whereas in the rabbinic teaching it is considered meritorious to perform these on the Sabbath (BK 82a, Ket. 62b).

In Rabbinic Literature. The rabbis wax eloquent on the value of Sabbath observance. "If Israel keeps one Sabbath as it should be kept, the Messiah will come. The Sabbath is equal to all the other precepts of the Torah" (Ex. R. 25:12). "God said to Moses: 'Moses, I have a precious gift in My treasury whose name is the Sabbath and I want to give it to Israel. Go and tell them'" (Beẓah 16a). "The Sabbath is one sixtieth of the world to come" (Ber. 57b). "The Sabbath increases Israel's holiness. 'Why does so-and-so close his shop?' 'Because he keeps the Sabbath.' 'Why does so-and-so refrain from work?' 'Because he keeps the Sabbath.' Furthermore, whoever keeps the Sabbath testifies of Him at whose word the world came into being; that He created the world in six days and rested on the seventh" (Mekh. SbY to Ex. 31:14). The juxtaposition of the instructions to build the Sanctuary and the prohibition of Sabbath work caused the rabbis to deduce that it was forbidden on the Sabbath to do any work that was required for the Sanctuary. The rabbinic definition of forbidden Sabbath work is, therefore, that which was needed for the Sanctuary (Mekh. SbY. to Ex. 35:1; Shab. 49b). Any work analogous to those types used for the building of the Sanctuary is classified as being biblically forbidden. There are thus 39 main classes of work ("fathers of work," *avot*) used in the building of the Sanctuary, and many others derived from these ("offspring," *toledot*), with only slight technical differences between "father" and "offspring" (BK 2a). Watering of plants, for instance, is a *toledah* of sowing; weeding, of plowing; adding oil to a burning lamp, of lighting a fire. The Mishnah (Shab. 7:2) gives a list of the 39 main classes of work. (It has been noted that the number 39 is a standard number in rabbinic literature and that these types of work are all of a kind obtaining in the rabbinic period.) The Mishnah (Ḥag. 1:8) also states that the laws of forbidden work on the Sabbath are as mountains hanging by a hair, for there is little on the subject in the Scriptures yet the rules are many. In addition

Miniature oven used on the Sabbath for keeping food warm.
Amsterdam, Collection of the Jewish Historical Museum.

to the biblical prohibitions, there are various rabbinic prohibitions introduced as a "fence to the Torah" (Avot 1:1), such as the handling of tools or money *(mukzeh)*, riding a horse, instructing a gentile to do work. These rabbinic prohibitions are known as *shevut* ("rest"; Bezah 5:2). One who profanes the Sabbath in public is treated as an idolator (Ḥul. 5a). Conversely, whoever observes the Sabbath as it should be, is forgiven his sins, (Shab. 118b).

The Sabbath is a festive day and three meals should be eaten on it (Shab. 118a). It was considered meritorious for a man to make some preparations for the Sabbath himself, even if he had servants to do it for him (Kid. 41a). R. Safra used to singe the head of an animal, R. Huna used to light the lamp, R. Papa to plait the wicks, R. Ḥisda to cut up the beets, Rabbah and R. Joseph to chop the wood, R. Zera to kindle the fire (Shab. 119a). R. Ḥanina would say on the eve of the Sabbath: "Come let us go out to meet the Bride, the Queen." R. Yannai used to adorn himself and say: "Come O Bride, come O Bride" (*ibid.,* BK 32a–b). Out of respect for the sacred day, it was forbidden to fast on the eve of the Sabbath (Ta'an. 27b). In a well-known passage (Shab. 119b), it is said that on the eve of the Sabbath two ministering angels accompany a man from the synagogue to his home. If, when he arrives home, he finds the lamp burning, the table laid, and the couch covered with a spread, the good angel declares, "May it be thus on another Sabbath too" and the evil angel is obliged to answer "Amen." But if not, the evil angel declares, "May it be thus on another Sabbath too" and the good angel is obliged to answer "Amen." At the beginning of the Sabbath, the special sanctification (*Kiddush*) is recited (Pes. 106a), and after the termination of the Sabbath the *Havdalah* ("distinction") benediction (which signifies the separation of the Sabbath from the weekday) is recited (Ber. 33a), both over a cup of wine. A man should wear special garments in honor of the Sabbath; he should walk differently from the way he does on a weekday, and even his speech should be different (Shab. 11a–b).

In Jewish Thought. From an early period, the Sabbath became a day of spiritual refreshment. Philo (II Mos. 216) and Josephus (Apion, 2:175) refer to the practice of public discourses on the Torah on this day, as do the rabbis (Yal., Ex. 108). Philo (Decal. 96) sees the Sabbath as an opportunity for man to imitate his Creator who rested on the seventh day. Man, too, should rest from his weekday labors in order to devote himself to comtemplation and to the improvement of his character. The Midrash (Mekh. SbY to 20:11) similarly states that if God, who exerts no effort, "writes about Himself" that he rested how much more should man rest of whom it is said that he was born to toil. The benediction for the Sabbath afternoon service sums up the rabbinic attitude to the Sabbath as a precious gift from God, and as a sacred day kept even by the Patriarchs: "Thou art One and Thy Name is One, and who is like Thy people a unique nation upon the earth? Glorious greatness and a crown of salvation, even the day of rest and holiness, Thou hast given unto Thy people—Abraham was glad, Isaac rejoiced, Jacob and his sons rested thereon—a rest granted in love, a true and faithful rest, a rest in peace and tranquillity, in quietude and safety, a perfect rest wherein Thou delightest. Let Thy children perceive and know that this their rest is from Thee and by their rest may they hallow Thy Name."

The medieval Jewish philosophers tend to dwell on the symbolic nature of the day. For Maimonides (*Guide*, 2, 31), the Sabbath has a twofold significance: It teaches the true opinion that God created the world, and it provides man with physical rest and refreshment. According to Isaac Arama (*Akedat Yizḥak*, 55 ed. Bialystok (1849), 285–89), the Sabbath teaches the three fundamental principles of Judaism: belief in *creatio ex nihilo*, in revelation (because the Sabbath is a time when the Torah is studied), and in the world to come (of which the Sabbath is a foretaste). Judah Halevi looks upon the Sabbath as a God-given opportunity for men to enjoy complete rest of body and soul for a sixth part of their lives, in a way denied even to kings, who know nothing of this precious boon of complete cessation from toil and distraction (*Kuzari*, 3, 10).

Samson Raphael Hirsch (*Horeb*, section 2:21; tr. by I. Grunfeld, 1 (1962), 61–78) understands the prohibition of creative activity on the Sabbath (the types of forbidden work do not so much involve effort, as they are creative) to be a lesson for man to acknowledge his Creator as Creator of everything there is. Man is allowed to rule over the world for six days by God's will, but is forbidden on the seventh day to fashion anything for his own purpose. On each Sabbath man restores the world to God, as it were, and thus proclaims that he enjoys only a borrowed authority.

The Laws and Customs of the Sabbath. The mistress of the house kindles at least two candles before the advent of the

"The Blessing over the Candles" by Isidor Kaufmann (1853–1921). New York, Oscar Gruss Collection. Photo Frank J. Darmstaedter, New York.

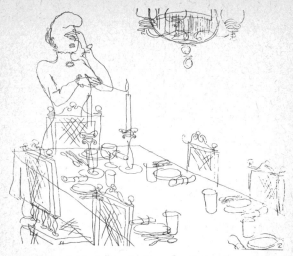

"Lighting the Sabbath Candles," a pencil drawing by Imre Szigeti (1897–). Jerusalem, Courtesy S. Gorr.

Sabbath, one corresponding to "remember the Sabbath day" (Ex. 20:8), the other to "observe the Sabbath day" (Deut. 5:12). For each meal two whole loaves of bread are placed on the table, covered by a cloth, to correspond to the double portion of manna for the Sabbath (Ex. 16:22–26). Before the *Kiddush* is recited, the parents bless the children. During the festive meals of the day, special table hymns (*zemirot*) are chanted. Whenever possible, guests should be invited to participate in the Sabbath meals. There is a special order of service for Sabbath in the synagogue. Psalms are recited before the evening service on Friday night and the morning service includes the weekly readings from the Torah, as well as a *Musaf Amidah*. The afternoon service also includes a Torah reading from the portion to be read on the following Sabbath. When the Sabbath is over, the *Havdalah* benediction is recited, together with a

"Ushering in the Sabbath," a painting by Moritz Oppenheim, Frankfort, 19th century. New York, Oscar Gruss Collection. Photo Frank Darmstaedter, New York.

benediction over spices (to restore the soul saddened by the
departure of the day), and over light (which could neither
be lit nor blessed on the Sabbath). Where there is danger to
life (*pikku'ah nefesh*), the Sabbath must be set aside and
Sabbath profanation in such circumstances is meritorious
in the extreme. Unlike the Karaites, who took the verse

Silver-gilt Sabbath candlesticks from Danzig, c.1680, chased with biblical scenes and engraved in Hebrew with the names Naphtali and Zipporah Herz. Cleveland, Ohio, Joseph B. Horwitz Judaica Collection.

"let no man go out of his place on the seventh day" (Ex. 16:29) literally, the rabbis placed no restrictions on freedom of movement within one's town, but they prohibited any walking outside the town beyond a distance of 2,000 cubits (a little more than half a mile). This boundary is known as the *tehum shabbat* (Sabbath limit). It is, however, permitted to place, before the Sabbath, sufficient food for two meals at the limits of the 2,000 cubits; then, by a legal fiction know as *eruv,* this place becomes one's "abode" for the duration of the Sabbath, so that the 2,000 cubits may then be walked from there. It is forbidden to instruct a non-Jew to do any work on the Sabbath which is not permitted to a Jew, unless it is for the sake of health. In cold climes, the heating of the home by a non-Jew falls under the heading "for the sake of health."

Modern inventions have produced a host of new questions regarding Sabbath observance. Orthodox Judaism forbids travel by automobile on the Sabbath, Reform Judaism permits it. Conservative Judaism has differing views on this question, but generally permits travel by automobile on the Sabbath solely for the purpose of attending synagogue. The basic legal question regarding the switching on of electric lights is whether the noncombustive type of burning produced by electricity falls under the prohibition of making a fire or any of the other prohibitions listed above. Orthodox Jews refrain from the use of electrical appliances on the Sabbath, with the exception of the refrigerator, which may be opened and closed on the grounds that any electrical current produced in the process is incidental and without express intention. It has, however, become the practice for observant Jews to use electrical appliances on the Sabbath which are operated by time switches set before the Sabbath. In Israel, on religious kibbutzim, the same procedure is used to milk the cows on the Sabbath. Israel also has local bylaws forbidding certain activities on the Sabbath. There is, however, no comprehensive law covering the whole country. Thus, whereas the public transport does not operate on the Sabbath in Jerusalem and in Tel Aviv, it does in Haifa. Except for specifically non-Jewish sections of the country, the Sabbath is the official day of rest on which all business and stores must close, but there is some doubt as to what is a business for this law.

4 FESTIVALS

The Hebrew for festival is חַג , *ḥag;* מוֹעֵד , *mo'ed;* or
יוֹם טוֹב , *yom tov.*

Introduction. The root of חַג is חָגַג *ḥagog,* to celebrate, or
possibly חוּג *ḥug,* to go round. It is related to the Arabic *ḥajja*
which means to go on a pilgrimage from which comes ḥajj,
the pilgrimage to Mecca. The term *mo'ed* means an
appointed place, time, or season.

The festivals can be divided into two main categories
each of which can be subdivided: (1) those commanded by
the Pentateuch, and (2) those added later. The Pentateuchal
festivals are: a) the Sabbath (not strictly a festival), b) the
three pilgrim festivals, Passover, Shavuot, and Sukkot,
with Shemini Aẓeret which is considered in some respects a
festival in its own right, c) the New Year (Rosh
Ha-Shanah) and the Day of Atonement, d) Rosh Ḥodesh,
the first day of the day of the new month. These divisions
can however be still further divided. Rosh Ha-Shanah and
the Day of Atonement, while obviously belonging to a
single pattern, nevertheless differ from each other completely. The three pilgrim festivals, too, although similar in
many aspects differ in detail. There is, furthermore, a
decided difference between the first and last festival days
and the middle days termed *ḥol ha-mo'ed* (see below). The
second category too can be subdivided: Purim and
Ḥanukkah; the first being biblical (Book of Esther) and
the second from the Hasmonean period; memorial days
such as Lag Ba-Omer (medieval) and the 15th of Av
(mishnaic) to which may be added Tu bi-Shevat; thirdly,
certain festival days added in modern times to mark historic
events of Jewish importance. Apart from the above are also

festival days of individuals or communities to record salvation or a similar event.

A festival is characterized by three factors: (1) rejoicing, which mostly takes the form of ceremonial meals (with the exception of the Day of Atonement), and, on the more important biblical festivals, the prohibition of work; (2) the liturgy (or in Temple times, the special sacrificial service); and (3) special ceremonials of the festival, such as eating of *mazzot* on Passover (biblical injunction), lighting of the candles of Ḥannukah (talmudic), and the planting of saplings on Tu bi-Shevat (custom).

The liturgy is in effect dictated by the type of festival. The main changes from everyday prayer are mainly in: a) the *Amidah,* b) the addition of *Hallel,* c) the reading of the Torah, d) the *Musaf* service representing the special sacrifices of the day (for details, see above— Prayer). It can generally be stated that the less important the festival, the less changes are made in the liturgy. On Sabbath, the pilgrim festivals, and the high holidays, it is customary for the woman to light candles accompanied by a special benediction, and (except Sabbath) also by the *she-heḥeyanu,* whereas the man makes sanctification *(Kiddush)* over wine (except on the Day of Atonement). It is interesting to note that the national day of mourning, Ninth of Av, is also regarded in a sense as a festival, as it is termed *"mo'ed"* in Lamentations (1:15), and, according to tradition, will be the greatest festival in the time to come (with reference to Jer. 31:13).

In the Bible. The festivals mentioned in the Pentateuch as "feasts" *(חַגִּים haggim)* are Passover (Ex. 12:14), also called "the feast of unleavened bread"; Shavuot, otherwise "the feast of harvest" (Ex. 23:16) or the "day of the first fruits"; and Sukkot, also known as "the feast of ingathering" *(ibid.)* and sometimes called simply "feast" *(ḥag)* in the Bible. The sages, too, mostly use the term *ḥag* by itself to refer to Sukkot. Common to all three festivals is the pilgrimage to Jerusalem from which the term (שָׁלֹשׁ רְגָלִים "the three pilgrim festivals") is derived. The term "appoint-

Hoshana Rabba at the Amsterdam Portuguese Synagogue by Bernard Picart. Amsterdam, Stedelijk Museum.

ed seasons" *(mo'adim)* in the Pentateuch, however, includes also Rosh Ha-Shanah and the Day of Atonement, as in the verse "These are the appointed seasons of the Lord, even holy convocations, which ye shall proclaim in their appointed season" (Lev. 23:4). At times the term "appointed seasons" is used for all the days which are "holy convocations," including the Sabbath. Rosh Ḥodesh, on which work is not forbidden by biblical injunction and which is not mentioned at all with the festivals in Leviticus, is nevertheless included among "the appointed seasons" in the section on sacrifices (Num. 28:11). It seems that the prophets, too, sometimes use "appointed seasons" to refer to the Sabbath and Rosh Ḥodesh though mostly these days are not indicated. In one instance only the three pilgrim festivals are included "on the appointed seasons, three times in the year" (II Chron. 8:13). Thus the term "season" generally has a wider meaning in the Bible than "feast" because only the three pilgrim festivals are called "feast," whereas "season" usually comprises also Rosh Ha-Shanah and the Day of

"In the Sukkah" by Moritz Daniel Oppenheim, oil on canvas. N.Y., Oscar Gruss Collection. Photo Frank Darmstaedter.

Atonement. A day of feasting and joy, whether fixed by individuals or established by the whole people to be observed by succeeding generations, which does not entail special sacrifices, is called *yom tov* (I Sam. 25:8; Esth. 8:17).

The festivals, like the Sabbath, have their origin in Divine commandments. Leviticus commands not only "it is a Sabbath unto the Lord" (23:3) and "the Sabbaths of the Lord," but also "the appointed seasons of the Lord" (23:4, 44). In the Bible the common expression "feast of the Lord" (see Hos. 9:5) or "a feast to the Lord" refers to Passover as well as to Shavuot and to Sukkot. Similarly, the festival which the children of Israel were to celebrate with sacrifices to the Lord in the wilderness is termed "feast." Aaron, too, at the incident of the golden calf, proclaims "Tomorrow shall be a feast to the Lord" (Ex. 32:5).

The Source of the Festivals. In the pagan religions of the ancient East, the festivals were established by man in order to find favor with the deity and prevent disasters. It was against this concept that the prophets so trenchantly militated. The biblical concept, on the other hand, is the exact antithesis, for not only are the festivals commanded by God but the service on these days as well. The festival sacrifices (*Musaf*) are not offered for any material reward, but in obedience to the Divine commmand. Among the sins of Jeroboam is mentioned his ordainment of a feast "like unto the feast that is in Judah" on the 15th of the eighth month "in the month which he had devised of his own heart," and his bringing sacrifices on it (I Kings 12:32–33). Apart from this incident, there is no mention in the Bible of alterations to the festivals as stated in the Pentateuch or the creation of new ones; "the feast of the Lord from year to year in Shiloh" (Judg. 21:19) is seemingly one of the festivals mentioned in the Pentateuch. In the Bible various reasons are given for the festivals. Some are specifically connected with the exodus from Egypt. Passover, the feast of unleavened bread, is celebrated on the anniversary of the day that God led the children of Israel out of Egypt. The paschal lamb was commanded for all generations to commemorate "that He passed over the houses of the children of Israel in Egypt" (Ex. 12:27) and the unleavened bread is in memory of the haste with which the Israelites left Egypt. Similarly, the reason for dwelling in tabernacles on Sukkot is "that your generations may know that I made the children of Israel to dwell in booths when I brought them out of the land of Egypt" (Lev. 23:43); and even for Shavuot it is said "And thou shalt remember that thou wast a bondman in Egypt; and thou shalt observe and do these statutes" (Deut. 16:12; cf. Naḥmanides ad loc.; cf. Deut.

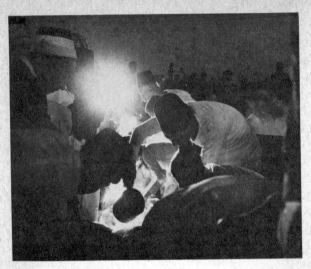

The sacrifice of the paschal lamb by the Samaritans on Mt. Gerizim, 1968. A sheep is being plucked with the aid of boiling water. Courtesy Government Press Office, Tel Aviv.

5:15 on Sabbath). The recital on the offering of the first fruits also testifies to the exodus from Egypt (Deut. 26:5–10). Together with their theological-historical sources, the festivals are also connected with the annual agricultural cycle. Shavuot is the festival "of the first fruits of wheat harvest" (Ex. 34:22) on which two loaves made from the new wheat crop were offered; hence its names: "the harvest feast" and "the day of the first fruits." Sukkot is "the feast of the ingathering" at the end of the agricultural year when the ingathering from the threshing floor and the winepress is completed. Even Passover, in the spring, apart from the commemoration of the exodus, has an agricultural basis. The *omer* sacrifice of the new barley was offered on the second day of the festival and permitted the partaking of the new grain crop.

The festivals thus seem to be rooted in two distinct

sources which, according to some scholars, are independent of each other. They claim that the agricultural festivals antedate their theological-historical source, specifically pointing to the fact that Passover and Sukkot are celebrated in seasons when night and day are roughly of equal length. Their contention, however, is unacceptable since each festival in the Pentateuch is based on two distinct types of reasons stated sometimes even in the same paragraph. In the case of Passover, the agricultural motif is added to the clearly historical aspect of the festival, while with Sukkot, the historical aspect of the festival is added to the agricultural although this historical aspect is not specifically connected with the time of the year of Sukkot. At any rate the distinction between "the ancient folk festivals" and the later "theological festivals" is doubtful. Contrary to the three pilgrim festivals which are mentioned in the Bible together with their double motifs, no reason, save it being a Divine precept, is given for the day of "memorial proclaimed with the blast of horns" (i. e., the later Rosh Ha-Shanah), celebrated on the first day of the seventh month. The Day of Atonement, however, was inaugurated for the atonement of sins.

Celebration of the Festival. The Pentateuch cites two specific commandments in connection with the "seasons of the Lord, holy convocations": work is forbidden and, as a remembrance, sacrifices are to be brought to the accompaniment of trumpet blowing before the Lord (Num. 10:10). The Bible also specifically commands rejoicing on Shavuot (Deut. 16:11) and especially on Sukkot (Lev. 23:40; Deut. 16:14–15; cf. Neh. 8:17). Such commandments, however, were common to all the festivals, as is proven for instance by the great rejoicings on Passover (Ezra 6:22; II Chron. 30:21ff.) and those "on the first day of the seventh month" (Neh. 8:2, 9ff.). These celebrations, especially when the people gathered in the Temple, are testified to by Isaiah "Ye shall have a song as in the night when a feast is hallowed; And gladness of heart, as when one goeth with a pipe to come into the mountain of the Lord to the Rock of Israel" 293

(30:29). The festivals are therefore referred to as days of mirth, gladness, and joy. It seems that the rejoicing of the people at the golden calf "[they] offered burnt offerings, and brought peace offerings and the people sat down to eat and drink and rose up to make merry" (Ex. 32:6) was typical of all festive celebrations, in which the huge feast as well as dancing occupied a prominent place. The celebrations were, however, limited by the sanctity of the festival, and there is no hint in the Bible of the orgies, wildness, and promiscuous abandon connected with the pagan festivals in the ancient Near East. The Pentateuch even stresses the fact that the rejoicings are of the whole community, including slaves, and commands not to forget the levite, the proselyte, the orphan, or the widow (Deut. 16:11, 14). During the early Second Temple period it was customary to send presents to the needy on the festivals (Neh. 8:10–12).

In the Apocrypha and Hellenistic Jewish Literature. During the early Second Temple period the laws of the Sabbath and festivals came to be very strictly observed. The festivals were celebrated with great rejoicings and it was customary to invite the poor to the feasting (Tob. 2:1–2). Many would go up to Jerusalem on all the festivals. During the persecutions of Antiochus, observance of the Sabbath and festivals was forbidden. Demetrius, however, declared the Sabbaths, New Moons, and festivals, including three days before and after, to be holidays for all Jews in the Seleucid kingdom (testified to in his letter to Jonathan the Maccabee; I Macc. 10:34).

In contrast to the Greek and Roman festival celebrations which were accompanied by gluttonous, drunken, and bacchanalian revelries, Hellenistic Jewish writers stressed the uniqueness of the Jewish festivals. Philo claims that the cessation of work on the festival was a possible danger since eating and drinking arouse lust and other low instincts. Giving vent to these feelings without restriction could lead to vice and limitless evil since the festival would serve as a protective means against retribution. The lawgiver therefore did not permit his people to celebrate their festivals in the way of other nations but commanded them first to purify themselves through the restriction of their desires for pleasure at the very time of their celebrations. Then they were to gather at the Temple to participate in the hymns, prayers, and sacrifices so that the place, the sight, and the service would influence their finer senses—sight and hearing—with a spirit of piety. Last but not least, by commanding the sacrifice of a sin-offering, he warned the people to stop sinning; for it seems that a person would not transgress at the very time he asks for forgiveness. Those gathered for the festive banquet do not come to stuff themselves with meat and wine like other nations, but through prayers and psalms follow the tradition of their forefathers. Therefore the Day of Atonement is also a festival though the partaking of food is forbidden and there is no wild rejoicing, merrymaking, and dancing accompanied by song and music which arouse uncontrollable desires. Ignorance of the nature of true happiness leads people to assume that on the festivals joy is to be achieved through physical indulgences (Philo, Spec. 2:193–4). Philo further states that the true significance of the festival is to find pleasure and enjoyment through meditation about the world and the harmony existing in it (*ibid.*, 2:52). Were man's virtue constantly to rule his desires, his whole life, from his birth to the day he dies, would be one long festival (*ibid.*, 2:42).

In Talmudic Literature. The term *ḥaggim,* as referring to Jewish festivals, hardly occurs in rabbinical literature (except in prayers which are in an archaic language). Instead, the festivals mentioned in the Bible are called *mo'adot. Mo'ed* (though not *ha-mo'ed*) in the singular is mostly applied to the intermediate days, especially to distinguish them from festival days on which no work at all is allowed. These are usually called *yom tov.* As in the Bible, *yom tov* was also applied in rabbinic literature to days of rejoicing (general or private) not mentioned in the Pentateuch, and on which work was allowed. These were either new festivals ordained for all times or days of rejoicing for certain events. It is doubtful whether the Day of Atonement was included in the term *yom tov* (but see Ta'an. 4:8).

The commandment concerning the feast of unleavened bread, that " ... no manner of work shall be done in them ..., save that which every man must eat, that only may be done by you" (Ex. 12:16), was interpreted by the sages to mean that work, for purposes of eating, is allowed on all those festivals (Sif. Num. 147) on which "servile work" is prohibited by the Pentateuch. (In contrast to the Sabbath and the Day of Atonement where it is ordained "ye shall do no work.") The types of work forbidden on the Sabbath but allowed on *yom tov* for the purpose of eating (Beẓah 5:2) are: kneading, baking, slaughtering, skinning, salting, cutting, burning, and carrying (the last two are also permitted for purposes other than eating; Beẓah 12a–b). Hunting, reaping, sheaf binding, threshing, winnowing, selecting, and grinding are forbidden (as to sifting, opinion is divided). Types of work for the indirect preparation of food (מכשירי אוכל נפש) are permitted. The differentiation between the types of work allowed and those forbidden is apparently based on customs prevalent at the time. Except for the work permitted for the sake of food and some other minor allowances made (see Beẓah 5:1), everything forbidden on the Sabbath is also forbidden on the festivals. Moreover, the prohibition of handling *mukẓeh* (non-usable) objects is stricter on the festivals than on the Sabbath so that the festival prohibitions should not be taken lightly (Beẓah 2a–b).

The festivals are also similar to the Sabbath in rejoicing and in honoring the day. All halakhic Midrashim interpret the term "holy convocation" to mean that the festivals are to be sanctified "with food and drink and clean clothes" and "the Day of Atonement, on which there is no food or drink, the Torah states that one must honor it with clean clothes" (Shab. 119a). It was usual to cut one's hair before the festivals. Similarly, it was the custom, later incorporated

Passover *seder* of Kurdish Jews in Jerusalem. The ceremonial *seder* plate is being raised. Photo David Harris, Jerusalem.

in the *halakhah*, not to work or eat in the late afternoon preceding the festival. In the Middle Ages, it became customary to light a candle on the eve of the festival and to recite a blessing, as on the Sabbath. Rejoicing on the festival involved eating and drinking (concerning the prohibition of fasting see Judith 8:6; TJ, Ta'an. 2:12) and giving presents to the women and children. During the tannaitic period the sages disputed the question as to how a person should spend the festival: "R. Eliezer says that a person should either eat and drink or sit and study on the festival; R. Joshua declares that a person's time should be divided between eating and drinking and the house of learning." R. Johanan, the *amora*, found support in the Scriptures for both opinions (Pes. 68b; cf. Beẓah 15b; Sif. Deut. 135, is similar to R. Joshua's opinion). The *amoraim* also disagreed on the similar question as to whether the festivals were meant for the study of Torah, or whether eating and drinking was the main reason and permission to study the Torah on them but a secondary consideration (TJ, Shab. 15:3). According to the sources it seems that it was customary to go to the *bet ha-midrash* both on the eve of the festival as well as in the morning. Prayers, however, were shortened because of the festive meal. The sages, while stating that "the festivals were given to Israel only for their own pleasure" (S. Buber (ed.), *Midrash Tanḥuma* (1885), Mid. Tanḥuma Gen. 4), nevertheless noted the difference between Israel and the nations: "You grant the nations many festivals and they eat, drink, and are wanton, they go to the theater, the circus, and anger You by word and deed; but Israel is not so. You grant them festivals and they eat, drink, and rejoice, and go to the synagogues and *battei midrash* ("houses of learning") and multiply their prayers, their festival offerings, and their sacrifices" (PdRK 340–1). It seems that R. Joshua's opinion "half to the Lord and half for yourselves" was practiced and became *halakhah*. However, practices of drunkenness and licentiousness are also mentioned (Beẓah 4a; Kid. 81a); R. Abba bar Memel, a Palestinian *amora*, states "Did they not forbid work on the intermediate days only in order that people should eat, drink, and diligently study the Torah? But they eat, drink, and are wanton" (TJ, MK 2:3)—exactly as the Midrash describes the gentile nations.

Paul opposed the observance of the Sabbath and the festivals (Gal. 4:10; Col. 2:16). Traces of the Jewish-Christian dispute concerning the festivals are found in the Midrash (S. Buber (ed.), *Midrash Tanḥuma* (1885), *Pinḥas*, para. 17). The sharp condemnation by the sages of "he who despises the festivals" (Avot 3:12; Pes. 118a) is probably directed against the Christian heretics, and probably because of them the observance of the Sabbath and the festivals was stressed so strongly in Ereẓ Israel. Later, in the Middle Ages, Judah Halevi states that the festivals were the main factor which upheld Israel in its exile (*Kuzari* 3:10).

The Intermediate Days. Apart from the laws governing the *musaf* sacrifices on the festivals, nothing is stated about the festival days following the first day of Passover and Sukkot, respectively, which the sages called *ḥolo shel mo'ed* or just *mo'ed*. They taught that these days are also to be considered as days of "holy convocation." Only partial work is permitted on them for "the Torah gave the sages the power of determining on which day it is forbidden to do work and on which day it is allowed; which work is forbidden and which allowed" (Sif. Deut. 135). Generally, work which prevents deterioration or loss is permitted on the intermediate days; where this is not the case, work is forbidden. It is forbidden to delay work in order to do it on the intermediate days except for public works. In Erez Israel stringent laws were imposed whereby no work at all was done, even if it was required for the festival itself. The *halakhah*, however, conformed to the Babylonian practice which allowed some work (as mentioned above). All must rejoice on the intermediate days; thus marriage is not permitted on these days as rejoicing should not be mixed, *ein me'arevim simḥah be-simḥah* (MK 8b).

Second Days of Festivals. In the Diaspora an extra day (in Heb. *yom tov sheni shel galuyyot*) is added to each of the biblical festival days, except for *ḥol ha-mo'ed* and the Day of Atonement. The practice originated because of the uncertainty in the Diaspora of the day on which the Sanhedrin announced the New Moon. Later, when astronomical calculations were relied upon, the sages declared that the custom should nevertheless be accepted as permanent. Although the Day of Atonement was an exception, as a double fast day was considered too difficult, there were individuals who observed two days. Rosh Ha-Shanah, on the other hand, gradually came to be observed as a two-day festival even in Erez Israel; beginnings of the custom here, too, are to be found in the Second Temple period (RH 4:4), although it became unanimous only in the Middle Ages. With regard to Passover and Sukkot, the first day of *ḥol ha-mo'ed* was observed as a full festival day in the Diaspora while an additional day was added at the end. Thus on Passover a second *seder* is held on the second night and an eighth day is added. The day following Shemini Aẓeret at the completion

"The Rejoicing of the Law in the Ancient Synagogue of Leghorn" by Solomon Alexander Hart, 1841/42, oil on canvas. New York, Jewish Museum, Oscar Gruss Collection.

of Sukkot became known as Simḥat Torah, the "Rejoicing of the Law." As long as the new moon was determined by visual evidence there was no fixed date for Shavuot, so that the day of the festival was not in any doubt as it was always on the 50th day counting from the second day of Passover, which day would have been ratified in good time by the Sanhedrin messengers. Despite this, a second day was observed in the Diaspora for Shavuot as well. It would appear that certain sources regard the second day as a punishment and that for its observance no reward is to be expected (TJ, Eruv. 3:9). The only difference in observance between the additional days and regular festival days is in the practice concerning burial, the use of medicine (Sh.Ar., OḤ, 496:2), and laws regarding *nolad* (the appearance or creation of something not previously in existence). An egg, for instance, which was laid on the first day of the festival remains forbidden all that day but may be eaten on the second day (*ibid.* 513:5). On the second day of Rosh Ha-Shanah, however, *nolad* is not permitted to be used because the two days are considered one long day. Certain trends in Conservative Judaism have made the second festival day optional while the Reform have abolished it altogether, even for Rosh Ha-Shanah.

A person from Erez Israel who temporarily visits the Diaspora has to observe the additional day when in company, so as not to arouse controversy (*ibid.* 496:3, cf. Pes. 4:1). A visitor to Erez Israel, however, observes only one day if he has any intention of staying. According to Zevi Hirsch Ashkenazi, even without such intention he observes one day only (*Ḥakham Zevi,* resp. no. 167).

Part Six:

HISTORY

1 ISRAEL AND JERUSALEM

There is no other faith in the world which is attached to a specific territory as is Judaism. There is in this fact a double element of paradox. On the one hand, Judaism rightly claims that its religious values are universal and that it looks forward to the time when universal peace and justice will prevail, when "The world will be perfected under the kingdom of the Almighty and all mankind will call upon Thy name; . . . when they will prostrate themselves before thee and give honour to the glory of thy kingdom and thou will reign over them for ever" (*Alenu* prayer). On the other hand, the Jewish people have maintained a particularistic, permanent bond with the Land of Israel, despite the fact that they have been fated to be in exile for a longer period than they enjoyed independence in their own territory. The paradox was partly resolved in two ways: negatively, in that for centuries the Jews had none of the privileges and prerogatives of citizenship in the countries of their sojourn; and positively, by their doctrinal faith, expressed in teaching as in prayer, which made them regard themselves as sojourners, robbed for a while of the only land they might lawfully claim to be their own. For them. it was God's inscrutable will that they should do atonement in exile. But it was equally the Divine Promise that they would be led home again. In spirit, as in fact, they lived out their lives as expatriates, their hopes never dying nor even dormant.

Jewish memory of and attachment to the Land of Israel were unbroken. Three times every day, wherever he found himself, every Jew turned toward Jerusalem and entreated: "And may our eyes behold when Thou returnest to Zion in mercy." Partaking of food, every Jew thanked God for the "pleasant, goodly and ample land which Thou hast caused our fathers to inherit." Every Jew besought his Maker for "mercy upon Jerusalem Thy city, upon Zion the dwelling place of Thy glory, upon the kingdom of David and the Temple, and for the building of Jerusalem," that "the All-Merciful may bring us upright to our Land."

At festivals, a Jew would pray: "For our sins we have been exiled from our Land, and thrust away from our country.... May it be Thy will, O Lord our God and God of our fathers, that Thou again have mercy upon us .... bring near those of us who are scattered among the nations and gather our dispersed from the four corners of the earth. Bring us to Zion, Thy city, in gladness and to Jerusalem, the site of Thy Temple, with everlasting joy."

When a Jew in exile prayed for rain, it was at the season when the far-off soil of the Holy Land stood in need of it; the seasons of the country in which he found himself mattered not at all. When he rejoiced in the harvest festival, it was to mark harvest time in Israel. And when he could not conceive of salvation to come about by natural means, he waited for it to come by a miracle. This place of the Land of Israel as part of the Jewish religion, as distinct from the purely national aspect, had a dual importance. On the one hand there was a positive religious injunction per se to dwell in the Land. It is incorporated in all the classical codes: Maimonides formulated it thus: "It is forbidden to emigrate from the Land of Israel and go abroad, unless one goes abroad to study the Torah, or to marry, or to rescue one's property, and one must then return to the Land.... But one is forbidden to make one's permanent home abroad, unless famine prevails in the Land of Israel.... But though it is permitted, it is not in conformity with a noble conception of conduct ...

"The greatest of our Sages used to kiss the very stones of the Land and roll in its dust.... The Rabbis declared that the sins of him who lives in the Land of Israel are forgiven.... Even if one walks four cubits in it, one is assured of the life of the world to come.... At all times one should live in the Land of Israel even where the majority of the inhabitants are heathen, rather than outside the Land even where the majority of the inhabitants are Jewish. For he who dwells outside the Land of Israel is regarded as one who worships idols'' (Yad, Melakhim 5:9-12). The significance of the religious duty to dwell in the Land of Israel was broadened, and made more compelling, by emphasizing the fact that there are a large number of biblical commandments, particularly those connected with agriculture, which can be observed only within the territory of the Land of Israel. During the 13th century, when there was a ferment among the Jews of Western Europe to fulfill the religious commandment of living in the land of Israel, one French rabbi, Ḥayyim Cohen, expressed his opinion that this duty was no longer operative, because of the difficulty of fulfilling those laws (Tos. Ket. 110b) but his opinion remained an isolated one.

This belief in the religious duty to dwell in the Land of Israel, and the central and dominant place which the country in general, and Jerusalem in particular, held in the sentiments of the Jewish people remained an unchallenged element of Jewish thought throughout the ages of exile. It infused all aspects of his everyday life and his creativity. It was only in the 19th century that for the first time an attempt was made to displace it by a serious and powerful rival, and it is interesting that the challenge of the denial of the centrality of Israel became part of the doctrine of a Jewish religious, and not a political, schism.

It was strongly backed, and was sponsored by an appealing ideology: the doctrine of Liberty, Equality and Fraternity proclaimed by the French Revolution was the slogan in the new battle for democracy, for the abolition of privilege and the equality of all men before the Law. Its impact upon the Jews was electrifying. They were determined that these ideals should embrace them as

Priestly Blessing at the Western Wall, Jerusalem, 1971. Photo K. Weiss, Jerusalem.

well, that the Rights of Man belonged to all mankind. With Moses Mendelssohn, a man of scintillating intellect who first broke through the social barriers of his German periphery in the latter part of the 18th century, there began the fight for Jewish emancipation that was to monopolize the energy and talents of public-minded Jews during the whole century.

As, stage by stage, success was won, as Jews began to penetrate into society and take their places in public life, a new doctrine gained ground; total emancipation would constitute the true Messianic Age. The attachment of full civic rights for the Jews would be the end of the road. Not by a return to the ancient Homeland, but as citizens of the countries where they lived, each contributing his share towards the common weal, would Jews fulfill their own nation's destiny. Some went as far as entire assimilation, loss of Jewish identity. Even the less extreme among them

307

stripped Judaism of all its national content, avowing it to be merely a faith and a form of worship: the only dividing line between the Englishman or the Frenchman or German who was a Jew and his Christian fellow-national was in his mode of worship. The Jewish Reform Movement, largely influenced by these ideas, rationalized the doctrine by expunging from the prayer book every allusion to Zion and its eventual restoration.

In Eastern Europe, where the compact masses of Jewry still lived, the old loyalties held their ground, entrenched as they were within an adamant religious allegiance; nor had civic emancipation yet penetrated into those countries.

It was only under the impact of the State of Israel that this denial of the central place of Israel in certain trends of Jewish religious thought was finally expunged. Reform Jews today are as fully committed to the doctrine of the centrality of Israel in Jewish thought as are their Orthodox and Conservative coreligionists, and some of the outstanding leaders of the movement have come from their ranks. If on the one hand there is still a dwindling fringe element of Reform Jews who cling obstinately to the disassociation of Reform Judaism from the Land of Israel, there are at the other extreme the supporters of the fanatically extreme Satmar Ḥasidim who not only expound the isolated statement of Ḥayyim Cohen but go further and regard the State of Israel as a flaunting rejection of the Divine Will. But both these are backwaters of the powerful communal current of modern Jewish thought.

On the other hand, it was in Eastern Europe in the latter part of the 19th century that there arose a number of secular trends that also denied the central place of Israel in Jewish thought, but retained the principle of a distinct Jewish identity. In the scholarly sphere, Simon Dubnow evolved the theory of the autonomism of Jewish communities in the Diaspora as the basis of survival in the past and in the future. In the political sphere, the once-powerful Bund organization placed its faith in the ideal of the Yiddish-speaking proletariat as a distinctive element in the struggle for the emergence of world socialism. Mention should also be made of the various movements of which the Jewish Territorial Organization was the most important, which, while seeking a national solution for the Jewish problem, did not see Erez Israel as its only or even essential homeland.

A word must be said about Religious Zionism, especially the movement originally called the Mizrachi and now the National Religious Movement. This movement, unlike the more extreme Agudat Israel, has always been an integral part of the otherwise secular Zionist movement and as such it can be said that its main thrust has been in the direction of the national aspirations of the Jewish people to establish an independent sovereign Jewish State. In addition to that however, the main plank of their platform is a religiously observant state faithful to the principles and way of life of orthodox Judaism. In addition to the religious duty of living in the Land of Israel and the opportunities of living a full Jewish life which is possible only in an independent Jewish State, they see in the State, in the formulation of the prayer for Israel drawn up by the late Chief Rabbi of Israel, Rabbi Yitzhak Isaac Herzog, the "beginning of the florescence of our Redemption," a definitive and important stage in the realization of the Messianic age and all that is implied by it. But over and above all these aspects of the place of the State of Israel in terms of Jewish values, there is an overriding consideration which serves to resolve the paradox mentioned at the beginning of this article, of the "particularism" which seems to characterize the predominant place held by the Land of Israel and the universal aspect of Judaism referred to in the previous sections of this volume. It is the fulfillment of the most glorious of all universalist visions to be found in the Bible, repeated in almost identical words by both Isaiah (2:2-4) and Micah (4:1-3):

"But in the last days it shall come to pass, that the mountain of the house of the Lord shall be established in the top of the mountains, and it shall be exalted above the hills: and people shall flow unto it. And many nations shall come, and say, Come, and let us go up to the mountain of the Lord, and to the house of the God of Jacob, and he will teach us of his ways, and we will walk in his paths: for the law shall go forth of Zion, and the word of the Lord from Jerusalem. And he shall judge among many people, and rebuke strong nations afar off: and they shall beat their swords into plowshares, and their spears into pruninghooks: nation shall not lift up a sword against nation, neither shall they learn war any more.''

This sublime synthesis of particularistic and universal, of national redemption in the Land of Israel and the blessing of civilization as a whole, is the Jewish vision.

BIOGRAPHICAL INDEX

ABRABANEL, ISAAC BEN JUDAH (1437–1508)—statesman, philosopher and biblical exegete. Lived in Portugal, Spain and Italy.

ABRABANEL, JUDAH (called Leone Ebreo or Leo Hebraeus; c. 1460–after 1523)—Italian poet, physician, and one of the foremost philosophers of the Renaissance.

ABRAHAM BAR ḤIYYA (ḤAYYA; d.c. 1136)—Spanish philosopher, mathematician, astronomer and translator.

ADRET, SOLOMON BEN ABRAHAM (known from his initials as RaShBa; c. 1235–c. 1310)—Spanish rabbi and one of the foremost Jewish scholars of his day.

AḤAD HA'AM (Asher Hirsch Ginsberg; 1856–1927)—Hebrew essayist, thinker and leader of the Ḥibbat Zion movement; wrote under the name of Aḥad Ha'am ("One of the People").

ALBO, JOSEPH (d. 1444)—Spanish philosopher and preacher; author of *Sefer ha-Ikkarim* ("Book of Principles"), a famous treatise on Jewish articles of faith in 1425.

AL-FARABI, ABU NASR MUHAMMAD (c. 870–c. 950)—one of the greatest Islamic philosophers of the medieval Islamic world; had considerable influence on Jewish philosophers, particularly Maimonides.

AL-GHAZALI, ABU HAMID MUHAMMAD IBN MUHAMMAD AL-TUSI (1058–1111)—Persian Muslim theologian, jurist, mystic and religious reformer.

ARAMA, ISAAC BEN MOSES (c. 1420–1494)—Spanish rabbi, philosopher and preacher.

AVERROES (ABU AL-WALID MUHAMMAD IBN RUSHD; 1126–1198)—one of the greatest Islamic philosophers and a noted physician; primarily known as commentator on Aristotle's works; lived in Spain.

AVICENNA (Abu Ali Al-Hussein ibn Abu Abdallah ibn Sina; 980–1037)—physician, scientist, man of affairs, and an outstanding Muslim philosopher.

BAAL SHEM TOV—see Israel ben Eliezer.

BAECK, LEO (1873-1956)—German rabbi and religious thinker; leader of Progressive Judaism.

BAHYA BEN JOSEPH IBN PAQUDA (11th century)—Jewish moral philosopher and author of the most important ethical work of the medieval period, *Duties of the Heart (Hovot ha-Levavot)*.

BUBER, MARTIN (1878-1965)—philosopher and theologian; Zionist thinker and leader; lived in Germany and Israel.

CARO, JOSEPH (1488-1575)—halakhist and codifier of *Shulḥan Arukh*.

COHEN, HERMANN (1842-1918)—German idealist philosopher and noted Jewish philosopher.

CORDOVERO, MOSES (known as the Remak; 1522-1570)—Kabbalist of the 16th century Safed school.

CRESCAS, HASDAI (d. 1412?)—Spanish philosopher, theologian and statesman; leading Jewish critic of medieval Aristotelianism.

DELMEDIGO, ELIJAH BEN MOSES ABBA (c. 1460-1497)—philosopher and talmudist; born in Crete.

DELMEDIGO, JOSEPH SOLOMON (1591-1655)—rabbi, philosopher, mathematician and astronomer; also known as Joseph Solomon Rofe (acronym YaSHaR) of Candia (Crete).

DURAN, SIMEON BEN ZEMAH (RaSHBaZ, Hebrew acronym of Rabbi SHimon Ben Zemaḥ; 1361-1444)—rabbinic authority, philosopher and scientist.

ELIJAH BEN SOLOMON ZALMAN (the "Vilna Gaon" or "Elija Gaon"; 1790-1797)—one of the greatest spiritual and intellectual leaders of Jewry in modern times. A leading opponent of Hasidism.

FALAQUERA (Ibn Falaquera, Palaquera), SHEM TOV BEN JOSEPH (c. 1225-1295)—Spanish philosophical author and translator.

FORMSTECHER, SOLOMON (1808-1889)—German idealist philosopher and rabbi.

GEIGER, ABRAHAM (1810-1874)—one of the leaders of the Reform movement in Judaism and an outstanding scholar of the *Wissenschaft des Judentums* (Science of Judaism).

GORDON, AHARON DAVID (1856-1922)—Hebrew writer and spiritual mentor of the Zionist labor movement which emphasized self-realization through settlement on the land (*ha-lutziut*); born in Troyanov (Russia); moved to Erez Israel.

HESCHEL, ABRAHAM JOSHUA (1907-1973)—German-born

American scholar and philosopher.

HIRSCH, SAMSON RAPHAEL (1808-1888)—rabbi and theologian; leader and foremost exponent of orthodoxy in Germany in the 19th century; critic of the Reform movement.

IBN DAUD, ABRAHAM BEN DAVID HALEVI (c. 1110-1180) —Spanish historian, physician and astronomer; first Jewish Aristotelian of the medieval period.

IBN EZRA, ABRAHAM (1089-1164)—poet, grammarian, biblical commentator, philosopher, astronomer and physician.

IBN GABIROL, SOLOMON BEN JUDAH (c. 1020-c. 1057)— Spanish poet and neo-Platonic philosopher; influenced medieval Christian thought.

IBN ZADDIK, JOSEPH BEN JACOB (d. 1149)—philosopher and poet.

ISAAC BEN SHESHET PERFET (known as RIBaSH from the initials of Rabbi Isaac Ben SHeshet; 1326-1408)—Spanish rabbi and halakhic authority.

ISRAEL BEN ELIEZER BA'AL SHEM TOV (known by the initials BESHT = Ba'al SHem Tov; c. 1700-1760)—charismatic founder and first leader of the Ḥasidic movement.

ISRAELI, ISAAC BEN SOLOMON (c. 855-c. 955)—physician and neo-Platonic philosopher; North African.

JABEZ, JOSEPH BEN ḤAYYIM (d. 1507)—Hebrew homilist and exegete.

JUDAH BEN BARZILLAI OF BARCELONA (late 11th to early 12th century)—Spanish talmudist and halakhic codifier.

JUDAH BEN SAMUEL HE-ḤASID (d. 1217)—author of Sefer he-Ḥasidim; mystic and talmudist; leader of German Ḥasidei Ashkenaz.

JUDAH HALEVI (before 1075-1141)—Spanish Hebrew poet and philosopher; one of the most important figures in medieval Jewish literature.

KAPLAN, MORDECHAI MENAHEM (1881-)—U.S. rabbi and founder of the Reconstructionist movement; theologian.

KIMḤI, DAVID (known as RADAK from the acronym of Rabbi David Kimḥi; 1160?-1235?)—grammarian and exegete of Narbonne, Provence.

KOOK, ABRAHAM ISAAC (1865-1935)—rabbinical authority and mystical thinker; first Ashkenazi Chief Rabbi of modern Israel.

KROCHMAL, NACHMAN (1785-1840)—philosopher and historian; one of the founders of the "science of Judaism"

(*Wissenschaft des Judentums*); a leader of the Haskalah movement in Eastern Europe.

LEVI BEN GERSHOM (acronym: RaLBaG; 1288–1344)—mathematician, astronomer, Aristotelian philosopher and biblical commentator; born probably in Languedoc, France.

LURIA, ISAAC BEN SOLOMON (referred to as Ha-Ari ("The[Sacred]Lion")1534–1572)—a great kabbalist; one of the outstanding figures in the Jewish mystical tradition; led the mystical community in Safed in Erez Israel.

LUZZATTO, MOSES ḤAYYIM (RAMḤAL; 1707–1746)—Italian kabbalist and moralist.

LUZZATTO, SAMUEL DAVID (often referred to by the acronym of SHaDaL or SHeDaL; 1800–1865)—Italian scholar, philosopher, Bible commentator and translator.

MAGNUS, ALBERTUS (c. 1206–1280)—medieval Christian theologian.

MAIMONIDES—see Moses Ben Maimon.

MENDELSSOHN, MOSES (1729–1786)—philosopher of the German Enlightenment in the pre-Kantian period and spiritual leader of German Jewry. First major modern Jewish philosopher.

MOSES BEN MAIMON (MAIMONIDES; known in rabbinical literature as "Rambam" from the acronym Rabbi Moses Ben Maimon; 1135–1204)—rabbinic authority, codifier, Aristotelian philosopher and royal physician. The greatest single figure in medieval Judaism in both philosophical and halakhic scholarship.

MOSES BEN NAḤMAN (NAḤMANIDES; RaMBaN = Rabbi Moses Ben Naḥman; 1194–1270)—Spanish rabbi and scholar; philosopher, kabbalist, biblical exegete, poet and physician; one of the leading authors of talmudic literature in the Middle Ages.

PHILO JUDAEUS (Philo of Alexandria; c. 20 B.C.E.–50 C.E.)—Hellenistic Jewish philosopher; credited with being the founder of the medieval philosophical movement.

RASHI (SOLOMON BEN ISAAC; 1040–1105)—leading commentator on the Bible and Talmud in the whole of the Jewish tradition. Lived in France.

ROSENZWEIG, FRANZ (1886–1929)—German Jewish theologian; one of the most influential of modern Jewish theologians.

SAADIAH (BEN JOSEPH) GAON (882–942)—scholar and author of the geonic period; important leader of Babylonian Jewry. The first medieval Jewish philosopher.

SCHOLEM, GERSHOM GERHARD (1897-   )—Jewish scholar;
pioneer and leading authority in the field of Kabbalah and
Jewish mysticism.

SHNEUR ZALMAN OF LYADY (1745–1813)—founder of
Ḥabad Ḥasidism.

STEINHEIM, SOLOMON LUDWIG (1789–1866)—German poet
and religious philosopher.

GLOSSARY

Aggadah, name given to those sections of Talmud and Midrash containing homiletic expositions of the Bible, stories, legends, folklore, anecdotes, or maxims. In contradistinction to *halakhah*.

Agunah, woman unable to remarry according to Jewish law, because of desertion by her husband or inability to accept presumption of death.

Aliyah, (1) being called to Reading of the Law in synagogue; (2) immigration to Erez Israel; (3) one of the waves of immigration to Erez Israel from the early 1880s.

Amidah, main prayer recited at all services; also known as *Shemoneh Esreh* and *Tefillah*.

Amora (pl. **amoraim**), title given to the Jewish scholars in Erez Israel and Babylonia in the third to sixth centuries who were responsible for the *Gemara*.

Asarah be-Tevet, fast on the 10th of Tevet commemorating the commencement of the siege of Jerusalem by Nebuchadnezzar.

Ashkenaz, name applied generally in medieval rabbinical literature to Germany.

Ashkenazi (pl. **Ashkenazim**), German or West-, Central-, or East-European Jew(s), as contrasted with Sephardi(m).

Avodah, divine worship.

Bar, "son of . . ."; frequently appearing in personal names.

Baraita (pl. **beraitot**), statement of *tanna* not found in Mishnah.

Bar mitzvah, ceremony marking the initiation of a boy at the age of 13 into the Jewish religious community.

Ben, "son of . . ."; frequently appearing in personal names.

Berakhah (pl. **berakhot**), benediction, blessing; formula of praise and thanksgiving.

Bet din (pl. **battei din**), rabbinic court of law.

Bet ha-midrash, school for higher rabbinic learning; often attached to or serving as a synagogue.

Conservative Judaism, trend in Judaism developed in the United States in the 20th century which, while opposing extreme changes in traditional observances, permits certain modifications of *halakhah* in response to the changing needs of the Jewish people.

Creatio ex nihilo, doctrine that world was created from nothingness, and not fashioned from preexistent matter.

Dayyan, member of rabbinic court.

Decisor, equivalent to the Hebrew *posek* (pl. *posekim*), the rabbi who gives the decision (*halakhah*) in Jewish law or practice.

Devekut, "devotion"; attachment or adhesion to God; communion with God.

Diaspora, Jews living in the "dispersion" outside Erez Israel; area of Jewish settlement outside Erez Israel.

Din, a law (both secular and religious), legal decision, or lawsuit.

Ein-Sof, "without end"; "the infinite"; hidden, impersonal aspect of God; also used as a Divine Name.

Erez Israel, Land of Israel; Palestine.

Exilarch, lay head of Jewish community in Babylonia (see also *resh galuta*), and elsewhere.

Gabbai, official of a Jewish congregation; originally a charity collector.

Galut, "exile"; the condition of the Jewish people in dispersion.

Gaon (pl. **geonim**), head of academy in post-talmudic period, especially in Babylonia.

Gaonate, office of gaon.

Gemara, traditions, discussions, and rulings of the *amoraim*, commenting on and supplementing the Mishnah, and forming part of the Babylonian and Palestinian Talmuds (see Talmud).

Get, bill of divorce.

Gilgul, metempsychosis; transmigration of souls.

Golem, automaton, especially in human form, created by magical means and endowed with life.

Ḥabad, initials of *hokhmah, binah, da'at*: "wisdom, understanding, knowledge"; hasidic movement founded in White Russia by Shneour Zalman of Lyady.

Haggadah, ritual recited in the home on Passover eve at *seder* table.

Halakhah (pl. **halakhot**), an accepted decision in rabbinic law. Also refers to those parts of the Talmud concerned with legal matters. In contradistinction to *aggadah*.

Ḥalizah, biblically prescribed ceremony (Deut. 25:9–10) performed when a man refuses to marry his brother's childless widow.

Ḥalutz (pl. **halutzim**), pioneer, especially in agriculture, in Erez Israel.

Ḥanukkah, eight-day celebration commemorating the victory of Judah Maccabee over the Syrian king Antiochus Epiphanes and the subsequent rededication of the Temple.

Ḥasidism, (1) religious revivalist movement of popular mysticism among Jews of Germany in the Middle Ages; (2) religious movement founded by Israel ben Eliezer Ba'al Shem Tov in the first half of the 18th century.

Haskalah, "Enlightenment"; movement for spreading modern European culture among Jews c. 1750–1880. An adherent was termed *maskil*.

Havdalah, ceremony marking the end of Sabbath.

Ḥerem, excommunication, imposed by rabbinical authorities for purposes of religious and/or communal discipline; originally, in biblical times, that which is separated from common use either because it was an abomination or because it was consecrated to God.

Ḥevra kaddisha, title applied to charitable confraternity (*ḥevrah*), now generally limited to associations for burial of the dead.

Kabbalah, the Jewish mystical tradition:
  Kabbalah iyyunit, speculative Kabbalah;
  Kabbalah ma'asit, practical Kabbalah;
  Kabbalah nevu'it, prophetic Kabbalah.

Kaddish, liturgical doxology.

Kahal, Jewish congregation; among Ashkenazim, *kehillah*.

Kalām (Ar.), science of Muslim theology; adherents of the Kalām are called *mutakallimūn*.

Karaite, member of a Jewish sect originating in the eighth century which rejected rabbinic (Rabbanite) Judaism and accepted only Scripture as authoritative.

Karet, divine punishment, specified in Bible for certain sins.

Kasher, ritually permissible food.

Kashrut, Jewish dietary laws.

Kavvanah, "intention"; term denoting the spiritual concentration accompanying prayer and the performance of ritual or of a commandment.

Kedushah, addition to the third blessing in the reader's repetition of the *Amidah* in which the public responds to the precentor's introduction and connecting text with verses praising God.

Kiddush, prayer of sanctification, recited over wine or bread on eve of Sabbaths and festivals.

Kiddush ha-Shem, term connoting martyrdom or act of strict integrity in support of Judaic principles.

318 **Levir,** husband's brother.

Levirate marriage (Heb. *yibbum*), marriage of childless widow (*yevamah*) by brother (*yavam*) of the deceased husband (in accordance with Deut. 25:5); release from such an obligation is effected through *halizah*.

Mamzer, bastard, according to Jewish law, the offspring of an incestuous relationship.

Marrano(s), descendant(s) of Jew(s) in Spain and Portugal whose ancestors had been forcibly converted to Christianity but who secretly observed Jewish rituals.

Maskil (pl. **maskilim**), adherent of Haskalah ("Enlightenment") movement.

Mezuzah (pl. **mezuzot**), parchment scroll placed in container and affixed to doorposts of rooms occupied by Jews.

Midrash, method of interpreting Scripture to elucidate legal points (*Midrash Halakhah*) or to bring out lessons by stories or homiletics (*Midrash Aggadah*). Also the name for a collection of such rabbinic interpretations.

Minhag (pl. **minhagim**), ritual custom(s); synagogal rite(s); especially of a specific sector of Jewry.

Mishnah, earliest codification of Jewish Oral Law.

Mitnagged (pl. **Mitnaggedim**), originally, opponents of Hasidism in Eastern Europe.

Mitzvah, biblical or rabbinic injunction; applied also to good or charitable deeds.

Musar, traditional ethical literature.

Musar movement, ethical movement developing in the latter part of the 19th century among Orthodox Jewish groups in Lithuania; founded by R. Israel Lipkin (Salanter).

Nasi (pl. **nesi'im**), talmudic term for president of the Sanhedrin, who was also the spiritual head and, later, political representative of the Jewish people; from second century a descendant of Hillel recognized by the Roman authorities as patriarch of the Jews. Now applied to the president of the State of Israel.

Omer, first sheaf cut during the barley harvest, offered in the Temple on the second day of Passover.

Orlah, fruit of tree prohibited in the first three years after planting.

Orthodoxy (Orthodox Judaism), modern term for the strictly traditional sector of Jewry.

Pardes, medieval biblical exegesis giving the literal, allegorical, homiletical, and esoteric interpretations.

Parnas, chief synagogue functionary, originally vested with both religious and administrative functions; subsequently an elected lay leader.

Rabbanite, adherent of rabbinic Judaism. In contradistinction to Karaite.

Reb, rebbe, Yiddish form for rabbi, applied generally to a teacher or ḥasidic rabbi.

Reconstructionism, trend in Jewish thought originating in the United States.

Reform Judaism, trend in Judaism advocating modification of Orthodoxy in conformity with the exigencies of contemporary life and thought.

Responsum (pl. **responsa**), written opinion (*teshuvah*) given to question (*she'elah*) on aspects of Jewish law by qualified authorities; pl. collection of such queries and opinions in book form.

Rosh Ha-Shanah, two-day holiday (one day in biblical and early mishnaic times) at the beginning of the month of Tishri (September–October), traditionally the New Year.

Rosh Ḥodesh, New Moon; first of the Hebrew month.

Sanhedrin, the assembly of ordained scholars which functioned both as a supreme court and as a legislature before 70 C.E. In modern times the name was given to the body of representative Jews convoked by Napoleon in 1807.

Savora (pl. **savoraim**), name given to the Babylonian scholars of the period between the *amoraim* and the *geonim,* approximately 500–700 C.E.

Seder, ceremony observed in the Jewish home on the first night of Passover (outside Ereẓ Israel first two nights), when the *Haggadah* is recited.

Sefer Torah, manuscript scroll of the Pentateuch for public reading in synagogue.

Sefirot, the ten, the ten "Numbers"; mystical term denoting the ten spheres or emanations through which the Divine manifests itself; elements of the world; dimensions; primordial numbers.

Sephardi (pl. **Sephardim**), Jew(s) of Spain and Portugal and their descendants, wherever resident, as contrasted with Ashkenazi(m).

Shabbatean, adherent of the pseudo-messiah Shabbetai Ẓevi (17th century).

Shavuot, Pentecost; festival of Weeks; second of the three annual pilgrim festivals commemorating the receiving of the Torah at Mt. Sinai.

Sheḥitah, ritual slaughtering of animals.

320 **Shekhinah,** Divine Presence.

Shema (*Yisrael*; "hear . . . (O Israel)," Deut. 6:4), Judaism's confession of faith, proclaiming the absolute unity of God.

Shemini Azeret, final festal day (in the Diaspora, final two days) at the conclusion of Sukkot.

Shofar, horn of the ram (or any other ritually clean animal excepting the cow) sounded for the memorial blowing on Rosh Ha-Shanah, and other occasions.

Shulḥan Arukh, Joseph Caro's code of Jewish law (1564–65) in four parts:

> *Oraḥ Ḥayyim,* laws relating to prayers, Sabbath, festivals, and fasts;
>
> *Yoreh De'ah,* dietary laws, etc;
>
> *Even ha-Ezer,* laws dealing with women, marriage, etc;
>
> *Ḥoshen Mishpat,* civil, criminal law, court procedure, etc.

Siddur, among Ashkenazim, the volume containing the daily prayers (in distinction to the *maḥzor* containing those for the festivals).

Simḥat Torah, holiday marking the completion in the synagogue of the annual cycle of reading the Pentateuch; in Erez Israel observed on Shemini Azeret (outside Erez Israel a separate celebration on the following day).

Sukkah, booth or tabernacle erected for Sukkot when, for seven days, religious Jews "dwell" or at least eat in the *sukkah* (Lev. 23:42).

Sukkot, festival of Tabernacles; last of the three pilgrim festivals, beginning on the 15th of Tishri.

Tallit (gadol), four-cornered prayer shawl with fringes *(ẓiẓit)* at each corner.

Tallit katan, garment with fringes *(ẓiẓit)* appended worn during the day by observant male Jews under their outer garments.

Talmud, "teaching"; compendium of discussions on the Mishnah by generations of scholars and jurists in many academies over a period of several centuries. The Jerusalem (or Palestinian) Talmud mainly contained the discussions of the Palestinian sages. The Babylonian Talmud incorporates the parallel discussion in the Babylonian academies.

Talmud torah, term generally applied to Jewish religious (and ultimately to talmudic) study; also to traditional Jewish religious public schools.

Tanna (pl. **tannaim**), rabbinic teacher of mishnaic period.

Targum, Aramaic translation of the Bible.

Tefillin, phylacteries, small leather cases containing passages from Scripture and affixed on the forehead and arm by male Jews during the recital of morning prayers.

Torah, Pentateuch or the Pentateuchal scroll for reading in synagogue; entire body of traditional Jewish teaching and literature.

Tosafist, talmudic glossator, mainly French (12th–14th centuries), bringing additions to the commentary by Rashi.

Tosafot, glosses supplied by tosafist.

Tosefta, a collection of teachings and traditions of the *tannaim*, closely related to the Mishnah.

YHWH, the letters of the holy name of God, the Tetragrammaton.

Zaddik, person outstanding for his faith and piety; especially a hasidic rabbi or leader.

Zizit, fringes attached to the *tallit* and *tallit katan*.

Zohar, mystical commentary on the Pentateuch; main textbook of Kabbalah.

ABBREVIATIONS

Ar.	Arabic.
Aram.	Aramaic.
b.	born; *ben, bar.*
B.C.E.	Before Common Era (= B.C.).
C.E.	Common Era (= A.D.).
Heb.	Hebrew.
Nov.	Novellae (Heb. *Ḥiddushim*).
R.	Rabbi or Rav (before names); in Midrash (after an abbreviation)—*Rabbah.*
Resp.	Responsa (Latin "answers," Hebrew *She'elot u-Teshuvot* or *Teshuvot*), collections of rabbinic decisions.
Yid.	Yiddish.

BIBLIOGRAPHIC ABBREVIATIONS

Ar.	*Arakhin* (talmudic tractate).
Assaf, Mekorot	S. Assaf, *Mekorot le-Toledot ha-Ḥinnukh be-Yisrael*, 4 vols. (1925–43).
Avot	*Avot* (talmudic tractate).
Av. Zar.	*Avodah Zarah* (talmudic tractate).
Baron, Community	S.W. Baron, *The Jewish Community, its History and Structure to the American Revolution*, 3 vols. (1942).
Baron, Social	S.W. Baron, *Social and Religious History of the Jews*, 3 vols. (1937); enlarged, 1–2(1952²), 3–14 (1957–69).
BASOR	*Bulletin of the American School of Oriental Research.*
BB	(1) *Bava Batra* (talmudic tractate).
Bek.	*Bekhorot* (talmudic tractate).
Ber.	*Berakhot* (talmudic tractate).
Beẓah	*Beẓah* (talmudic tractate).
Bik.	*Bikkurim* (talmudic tractate).
BJRL	*Bulletin of the John Rylands Library* (1914 ff.).
BK	*Bava Kamma* (talmudic tractate).
BM	(1) *Bava Meẓia* (talmudic tractate).
	(2) *Beit Mikra* (1955/56 ff.).
Dan.	Daniel (Bible).
Deut.	Deuteronomy (Bible).
Deut. R.	*Deuteronomy Rabbah.*
Eccles.	Ecclesiastes (Bible).
Eccles. R.	*Ecclesiastes Rabbah.*
Ecclus.	Ecclesiasticus or Wisdom of Ben Sira (or Sirach; Apocrypha).
EM	*Enẓiklopedyah Mikra'it* (1950 ff.).
ERE	*Encyclopaedia of Religion and Ethics*, 13 vols. (1908–26); reprinted.

Esth.	Esther (Bible).
Est. R.	*Esther Rabbah.*
ET	*Enẓiklopedyah Talmudit* (1947 ff.).
Ex.	Exodus (Bible).
Ex. R.	*Exodus Rabbah.*
Ezek.	Ezekiel (Bible).
Ezra	Ezra (Bible).
Gen.	Genesis (Bible).
Gen. R.	*Genesis Rabbah.*
Ginzberg, Legends	L. Ginzberg, *Legends of the Jews,* 7 vols. (1909–38; and many reprints).
Git.	*Gittin* (talmudic tractate).
Guide	Maimonides, *Guide of the Perplexed.*
Guttmann, Philosophies	
	J. Guttmann, *Philosophies of Judaism* (1964).
Hab.	Habakkuk (Bible).
Ḥag.	*Ḥagigah* (talmudic tractate).
Haggai	Haggai (Bible).
Ḥal.	*Ḥallah* (talmudic tractate).
HTR	*Harvard Theological Review* (1908ff.).
HUCA	*Hebrew Union College Annual* (1904; 1924ff.)
JAOS	*Journal of the American Oriental Society* (c. 1850ff.).
JBL	*Journal of Biblical Literature* (1881 ff.).
JJS	*Journal of Jewish Studies* (1948 ff.).
Job	Job (Bible).
Joel	Joel (Bible).
Josh.	Joshua (Bible).
JQR	*Jewish Quarterly Review* (1889 ff.).
Jub.	Jubilees (Pseudepigrapha).
Judg.	Judges (Bible).
Kaufmann Y., Religion	Y. Kaufmann, *The Religion of Israel* (1960), abridged tr. of his *Toledot.*
Kaufmann Y., Toledot	Y. Kaufmann, *Toledot ha-Emunah ha-Yisre'-elit,* 4 vols. (1937–57).
Kelim	*Kelim* (mishnaic tractate).
Ker.	*Keritot* (talmudic tractate).
Ket.	*Ketubbot* (talmudic tractate).
Kid.	*Kiddushin* (talmudic tractate).

KS	*Kirjath Sepher* (1923/4 ff.).
Lam.	Lamentations (Bible).
Lam. R.	*Lamentations Rabbah.*
Lev.	Leviticus (Bible).
Lev. R.	*Leviticus Rabbah.*
Ma'as.	*Ma'aserot* (talmudic tractate).
Ma'as. Sh.	*Ma'aser Sheni* (talmudic tractate).
I, II, III, and IV Macc.	Maccabees, I, II, III (Apocrypha), IV (Pseudepigrapha).
Maimonides, Guide	Maimonides, *Guide of the Perplexed.*
Maim., Yad	Maimonides, *Mishneh Torah (Yad Ḥazakah).*
Mak.	*Makkot* (talmudic tractate).
Makhsh.	*Makhshirin* (mishnaic tractate).
Mal.	Malachi (Bible).
Meg.	*Megillah* (talmudic tractate).
Me'il.	*Me'ilah* (mishnaic tractate).
Men.	*Menaḥot* (talmudic tractate).
MGWJ	*Monatsschrift fuer Geschichte und Wissenschaft des Judentums* (1851–1939).
Mid.	*Middot* (mishnaic tractate).
MK	*Mo'ed Katan* (talmudic tractate).
Nah.	Nahum (Bible).
Naz.	*Nazir* (talmudic tractate).
Ned.	*Nedarim* (talmudic tractate).
Neg.	*Nega'im* (mishnaic tractate).
Neh.	Nehemiah (Bible).
Nid.	*Niddah* (talmudic tractate).
Num.	Numbers (Bible).
Num. R.	*Numbers Rabbah.*
Obad.	Obadiah (Bible).
Or.	*Orlah* (talmudic tractate).
OTS	*Oudtestamentische Studien* (1942 ff.).
Par.	*Parah* (mishnaic tractate).
PdRK	*Pesikta de-Rav Kahana.*
Pes.	*Pesaḥim* (talmudic tractate).
Pritchard, Texts	J.B. Pritchard (ed.), *Ancient Near Eastern Texts . . .* (1970[3]).
REJ	*Revue des études juives* (1880 ff.).

RH	*Rosh Ha-Shanah* (talmudic tractate).
RHR	*Revue d'histoire des religions* (1880 ff.).
Ruth	Ruth (Bible).
Ruth R.	*Ruth Rabbah.*
I and II Sam.	Samuel, books I and II (Bible).
Sanh.	*Sanhedrin* (talmudic tractate).
Shab.	*Shabbat* (talmudic tractate).
Sh. Ar.	J. Caro, Shulḥan Arukh.
	OḤ — *Oraḥ Ḥayyim*
	YD — *Yoreh De'ah*
	EH — *Even ha-Ezer*
	ḤM — *Ḥoshen Mishpat.*
Shek.	*Shekalim* (talmudic tractate).
Shev.	*Shevi'it* (talmudic tractate).
Shevu.	*Shevu'ot* (talmudic tractate).
Sifra	*Sifra* on Leviticus.
Sif. Deut.	*Sifrei Deuteronomy.*
Singer, Prayer	S. Singer, *Authorised Daily Prayer Book* (1943[17]).
Ta'an.	*Ta'anit* (talmudic tractate).
Tam.	*Tamid* (mishnaic tractate).
TB	Babylonian Talmud or Talmud Bavli.
Tem.	*Temurah* (mishnaic tractate).
Ter.	*Terumah* (talmudic tractate).
TJ	Jerusalem Talmud or Talmud Yerushalmi.
de Vaux, Anc Isr	R. de Vaux, *Ancient Israel: its Life and Institutions* (1961; paperback 1965).
VT	*Vetus Testamentum* (1951 ff.).
Yad	Maimonides, *Mishneh Torah (Yad Ḥazakah)*
Yad.	*Yadayim* (mishnaic tractate).
YD	*Yoreh De'ah.*
Yev.	*Yevamot* (talmudic tractate).
Yoma	*Yoma* (talmudic tractate).
ZA	*Zeitschrift fuer Assyriologie* (1886/87 ff.).
Zav.	*Zavim* (mishnaic tractate).
ZAW	*Zeitschrift fuer die alttestamentliche Wissenschaft und die Kunde des nachbiblischen Judentums* (1881 ff.).
Zech.	Zechariah (Bible).

BIBLIOGRAPHY

Judaism: J. B. Agus, *The Evolution of Jewish Thought* (1959); Baron, *Social*[2]; I. Epstein, *Judaism, A Historical Presentation* (1959); M. Friedlaender, *The Jewish Religion* (1913[3]); A. Hertzberg (ed.), *Judaism* (1961); M. Joseph, *Judaism as Creed and Life* (1958[4]); M. M. Kaplan, *Judaism as a Civilization* (1957[2]); K. Kohler, *Jewish Theology* (1918); Loewe, in ERE, 7 (1914), 581–609; G. F. Moore, *Judaism in the First Centuries of the Christian Era,* 2 vols. (1927); L. Roth, *Judaism, A Portrait* (1960); M. Steinberg, *Basic Judaism* (1947); Werblowsky, in: *The Concise Encyclopedia of Living Faiths* (1959), 23–50; L. Baeck, *The Essence of Judaism* (1961); M. Buber, *On Judaism* (1967).

Articles of Faith: Loew, *Gesammelte Schriften,* I (1889), 31–52, 133–76; Guttmann, *Ueber Dogmenbildung im Judentum* (1894); S. Schechter, *Studies in Judaism* (1896, repr. 1945), 147–81; J. Holzer, *Zur Geschichte der Dogmenlehre . . .* (1901), 5–42 (contains also *Mavo le-Perek Helek* in Arabic and Hebrew); Maimonides, *Commentary on Mishna,* ed. and tr. by Y. Kafaḥ (1965), 195–217; D. Neumark, *Toledot ha-Ikkarim be-Yisrael,* 2 vols. (1912); I. Scheftelowitz, in: MGWJ, 34 (1926), 65–75; L. Baeck, *ibid.,* 225–36; F. Goldmann, *ibid.,* 441–57; Julius Guttmann, *ibid.,* 35 (1927), 241–55; Guttmann, *Philosophies,* passim; A. Altmann, in: *Der Morgen* (Berlin-Amsterdam, 1937), 228–35; S. Heller-Wilensky, *Rabbi Yiẓḥak Arama u-Mishnato ha-Filosofit* (1956), 78–96; M. Goshen-Gottstein, in: *Tarbiz,* 26 (1957), 185–96; A. Hyman, in: A. Altmann (ed.), *Jewish Medieval and Renaissance Studies* (1967), 111–44; J. Petuchowski, in: A. Altmann (ed.), *Studies in Nineteenth Century Jewish Intellectual History* (1964), 47–64.

Tradition: S. Belkin, *In His Image* (1960), 290ff.; B. Cohen, *Law and Tradition in Judaism* (1959), 243ff.; I. Epstein, *Judaism* (1959), 49ff.; S. Freehof, *Reform Jewish Practices* (1944), 193ff.; S. R. Hirsch, *Judaism Eternal,* 2 (1956), 612ff.; L. Jacobs, *Principles of Faith* (1964), 473ff.; D. Rudavsky, *Emancipation and Adjustment*

(1967), 460ff.

Monotheism: Y. Kaufmann, *The Religion of Israel* (1960), index; Guttmann, *Philosophies*, index; A. Altmann, in: *Tarbiz*, 27 (1958), 301–9; G. Vajda, in: A. Altmann (ed.), *Jewish Medieval and Renaissance Studies* (1966), 49–74.

Idolatry: P. Scholz, *Goetzendienst und Zauberwesen bei den alten Hebraeern* (1877); G. d'Alviella, in: *RHR*, 12 (1885), 1–25; E. Schiaparelli, *Libro dei Funerali*, 1–3 (1882–90); H. Zimmern, *Beitraege zur Kenntnis der babylonischen Religion* (1894); A. Erman, *Life in Ancient Egypt* (1894), 259–305; Ch. Fossey, *La Magie Assyrienne* (1902); A. Moret, *Le Rituel du Culte Journalier en Egypte* (1902); G. Maspéro, *Causeries d'Egypte* (1907); E. A. W. Budge, *The Book of Opening of the Mouth*, 1–2 (1909); A. M. Blackman, in: *Journal of Egyptian Archaeology*, 10 (1924), 47–59; 11 (1925), 249–58; 12 (1926), 176–85; 21 (1935), 6–7; 27 (1941), 136–90; T. J. C. Baly, *ibid.*, 16 (1930), 173–86; G. A. Wainwright, *ibid.*, 19 (1933), 160–2; H. W. Fairman, *ibid.*, 32 (1946), 84ff.; Kaufmann Y., *Toledot*, 1 (1937); Kaufmann Y., *Religion*; H. Junker, *Die Goetterlehre von Memphis* (1940); E. D. Van Buren, in: *Orientalia*, 10 (1941), 65–92; J. A. Wilson, in: H. Frankfort et al. (eds.), *The Intellectual Adventure of Ancient Man* (1946), 62–71; R. Follet, in: *Recherches de science religieuse*, 38 (1951/54), 189–208; A. L. Oppenheim, *Ancient Mesopotamia* (1964), 171–227; J. Faur, in: *Tradition*, 9 (1968), 47–48; Y. Kaufmann, in: JBL, 70 (1951), 179–97. IN THE TALMUD: S. Lieberman, *Hellenism in Jewish Palestine* (1950), 115–38; idem, in: JQR, 37 (1946/47), 42–53.

God: IN THE BIBLE: Kaufmann Y., *Toledot* (incl. bibliography); Kaufmann Y., *Religion*; M. Buber, *I and Thou* (1937); EM, 1 (1950), 297–321; U. Cassuto, *The Documentary Hypothesis* (1961); A. J. Heschel, *The Prophets* (1962); R. Gordis, *The Book of God and Man* (1965). TALMUD: Ginzberg, *Legends*, index; M. Lazarus, *Ethics of Judaism*, 2 vols. (1900–01); G. F. Moore, *Judaism*, 2 vols. (1927), index; C. G. Montefiore and H. Loewe, *A Rabbinic Anthology* (1938), index; A. Marmorstein, *The Old Rabbinic Doctrine of God* (1927, repr. 1968); A. Cohen, *Everyman's Talmud* (1932), 1–71 and index; M. Guttmann, *Das Judentum und seine Umwelt* (1927); H. Cohen, *Religion der Vernunft aus den Quellen des Judentums* (1929²); P. Kuhn, *Gottes Selbsterniedrigung in der Theologie der Rabbinen* (1968). IN MODERN JEWISH PHILOSOPHY: J. B. Agus, *Modern Philosophies of Judaism* (1941); Guttmann, *Philosophies*, index; S. H. Bergman, *Faith and Reason: An Introduction to Modern Jewish Thought* (1961). ATTRIBUTES OF GOD:

D. Kaufmann, *Attributenlehre* (1875); idem, *Gesammelte Schriften*, 2 (1910), 1–98; H. A. Wolfson, in: *Essays and Studies in Memory of Linda R. Miller* (1938), 201–34; idem, in: *Louis Ginzberg Jubilee Volume* (1945), 411–46; idem, in: *Harvard Studies in Classical Philology*, 56–67 (1947), 233–49; idem, in: HTR, 45 (1952), 115–30; 49 (1956), 1–18; idem, in: *Mordecai M. Kaplan Jubilee Volume* (1953), 515–30; idem, in: JAOS, 79 (1959), 73–80; idem, in: *Studies and Essays in Honor of Abraham A. Neuman* (1962), 547–68; A. Altmann, in: BJRL, 35 (1953), 294–315; idem, in: *Tarbiz*, 27 (1958), 301–9; Guttmann, Philosophies, passim; S. Rawidowicz, in: *Saadya Studies* (1943), 139–65; A. Schmiedl, *Studien ueber juedische, insondere juedische-arabische Religionsphilosophie* (1869), 1–66; G. Vajda, *Isaac Albalag, Averroiste Juif, Traducteur et Annotateur d'Al-Ghazali* (1960), 34–129, and passim; idem, in: *Jewish Medieval and Renaissance Studies* (1966), 49–74.

Torah: Solomon Schechter, *Aspects of Rabbinic Theology* (1960²); C. G. Montefiore and H. Loewe, *A Rabbinic Anthology* (1960²), index; G. G. Scholem, *On the Kabbalah and its Symbolism* (1965), index; S. Y. Agnon, *Attem Re'item* (1959); A. J. Heschel, *Torah min ha-Shamayim ba-Aspaklaryah shel ha-Dorot*, 2 (1965); F. E. Urbach, *Hazal Pirkei Emunot ve-De'ot* (1969), index.

Holiness: G. van der Leuw, *Religion in Essence and Manifestation* (1938); A. L. Oppenheim, *Ancient Mesopotamia* (1964), 171–205; C. H. Gordon, *Ugaritic Textbook* (1965), glossary, no. 2210, s.v. *qdš*; C. F. Jean and J. Hoftijzer, *Dictionnaire des Inscriptions Sémitiques de l'Ouest* (1965), 253–4, s.v. *qdš* I, II, II, esp. III, 1; Pritchard, Texts, 428; J. Milgrom, *Studies in Levitical Terminology*, 1 (1970); B. A. Levine, in: JAOS, 85 (1965), 307–18; idem, in: *Religions in Antiquity*, ed. by J. Neusner (1967), 71–87; idem, in: *Eretz Israel*, 9 (1969), 88–96; idem, in: *Leshonenu*, 30 (1965–66), 3–4; M. Haran, in: HUCA, 36 (1965), 191–226; J. Pedersen, *Israel, its Life and Culture*, 1–2 (1926), 187–212, 244–59; 3–4 (1940), 150–534; Kaufmann Y., Toledot, vols. 1 and 2, index, s.v. *Kedushah*, esp. vol. 1, 537–59; J. Liver, in: EM, 5 (1968), 507–8, 526–31; R. Otto, *The Idea of the Holy* (1943³), 30–41, 52–84; M. D. Cassuto, in: EM, 2 (1954), 354–8; J. Reenger, in: *Zeitschrift fuer Assyriologie*, 58 (1967), 110–88; R. Stadelmann, *Syrisch-Palaestinensische Gottheiten in Aegypten* (1962), 110–23; de Vaux, Anc Isr 221–9, 345–57, 406–13. IN RABBINIC LITERATURE: S. Schechter, *Some Aspects of Rabbinic Theology* (1909), index s.v. *holiness;* G. F. Moore, *Judaism* (1927), index, s.v. *holiness;* A. Buechler, *Types of Jewish-Palestinian Piety*

(1922); M. Kadushin, *The Rabbinic Mind* (1952), 167–88; E. E. Urbach, *Ḥazal, Pirkei Emunot ve-De'ot* (1969), index s.v. *Kadosh, Kedushah;* Montefiore and Loewe, *Rabbinic Anthology* (1960²), index s.v. *holiness.*

Ethics: IN THE BIBLE: F. Wagner, *Geschichte des Sittlichkeitsbegriffs* (1928–36); A. Weiser, *Religion und Sittlichkeit der Genesis* (1928); W. I. Baumgartner, *Israelitische und altorientalische Weisheit* (1933), 4–7, 24–30; F. R. Kraus, in: ZA, 43 (1936), 77–113; Kaufmann Y., Toledot, 1 (1937), 27ff., 31ff., 431–3; 2 (1945), 68–70, 557–628; J. Hempel, *Das Ethos des Alten Testaments* (1938); H. Duesberg, *Les scribes inspirés,* 1 (1938), 92–126, 481–500; H. Frankfort, *Ancient Egyptian Religion* (1948), 56–80; N. W. Porteous, in: H. H. Rowley (ed.), *Studies in Old Testament Prophecy* (1950), 143–56; E. Neufeld, *The Hittite Laws* (1951), 53; A. Gelin, *Morale et l'Ancient Testament* (1952), 71–92; H. Kruse, in: *Verbum Domini,* 30 (1952), 3–13, 65–80, 143–53; H. Bonnet, *Reallexikon der aegyptischen Religionsgeschichte* (1952); W. G. Lambert, in: *Ex Oriente Lux,* 15 (1957–58), 184–96; idem, *Babylonian Wisdom Literature* (1960); S. E. Loewenstamm, in: *Sefer S. Dim* (1958), 124–5; idem, in: BM, 13 (1962), 55–59; E. Jacob, in: VT Supplement, 7 (1960), 39–51.

Labor: IN THE BIBLE: S. Kalischer, in: *Festschrift Hermann Cohens* (1912), 579ff.; J. Husslein, *Bible and Labor* (1924); H. L. Ginsberg, in: VT Supplement, 3 (1955), 138ff.; I. Mendelsohn, in: BASOR, 143 (1956), 17ff.; L. Finkelstein, *The Pharisees,* 1 (1962), 219ff.; S. Talmon, in: BASOR, 176 (1964), 29ff. LATER RABBINIC WRITINGS: Shillem Warhaftig, *Dinei Avodah ba-Mishpat ha-Ivri* (1969), 2 vols.; N. Shemen, *Baziung zu Arbet un Arbeter* (1963), 2 vols.

Cruelty to Animals: Dembo, *Jewish Method of Slaughter* (1894); Wohlgemuth, in: *Jeschurun,* 14 (1927), 585–610; 15 (1928), 245–67, 452–68; S. H. Dresner, *Jewish Dietary Laws, their Meaning for Our Time* (1959); S. D. Sassoon, *Critical Study of Electrical Stunning and the Jewish Method of Slaughter* (1955³); E. Bar-Shaul, *Mitzvah va-Lev* (1960), ch. 1; A. Chafuta, in: *No'am,* 4 (1961), 218–25; N. Z. Friedman, *ibid.,* 5 (1962), 188–94.

Law and Morality: Fassel, *Tugend- und Rechtslehre . . . des Talmuds . . .* (1848, 1862²); M. Bloch, *Die Ethik in der Halacha* (1886); S. Schaffer, *Das Recht und seine Stellung zur Moral nach talmudischer Sitten- und Rechtslehre* (1889); M. Lazarus, *Die Ethik des Judentums,* 2 vols. (1904–11); I. S. Zuri, *Mishpat ha-Talmud,* 1 (1921), 86f.; S. Federbusch, *Ha-Musar ve-ha-Mishpat be-Yisrael*

(1947); S. Pines, *Musar ha-Mikra ve-ha-Talmud* (1948); J. Z. Lauterbach, *Rabbinic Essays* (1951), 259–96; ET, 1 (1951³), 228–30, 334f.; 7 (1956), 382–96; E. Rackman, in: *Judaism,* 1 (1952), 158–63; Y. Kaufmann, *The Religion of Israel* (1960), 122–211, 291–340; M. Silberg, *Kakh Darko shel Talmud* (1961); M. Elon, in: *De'ot,* 20 (1962), 62–67; Z. J. Melzer, in: *Mazkeret ... le-Zekher ... ha-Rav Herzog* (1962), 310–5; B. Cohen, in: *Jewish and Roman Law,* 1 (1966), 65–121; 2 (1966), 768–70; E. Urbach, *Ḥazal—Pirkei Emunot ve-De'ot* (1969), 254–347.

The 613 Commandments: Bloch, in: REJ, 1 (1880), 197–211; 5 (1882), 27–40; J. M. (Michael) Guttmann, *Beḥinat ha-Mitzvot* (1928); Halper, in: JQR, 4 (1913/14), 519–76; 5 (1914/15), 29–90; H. Heller (ed.), *Sefer ha-Mitzvot le-R. Moshe b. Maimon* (1914); Maimonides, *The Book of Divine Commandments,* tr. by C. B. Chavel (1940).

Reasons for Commandments: Heinemann, *Ta'amei ha-Mitzvot be-Sifrut Yisrael* (1949–56²); A. Marmorstein, *Studies in Jewish Theology* (1950), passim; W. Bacher, *Die exegetische Terminologie der juedischen Traditionsliteratur,* 1 (1899), 66–67, 113; 2 (1905), 69–73; C. Siegfried, *Philo von Alexandria* (1875), 20ff., 182ff., and passim; A. Altmann, in: *Rav Sa'adyah Ga'on* (1943), 658–73; idem. in: BJRL, 28, no. 2 (1944), 3–24; G. Golinski, *Das Wesen des Religionsgesetzes in der Philosophie des Bachja* (1935); D. Rosin, in: MGWJ, 43 (1899), 125ff.; idem, *Die Ethik des Maimonides* (1876), 92ff.; C. Neuberger, *Das Wesen des Gesetzes in der Philosophie des Maimonides* (1933); Miklishanski, in: *Ha-Rambam* (1957), 83–97; S. Poznański, *Perush al Yeḥezkel u-Terei Asar le-Rabbi Eli'ezer mi-Belganzi* (1913), 68, and passim; G. Vajda, *Recherches sur la philosophie et la kabbale* (1962), 161ff.; J. Wohlgemuth, *Das juedische Religionsgesetz in juedischer Beleuchtung,* 2 vols. (1912–19); Guttman, Philosophies, index; A. Barth, *The Mitzvoth, Their Aim and Purpose* (1949). KABBALAH: I. Tishby, *Mishnat ha-Zohar,* 2 (1961), 429–578; A. Altmann, in: KS, 40 (1964/65),

Prayer: K. Kohler, *The Psalms and Their Place in the Liturgy* (1897); A. Greiff, *Das Gebet im Alten Testament* (1915); F. Heiler, *Das Gebet* (1923); A. Wendel, *Das freie Laiengebet im vorexilischen Israel* (1932); Idelsohn, Liturgy; P. A. H. de Boer, in: OTS, 3 (1943); S. H. Blank, in: HUCA, 21 (1948), 331–54; 32 (1961), 75–90; idem, *Jeremiah, Man and Prophet* (1961), 92–93, 105ff., 234ff.; F. Hesse, *Die Fuerbitte im Alten Testament* (1951); M. D. Goldmann, in: *Australian Biblical Review,* 3 (1953), 1ff.; D. R. Ap-Thomas, in: *Scottish Journal of Theology,* 9 (1956), 422–9; idem, in: VT, 3 (1956), 225–41; J. Scharbert, in: *Theologie und*

Glaube, 50 (1960), 321–38; J. Has-Paecker, in: *Bibel und Leben,* 2 (1961), 81–92, 157–70; E. A. Speiser, in: JBL, 82 (1963), 300–6; H. Hamiel (ed.), *Ma'yanot* (1964); H. A. Broncers, in: ZAW, 77 (1965), 1–20; L. Krinetzki, *Israels Gebet im Alten Testament* (1905); A. Gonzáles, *La oración en la Biblia* (1968); M. Kadushin, *Worship and Ethics: A Study in Rabbinic Judaism* (1964); R. Schatz-Uffenheimer, in: *Studies in . . . Gershom G. Scholem* (1967), 317–36.

Study: Sh. Ar., Y. D. 246; G. F. Moore, *Judaism,* 2 (1927), 239–47; S. Zevin, *Le-Or ha-Halakhah* (1946), 159–64; E. E. Urbach, *Ḥazal, Pirkei Emunot ve-De'ot* (1969), index s.v. *Torah;* Assaf, Mekorot; A. Shoḥat, in: *Ha-Ḥinnukh,* 28 (1957), 404–18; Baron, Community, index s.v. *Education.*

Sabbath (Shabbat): E. Millgram, *Sabbath: The Day of Delight,* (1944, incl. full bibl.); U. Cassuto, *From Adam to Noah* (1961), 165–9; de Vaux, Anc Isr, 475–83 (incl. bibl.); H. J. Kraus, *Worship in Israel* (1966), 78–88; see also Maim. Yad, Shabbat; Sh. Ar., OḤ, 242–344; J. Z. Lauterbach, *Rabbinic Essays* (1951), 437–70; H. Biberfeld, *Menuḥah Nekhonah* (1965³); A. J. Heschel, *The Sabbath* (1951); S. Goldman, *Guide to the Sabbath* (1961); Y. L. Baruch, *Sefer ha-Shabbat* (1956).

Festivals: G. F. Moore, *Judaism,* 2 (1927), 40–54; E. Rackman, *Sabbath and Festivals in the Modern Age* (1961); Y. Vainstein, *Cycle of the Jewish Year* (1961²); H. Schauss, *Guide to Jewish Holy Days* (1962); S. Y. Zevin, *Ha-Mo'adim ba-Halakhah* (1963¹⁰); Y. L. Barukh and Y. T. Levinsky (eds.), *Sefer ha-Mo'adim,* 8 vols. (1963–65⁶); S. Goren, *Torat ha-Mo'adim* (1964); E. Kitov, *Book of Our Heritage,* 1 (1968). On Second Days of Festivals: *Conservative Judaism,* vol. 24, 2 (Winter 1970), 21–59.

INDEX